WEEDEN & CO.

the New York Stock Exchange
and the Struggle Over a National
Securities Market

1922–2002

Donald E. Weeden
Chairman, Weeden Securities Corp.

ISBN 0-9727789-0-X

Editor/Production/Creative: Gary Avey
Designer: Hilary Wallace
Copy Editor: Deborah Paddison

Consultant: Joel Harnett

*This book was printed in Tempe, Arizona by Ironwood Lithographers
on 70# Accent Opaque Smooth Text. Text is in Garamond.*

To my colleagues at Weeden & Co.,
past and present

Contents

Illustrations

than a touch of fall in it," May 1970
9. William McChesney Martin, *Institutional Investor* Magazine, 1971
10. Weeden & Co. advertisement: "The 10 most active stocks of 1971"
11. Weeden & Co. tombstone: 300,000 shares of common stock, October 14, 1970

Portfolio III *Following page 150*

1. SEC Advisory Committee for a comprehensive market disclosure system for listed securities, April 1972
2. Weeden & Co. advertisement: "When the blue chips were down," fourth quarter 1973
3. Weeden & Co. advertisement: "The Third Market. The 12 billion dollar stock market competition built," 1973
4. New York Stock Exchange Chairman James Needham on cover of *Institutional Investor* Magazine, "The Big Board Takes the Offensive," March 1973
5. Weeden & Co. advertisement: "One of the largest markets in listed securities is a firm," 1973
6. Weeden & Co. trading floor, Jersey City, New Jersey, 1976
7. Chart: Dow Jones Industrial Average monthly closes and NYSE average daily volume, 1960–1980
8. Chart: 90-day T-bill vs. 30-year bond yield, 1960–1980
9. Reprint of folder cover, "Cincinnati/NMS, an invitation to participate," 1978
10. Cover of *Institutional Investor* Magazine featuring article "The Tragedy of Don Weeden," June 1978

Portfolio IV *Following page 174*

1. Weeden & Co. tombstone, 1986
2. Weeden & Co. board of directors, 1986
3. Don and Pat Weeden, 1996
4. Weeden & Co. trading floor, Greenwich, Connecticut, 2002
5. Weeden & Co. advertisement: Reprint from *Pensions & Investments* describing results of a U.S. equity trading survey using the Plexus Broker Universe for the four quarters ending September 30, 2001

Endpapers: *San Francisco — Bird's-eye View*
Drawn and lithographed by Charles B. Gifford. Printed by Louis Nagel of San Francisco. Published July 1, 1864 by Robinson & Snow, Washington & Sansome Street. 25½ in. x 40 in.

Foreword

There has been for at least 27 years a vision of a National Securities Market or, as it is sometimes called, a National Market System. The vision still exists, but the reality has proved elusive. In the Securities Acts Amendments of 1975, Congress directed the U.S. Securities and Exchange Commission to create a National Market System and to appoint a National Market Advisory Board to give them guidance. A member of that board, and perhaps the most influential advocate of a National Market System, was Don Weeden, for many years a principal of Weeden & Co. No one seemed better equipped than he to understand the vision and to lead the struggle to create one.

For other reasons, an adversarial relationship between Weeden & Co. and the New York Stock Exchange existed long before 1975. Because the NYSE had a fixed minimum commission structure, non-member firms, such as Weeden, could effectively compete for the growing institutional business in listed stocks by offering a lower net price to them than could member brokers of the NYSE. This market, away from the NYSE, was called the Third Market, and Weeden was by far its largest dealer. At one time Weeden's share volume in those 300 stocks in which it made a market equaled approximately 10 percent of the NYSE volume.

The NYSE, like most business organizations, did not relish effective competition and tried to regulate and then legislate the Third Market out of existence. Neither effort was successful. Ironically, Don Weeden endorsed the abolition of fixed minimum commissions as being in the public interest, despite the fact that their elimination, achieved on May

1, 1975, greatly diminished the cost advantage enjoyed by his firm.

In National Market Advisory Board discussions, the arguments for and against a National Market System became explicit. Because the board represented a variety of points of view, especially by the industry representatives, its final report was less forceful than it would have been otherwise. Nevertheless, a majority of the board, including all of the non-industry members, favored the creation of a National Market System based upon a central limit order book (CLOB). Such an order book would achieve the central objective of a National Market System by giving priority to public orders over all dealer bids and offers. This would ensure that public investors wishing to sell stocks would be the first to receive the highest price, and that those buying stocks would be the first to pay the least that anyone was willing to accept.

The advantages of such a system seem obvious, and modern computer technology makes such a system feasible. Nevertheless, so far, the NYSE has been effective in blocking the creation of a National Market System. But the vision persists, and Don Weeden continues to be its leading advocate.

Don tells the story of this struggle clearly, and frequently in an entertaining way. We meet a varied cast of characters whose different roles are interpreted with great insight and sometimes with great humor. Anyone interested in the securities industry — and that's a very large number these days — and anyone interested in the lively controversy over a change in public policy will enjoy and be educated by this book.

James H. Lorie
Professor of Finance Emeritus
University of Chicago Graduate School of Business
National Market Advisory Board Member, 1975–1977

Introduction

"If the New York Stock Exchange could do it to someone else, they could do it to us. We did not want to pick a fight; we just wanted to get along and do our business. We were not trying to change the world. We merely wanted to compete."

—*Donald E. Weeden, from an interview for* Institutional Investor *Magazine's 20-year retrospective "The Way It Was," 1988.*

Beginning in the early 1960s, a number of events occurred that brought fundamental change to the securities markets in the United States. Weeden & Co., as the leading Third Market[1] firm, played a unique and often influential role in that process. As a second-generation member of this family firm, I became its principal spokesman, defending the way in which we traded listed stocks, then becoming an advocate for greater competition and use of modern technology and ultimately the principal supporter of a National Market System.

This book tells the story of those times: how the institutional investor changed the way stocks were bought and sold; the response of the New York Stock Exchange (NYSE; the Exchange) to the growth and influence of off-board market making; and the involvement of Congress, the courts and the regulatory agencies. All of this made for high drama in the otherwise mundane field of market structure. There were public charges and counter-charges amongst the protagonists, behind-the-scenes maneuvering and lobbying, passionate outcries on the fate of an industry and the future of the American capitalist system, even concern over potential harm to the world economy. From the viewpoint of this writer, there was plenty of excitement, uncertainty, frustration and humor throughout. This account tries to capture as much as I can remember.

This book also tells the story of Weeden & Co., from the firm's inception in 1922 through a merger in 1979 and then its reconstitution in 1986.

Finally, it tells the story of two generations of Weedens who found themselves, because of their firm's particular niche in the industry, thrust onto the public stage in a way none of them had envisioned, desired or were well trained for.

At first, our involvement was quiet, involving private and informal discussions with interested government regulators. Over time it expanded to include meetings with congressional committees and their staff members, and formal appearances before those committees and the commissioners of the U.S Securities and Exchange Commission (SEC; the Commission). As the differences between the NYSE and what came to be known as the Third Market became more vocal, publicly debated and intense, Weeden felt it necessary to counter what were increasingly inaccurate and misleading statements about the Third Market made by members and staff of the NYSE. We did this through articles, speeches, newspaper advertisements and interviews with the media. We also participated on several industry committees created to formulate changes in the equity markets. Reluctantly, the NYSE responded to criticism from the Justice Department, pressure from the SEC and legislation by Congress. But as the record will show, it was the growing effectiveness of the Third Market that brought about the more significant changes in the securities markets.

Two generations of Weedens — Frank, Norman, Alan, Jack and I — played significant roles during this time. It was their upbringing on a clipper ship captained by their father, Henry Frank Weeden, that imbued Frank and Norman with a certain moral fervor and tenacity to continue Weeden's Third Market business despite the persistent opposition of the NYSE. The effort was continuous for almost 20 years until 1978, when the firm, experiencing a severe loss of capital due to declining bond and stock markets, withdrew from its Third Market activities and from further public involvement in industry matters. Nevertheless, its influence continued into the 1980s. Instinet Corp., of which Weeden & Co. once owned more than 90 percent, ultimately grew to become the largest participant in the over-the-counter market. Our Weeden Holding Automated Market System (WHAM), introduced onto the Cincinnati Stock Exchange in 1976, became the Regional Market System (RMS) and then the Multiple Dealer Trading System (MDTS). MDTS was one of two systems authorized by the SEC in 1979 to serve as an experimental precursor to Congress' vision of a National Market System.

In the year 2002, a re-established Weeden & Co. still conducts a business little different from that which founders Frank (my father) and Norman Weeden began 80 years ago. Fueled by fresh young talent, Weeden is still dedicated to using its knowledge of the marketplace and the best in technology to service the institutional investor.

---

[1]Where stocks listed on a national securities exchange (principally the NYSE) are traded in the over-the-counter market.

The clipper ship *S.S. Marion Chilcott*, 1901

1

The Beginning
of Weeden & Co.

In the beginning, Weeden was strictly a bond house. The firm was started in San Francisco in 1922 by brothers Frank and Norman Weeden, who concentrated on dealing in securities they were familiar with from their prior firms. Frank had helped develop the municipal bond department for Blyth Witter, while Norman had been a municipal bond salesman for R.H. Moulton. California was growing rapidly, and so was the need for capital by the state, its cities and numerous irrigation districts.

The Weeden brothers had little capital at the beginning — $20,000 borrowed from their father, Henry Frank Weeden, a retired sea captain.

Their background precluded having a lot of rich friends. Thus, retail brokering was not their strong suit. They found a niche in a low-risk, conservative part of the market, where they concentrated their modest capital on buying up small lots of Liberty bonds and local municipal issues in the secondary markets away from the exchanges. When they had accumulated a reasonable block, they would try to sell it to one of the myriad small banks scattered up and down the state.

As their firm grew larger, the business became almost wholly institutional while expanding to include corporate bonds issued by California's fast-growing utilities. In a prospectus dated 1927, used in connection with a $300,000 issue of Weeden & Co. convertible preferred stock sold to friends and clients, they referred to themselves as "Dealers in Seasoned California Bonds" with the acronym DISCOB.

What was interesting about this was their decision to become a corporation, unusual in the securities industry at the time, in order to ensure that the capital would be permanent and not subject to withdrawal in difficult times.

Their early success encouraged them to open an office in Los Angeles in 1927. In the same year, because of the growing interest in California by the Eastern bank trust departments and insurance companies, they opened a two-man office at 14 Wall St. in Manhattan.

The market crash of 1929 had little effect on Weeden, because the firm was not involved in equities and conducted all of its business under the terms "delivery against payment." The firm continued its secondary trading and its underwriting of California bonds into the 1930s. Weeden also closely followed the investment trends of its major clients, the trust departments and insurance companies, and slowly began to trade preferred stocks, then utility common stocks. Eventually, the firm began to make markets in listed industrial common stocks. In the late 1940s, this trend brought Weeden into competition with the NYSE in its most actively traded stocks.

Weeden's trading of common stocks steadily grew, although well into the 1960s it was still secondary to the firm's primary activity of underwriting and trading municipal bonds of national interest.

This making of net markets in listed stocks, away from an exchange, soon to be dubbed the "Third Market" by the SEC, was the activity that pushed this California bond house into the national spotlight. As the 1950s wound down, Weeden & Co. had offices in Boston and Chicago as well as Los Angeles, San Francisco and New York. Both its bond and stock businesses were divided between institutional accounts and broker-dealers, some of whom were members of various exchanges and others who were not. Much of Weeden's business was conducted over private direct telephone lines. The ticker tape was essential for making a market in a listed stock. This was the situation when a telephone call came in from one of Weeden's friends in Dallas.

2

The Silver Case

In February 1959, Jim Jacques of First Southwest Corp. in Dallas called my father, Frank, to tell him "Some poor bastard down here just had his ticker tape yanked." That poor bastard was Harold Silver, whose firm, Municipal Securities Co., dealt in municipal bonds and over-the-counter securities. Silver had a number of direct phone lines to NYSE-member firms over which he conducted business. At the same time they removed the ticker tape, the NYSE told its members to pull their direct wires to Municipal Securities. No reason was given, either to their members or to Silver.

As Jim knew, this action against Municipal Securities would be of great concern to Weeden & Co., since our business of making markets in listed stocks was dependent upon access to the NYSE ticker tape. If the NYSE could remove Municipal Securities' ticker without giving any reason, they could do it to Weeden as well.

After Jim's telephone call, my father asked me to see what I could find out. At the time, I was making markets for Weeden in dollar-quoted municipal bonds. After graduating from Stanford, I had spent six months at Yale Law School, and this apparently qualified me as the family's expert in all legal matters. My father and uncle had little use for lawyers, and fortunately Weeden had never had to engage a law firm except for corporate matters, so I became the point man.

I first contacted a classmate from Yale who lived in New York City and whom I saw frequently, both of us having married European women. We enjoyed going together to Jones Beach on Long Island on the weekends and partying with mutual friends. I took the opportunity to explain our business as best I could. He was interested and said he'd do some investigating.

Unfortunately, my friend made the mistake of talking to his father, who was a retail broker for a NYSE firm. It was an innocent thing to do but very uncomfortable for us, as we did not want to draw the NYSE's attention to our interest in the matter.

I then called Bob Beshar, an associate at Casey Lane & Mittendorf and an upperclassman when I was at Yale. I explained why it was very important to Weeden: "If the NYSE need not justify their action to anyone, no matter how appropriate or inappropriate, then they could do the same to us. Not only would our Third Market business be affected, but our core business, trading in municipal bonds, would be significantly curtailed."

Municipal Securities had decided to fight back, and Bob soon learned that the case, *Silver, dba Municipal Securities Co., et al. v. New York Stock Exchange*, was being heard before Judge Frederick van Pelt Bryan in the U.S. District Court in Manhattan. Bob quietly followed its progress over the next two years. Judge Bryan finally delivered his decision in June 1961. We were ecstatic over his opinion. He plainly said that the NYSE had violated the Sherman Antitrust Act by propagating a "conspiracy in restraint of trade" by its individual members against Municipal Securities. He ordered a reversal of the action taken by the NYSE and a determination of damages.

The NYSE had argued that it was necessary and appropriate for them to take the action they did under the authority given them by the Securities Exchange Act of 1934. Judge Bryan concluded differently:

> "A registered stock exchange has neither the power nor authority to determine with whom its members may deal or to direct them to desist from dealing with non-member broker-dealers ... and if it does so, it is subject to such appropriate action as may be taken under the antitrust laws."

We felt the opinion was well reasoned and concluded that our Third Market business was no longer in jeopardy. So we had quite a surprise when, in April 1962, the Circuit Court of Appeals reversed the District Court by a vote of 2 to 1. We were not aware that the SEC had entered an *amicus curiae* brief in support of the NYSE. Essentially, they argued that the Securities Exchange Act of 1934 gave the SEC primary power over the activities of the securities industry and that the Sherman Act did not apply.

The SEC at the time viewed the NYSE as the main, if not only, effective self-regulatory body in the industry, and they felt nothing should restrict its ability to carry out its responsibilities. This was Weeden's first introduction to the SEC's thinking and leanings in the field of market regulation, and it put us on notice about their preference for the NYSE.

Prior to this, our dealings with the SEC had been minimal. One must remember that Weeden was primarily a bond house, while the SEC was almost exclusively focused on the activities of the stock market.

In fact, my father, as a member of the Investment Bankers Code Committee, an industry group, was concerned about the attempt by Congress to bring state and local securities (all bonds) under federal oversight. Frank actually made several trips to Washington to lobby members of Congress to keep state and local bonds from being included in the final writing of the Exchange Acts of 1933 and 1934. He also helped enlist a barrage of letters and telegrams from state and municipal governments arguing to keep their securities out of the hands of federal regulation.

Later, in 1938, during the passage of the Maloney Act (creating the National Association of Securities Dealers), Frank was the first to suggest that Wally Fulton, then securities commissioner for the State of California, become the first president of the NASD. Wally served in that capacity until his retirement in the 1960s.

Back to the Circuit Court decision: It was largely influenced by the *amicus curiae* brief written by the SEC, whose legal arguments were supported by the following language:

"The New York Stock Exchange is performing a vital public function. And its standing and reputation are important to the national economy."

"Exchanges are important public institutions."

"Such an important instrument in our economic welfare … must be surrounded by adequate safeguards."

The Circuit Court took this to mean that "when exchanges are acting other than in clear absence of all jurisdiction … they are secure from liability under antitrust laws to persons aggrieved by their actions, even if such action is *arbitrary or unreasonable*" (emphasis added).

You can imagine how troublesome and potentially injurious this was to our market making in NYSE-listed stocks. It became clear that the SEC considered itself dependent upon the self-regulatory powers of the NYSE and gave no consideration to their potential effect on competition. Joel Seligman, in *The Transformation of Wall Street: A History of the Securities and Exchange Commission and Modern Corporate Finance* (Boston: Houghton Mifflin, 1982), comments on the Commission at the end of the Eisenhower Administration.

"During the Eisenhower Administration, the Securities and Exchange Commission reached its nadir. Its enforcement and policy-making capabilities were less effective than at any other period in history" (p. 265).

"It was a time of budget-cutting and 'the assumption that business was over-regulated and that large institutions like the New York Stock Exchange could discipline themselves'" (p. 269).

This attitude was maintained by successive chairmen of the SEC: Ralph Demmler, J. Sinclair Armstrong and Edward Gadsby. The Commission's policy toward the NYSE was "hands off," according to minutes of a meeting of the commissioners in 1955 (ibid., p. 272). When Demmler became chairman, he told Exchange officials that "from here on they are on their own" and that the Commission "would express neither approval nor disapproval of any proposed rules."

It was in this atmosphere that the NYSE acted against Municipal Securities and instituted other anti-competitive acts, which will be described in a later chapter.

At Weeden, we discussed the Circuit Court opinion and what we could do about it. Unfortunately, there was little to be done. The court had decided.

While we worried, events took a strange twist. The NYSE literally fumbled the ball on the goal line and ultimately lost the case in the U.S. Supreme Court. Soon after the Circuit Court decision, Harold Silver died. His law firm, Dickstein, Shapiro and Galligan, had not been paid, and Municipal Securities Co. was out of business. As we were told, Silver's lawyer, David Shapiro, approached A. Donald MacKinnon of Milbank, Tweed, Hope & Hadley, the law firm for the NYSE, with a settlement proposition: "Pay us $75,000 to cover legal fees and there will be no appeal to the Supreme Court." MacKinnon thought it was a small price to pay to lock in law that was very favorable to the NYSE, and he recommended to the NYSE Board of Governors that the settlement proposition be accepted.

At the time, John Coleman was a past chairman and influential member of that board, a powerful member specialist known for his generosity to the Catholic Church and his arrogance to most everyone else. It is said that Coleman was "damned" if he would pay a cent to those "scoundrels." In consequence, David Shapiro and Harold Silver's widow, Evelyn Silver, a lawyer in her own right, appealed the decision to the Supreme Court.

Bob Beshar said that now was the time for Weeden & Co. to get involved.

3

Getting Involved

In 1958, I had finished my training in the back office, or "cage," as it was affectionately called in those days because of its restricted access, and had taken over trading of the dollar-quoted municipal bonds. Because of troublesome market conditions and considerable competition, this had become a marginal business for Weeden. I jumped at the challenge and managed to revitalize our business by making tighter markets, increasing turnover and spending a lot of time visiting the many municipal bond brokers around the country. In 1961, this business was turned over to Rick Ott, who had been hired from Drake & Co., an intra-dealer broker specializing in dollar bonds. I went over to the stock desk as a salesman introducing our Third Market business to corporations and institutional investors. It was in the latter part of 1962 that Bob Beshar and I high-tailed it down to Washington to see what we could do.

The judgment of the Circuit Court of Appeals had been entered on April 6, 1962. The petition for a writ of certiorari was filed on May 31, 1962 and was granted by the U.S Supreme Court on October 8, 1962.

Our efforts in Washington were twofold: first, contact the Justice Department, and then talk to whomever would listen at the SEC. With respect to the latter, we decided to call David Silver, who we knew had joined the SEC in December 1960 and also had been a clerk for Judge Frederick van Pelt Bryan back in 1959 when the Harold Silver/Municipal Securities case first came before him. What we didn't know was that David had joined the newly formed group preparing the Special Study of the Securities Markets, headed up by Milton Cohen. As we came to know David, we perceived him to be a curious-minded man with a keen intellect.

Bob called David and arranged for a meeting at Whyte's Restaurant on Fulton Street. It was a favorite hangout for those who loved good seafood and thick steaks. It was also midway between the Federal Building at Center Street on the north and Wall Street on the south. And, as we found out later, Fulton Street was the northern boundary of the NYSE's "exclusive territory." Member firms that didn't have an office south of Fulton had to give up a fair portion of their commissions to a member who had such an office.

David knew the case very well and agreed with Judge Bryan's decision. He was disturbed by the Circuit Court's reversal. He understood the implications to competition, but had absolutely no idea that there was an existing off-board market in listed securities that could well be affected by this decision.

David was also familiar with the SEC brief and had voiced his opposition, but others, more concerned with regulation than competition, prevailed. Following our dinner at Whyte's, David introduced us to others on the staff of the Special Study. (Later, David was the one who coined the phrase "the Third Market." When the Study first began, the staff had divided the market into two parts: the Exchange-listed stocks and those traded over the counter. The "Third Market" was where listed stocks were traded over the counter.)

Meanwhile, our efforts at the Justice Department were immediately fruitful. Bob had contacted the Antitrust Division and arranged for a meeting with their people, headed by Deputy Director Lionel Kestenbaum and including George Reycraft. (George later joined the law firm Cadwallader, Wickersham & Taft and became counsel to M.A. Schapiro & Co.) My memory is vague as to who from Weeden attended what meetings, but some combination of Bob, Frank and me met with various members of the Antitrust staff in Washington and at our New York City office at 25 Broad St. We described our business in detail and how it could be affected by a NYSE left to its own devices.

To the group of antitrust lawyers, this was a classic case the Sherman Act was designed to prevent. The only issue was whether the Act had been superseded by the Securities Exchange Act of 1934.

The Antitrust Division felt strongly that the Sherman Act did cover antitrust behavior within the securities industry despite the '34 Act, and prepared a brief supporting Harold Silver. Meanwhile, the SEC argued strongly for the NYSE.

Presented with totally different positions by the two agencies of the federal government, the then–Solicitor General, Archibald Cox, had the delicate job of melding them together.

While we were not privy to either the Justice Department brief or that of the SEC, it was clear that our meetings had helped to shape the final presentation by Solicitor General Cox before the Supreme Court. If nothing else, he well understood that a substantial volume of listed securities are also traded in the over-the-counter market, and that those dealers rely on the ticker tape and direct wires to obtain information and effect trades in a timely and efficient manner. In light of this, action taken by the NYSE and its collective members must be considered as to its effect on competition. The idea that such action could be exercised without any explanation to the affected parties, and especially to the agency overseeing their conduct, was contrary to the purpose of the Sherman Antitrust Act and not contemplated by the language of the '34 Securities Exchange Act.

There was nothing else for us to do but listen to the oral arguments before the Supreme Court and wait for its decision.

On May 20, 1963, the Supreme Court of the United States, by a vote of 7 to 2, reversed the Circuit Court ruling.

> "The duty of self-regulation imposed upon the Exchange by the Securities Exchange Act of 1934 did not exempt it from the Antitrust laws, nor justify it in denying petitioners the direct wire connections without the notice and hearing which they requested. Therefore, the Exchange's action in this case violated Section 1 of the Sherman Act, and the Exchange is liable to petitioners under Sections 4 and 16 of the Clayton Act."

We were jubilant. It was now the middle of 1963. The stock market had begun to recover from Kennedy's confrontation with U.S. Steel in May of 1962. Volume on the NYSE was increasing nicely, and our Third Market business as a percentage of NYSE volume had edged up to more than 1 percent overall. In the 200-odd stocks in which we made a net market, our percentage was significantly higher. It had become an important revenue source for Weeden.

The report of the Special Study of the Securities Markets had been made public, and the "Third Market" was, for the first time, described in great detail.

In his decision, Justice Arthur Goldberg alluded to the Special Study, which had detailed the presence of an active over-the-counter market in listed securities. Thus, we felt that his opinion understood the possibility of anti-competitive consequences when a powerful institution misuses its self-regulatory powers without adequate due process. Even the dissenting opinion by Justice Potter Stewart agreed that "had the NYSE action occurred in an ordinary commercial context" it would have constituted a violation of the Sherman Act.

One must take a moment to ponder why the NYSE did what it did, and in the arrogant manner displayed by NYSE President Keith Funston's dismissal of Harold Silver's entreaties, to know why they were putting him out of business.

"While I understand your position, I am sure you can also understand our position in declining to furnish such details. Before taking any such action, the Exchange always makes a very careful and very thorough investigation."

Edward C. Werle, then chairman of the NYSE Board of Governors, was more perfunctory.

"The Exchange does not furnish detailed reasons for its action in either approving or disapproving private wires or ticker service for non-members."

In retrospect, I believe the SEC should take some blame for NYSE's insensitivity and arrogance. For eight years it had said in effect to the NYSE "you are on your own" — "our policy going forward will be to express neither approval nor disapproval of proposed rules or other actions" (Seligman, *The Transformation of Wall Street*, p. 272).

The interesting question to us at Weeden was to what extent the NYSE action taken against Municipal Securities was an isolated one in which the only issue was the reputation and questionable activities of Harold Silver, and how much of this was part of a well-thought-out strategy aimed at the growing market in listed stocks away from the Exchange.

4

The Special Study

Our call to David Silver did not succeed in changing the SEC brief prepared for the Supreme Court, but it did catapult our off-board business into the middle of the Special Study of the Securities Markets. This study came about because some rather egregious acts of fraud, misrepresentation and self-dealing by Re and Re, a father-and-son specialist firm, and other members had come to light on the American Stock Exchange in 1957. While the colorful details of what took place and by whom are not part of this history, their actions were the catalyst that stirred up Congress to allocate funds for the first serious study of the securities markets since 1934.

The attitude of the SEC was part of the problem. As Joel Seligman points out in *The Transformation of Wall Street*, "Regulation of the American Stock Exchange (AMEX) by the SEC was largely passive" (p. 282) … "Between 1954 and 1959 the SEC *under investigated* (emphasis added) the Res, in spite of clear signals of serious wrongdoing at least as early as 1957" (p. 286). Not until May 1960 did they begin to look closely at the problem, and only in May 1961 did they "authorize a comprehensive staff investigation of the entire American Stock Exchange" (p. 288).

In a 1962 memorandum by Philip Loomis, director of the SEC's Division of Trading and Exchanges, he acknowledges that the SEC should have realized that something was seriously wrong in 1957, if not earlier (ibid.). Loomis went on to explain that the SEC was understaffed and was confronted with unprecedented enforcement problems which did not come from exchanges. "Exchange regulation was not considered an enforcement problem, it (the SEC) being assured that the Exchange was basically aware of its responsibilities and was honestly conducted" (ibid., p. 289).

In order to separate the Special Study from an SEC whose independence of the industry it was regulating was in question, a separate staff was created whose only requirement was to submit their report to the commissioners for final review before submitting it to Congress.

The Special Study staff, led by Milton Cohen and Ralph Saul, quickly included the Third Market on their agenda and devoted a full section to our business, which it described as "one of the more striking developments in the securities market" (Special Study of the Securities Markets, Part 2, Chapter 7, Section D, p. 870). It went on to say that its growth had been entirely outside the glare of publicity (ibid., p. 871).

For this reason, the staff literally had to start at the beginning: Who was involved? What kind of business was being done? What was its volume of trades and shares? How did it relate to the public? Were there regulatory issues that needed to be addressed?

We were anxious to help. Led by my father, Frank, we described Weeden's activity in great detail to several of the staff through meetings in Washington and their visits to our New York office. We took them step by step through a typical trade: who it was done with and why they did it, and how it related to the market on the NYSE at the time. We slowly built a case for our competitiveness, the absence of improper behavior and our value to the public. From these initial discussions, the staff created a series of questions that were sent to those broker-dealers who were acting as a market maker quoting two-sided net markets, and to the non-member broker-dealers who used the Third Market in executing retail orders. Questionnaires also went to institutions who were using the Third Market.

Frank became quite active in our discussions with the Special Study people. While he argued against openly challenging the NYSE, he was quite willing to become involved in a quiet non-public dialogue with our chief regulator. And he was very good at it, because he knew the business thoroughly and had nothing to hide.

From the quantity of data received and the answers to a variety of questions as to how, when and why, the study was able to present a detailed picture of the Third Market, past and present.

We were not surprised at the findings. They pointed out that the growth of Third Market activity had exceeded that of the NYSE for the past 20 years, accelerating from 1955 on to a rate that was three times NYSE's growth in 1961. A growing institutional interest in stocks was the principal reason, as their participation grew to more than 60 percent of total Third Market volume, a much higher percentage than their participation on the NYSE.

The study also pointed out how Third Market activity shifted from primarily financial, real estate and utility stocks in the 1940s toward the blue-chip industrial common stocks, which were gaining increasing attention from the institutions.

In 1961, Third Market activity by pension funds, insurance companies and common trust funds equaled 15 percent of their total business. For mutual funds it came to only 6 percent. (This difference became an issue later on when the SEC began scrutinizing member broker give-up practices and four-way tickets.[2])

The institutions queried in the study cited price and cost as the main reason for using the Third Market, with availability of size being secondary.

Individual investor use of the Third Market was also growing, and was seen in the activity of banks on behalf of their custodial accounts and through use by non-member brokers, of which at the time there were some 4,000 registered with the NASD throughout the country.

This growing interest in the price advantage of dealing in the Third Market (lower cost to the institution, increased commissions retained by the non-member broker) attracted a number of new market markers. The study counted 17 market makers in late 1962, compared to only three in the early 1940s and 12 in the '50s. A market maker was defined as someone advertising his willingness to make a two-sided market upon inquiry. Of the 17 market makers, seven accounted for 96 percent of the volume in 1961. Of the seven, half concentrated on servicing their institutional clients and half dealt almost exclusively with small broker-dealers (Weeden stood out as the only firm catering to both groups).

What was interesting was the minimal use made of the NYSE market by the Third Market dealers, totaling only 5 percent of their volume, and mostly on the buy side of the market. (Early on, Weeden had decided as a matter of policy not to sell on the NYSE, in order to counter the constant accusation that we dumped our excess inventory onto the central market, causing undue volatility and disruption.)

The market makers were truly that, acting as principal 93.3 percent

THE SPECIAL STUDY **15**

of the time. As a result, by 1961 the Third Market activity had risen to 4 percent of dollar volume on the NYSE and was clearly growing.

Very important to us was the study's conclusion that *the Third Market, whatever its effect on the depth of the primary market, provides the public customer with overall markets of greater depth. While the off-board may be viewed as competitive to the NYSE, from the reference point of the institutional customer it is complementary.*

Despite the plethora of data and information gathered from the half-dozen or so questionnaires and the myriad visits and interviews with the various participants, the report made it clear that they considered their efforts "less a definitive study than an exploratory survey" (Special Study, Part 2, p. 910).

As a result, one of the main recommendations was to secure information concerning the Third Market on a continuous basis from the market makers and from the broker-dealers acting as agents for public customers (ibid., p. 911).

The main conclusion of the study pointed out that "the rapid growth of the Third Market has made this an increasingly important segment of the national securities markets ... " (ibid., pp. 910–11).

Reading the chapter on the Third Market almost 40 years after it was written, one is struck by how well the study came to understand the mechanics of the market, as well as its purpose, function and value.

Actually, Frank Weeden deserves much of the credit for this result. Walter Werner had been given responsibility for writing the chapter on the Third Market. Walter came to the study late from the private sector and was well regarded as a competent businessman and lawyer of integrity. Walter had come to respect Frank's opinion and asked him to privately review the report as it was being written and to advise where he thought there were inaccuracies, confusions or misunderstandings about the Third Market.

For many years, Walter invited me to participate in seminars at Columbia University run jointly by him and Sidney Robbins on current market structure issues. Several times he mentioned to me how much help Frank had been and how much he trusted Frank's knowledge, objectivity and honesty about the marketplace.

The "discovery" of the Third Market was one of the surprises of the study. And for good reason — up to then, neither the NYSE nor the Third Market makers had wanted to bring attention to it, though for obviously different reasons.

A snapshot of Weeden & Co. as of December 31, 1961 is provided by a memo from Norman Weeden written in early 1962.

- As of 12/31/61, Weeden & Co. had $7,187,000 in capital. It had five offices and 132 employees, 30 of whom were traders and salesmen. Their average age was 35 and they had on average been with the company for 12 years.
- There were 96 employees engaged in cashiering, bookkeeping and administrative activities, 17 male and 79 female. Their average time with Weeden was four years.
- The company had 232 shareholders, 65 percent of whom were employees and ex-employees. The profit-sharing trust owned 7 percent of the company.
- After 39 years, the firm's business was the same as at its inception: the trading of seasoned securities of interest to institutional and other professional investors.

---

[2]Both practices involved a splitting of commissions with others not involved in the trade, usually at the request of a mutual fund or other institution. The practice pointed up the excessive commissions being charged on large trades because of the minimum commission rule.

5

The Third Market

The real beginning of what the Special Study dubbed the "Third Market" is hard to pinpoint, as no records have been kept from those times. In 1962, my brother Alan Weeden wrote the following in an article for the *Yale Daily News*:

"Active off-board markets in securities formerly traded exclusively on an exchange was not a new concept. An overwhelmingly large proportion of high-grade securities, including government bonds, state and municipal bonds, most corporate bonds, bank and insurance company stocks and most preferred stocks, came to be traded in greater volume over the counter than on the exchange."

Frank Weeden, in a presentation titled "The Third Market: Past, Present and Future," recounted the early days of Weeden & Co. and how the Third Market evolved out of our bond-trading.

"While the designation 'Third Market' is relatively new, the practice has existed for many years. I recall the early 1920s in California, at which time the institutions confined their investments almost exclusively to bonds. A fairly active bond market prevailed on the exchanges in San Francisco and Los Angeles, but it was difficult to buy in any kind of size without having to wait a considerable period of time. Our first venture in trading listed securities was to accumulate odd lots of bonds and present them to banks and other institutions when we were able to offer a block.

"By the mid 1920s, the bond market was largely on the street. Local utility companies, principally the Pacific Gas & Electric Co. and Southern California Edison Co., were selling their preferred stocks to their customers, and this gave us an opportunity to maintain a secondary or over-the-counter market in utility preferreds. We found this type of security was beginning to have some appeal to institutions.

"In the 1930s, the utility holding company empire had disintegrated and the operating companies were financing through the sale of their common stocks. This caused several large non-member underwriting houses to develop an interest in trading utility commons and many institutions to begin buying them in a small way. There was a definite emergence of the off-board or Third Market at this time. Our development and interest have paralleled the increased interest and growth of the institutional market. We have increased the list of securities we trade as the institutions have increased the scope of their holdings. Their buying interest has been the main factor in determining our activity. Today there is a tremendous institutional interest in many types of industrial stocks."

This off-board trading of utility common stocks that slowly developed in the 1930s was fueled not only by the growing institutional interest, but also by the several thousand non-member brokers throughout the country recommending the local utility stock to their retail accounts. The fixed commission made it difficult for them to make anything on a listed stock until firms like American Securities and Weeden made their net markets available in small amounts, which enabled them to earn a commission that otherwise would have been paid to a member firm.

At the time, this business in utility stocks did not seem to concern the NYSE. Most of the specialists were assigned only one or two utility stocks, had no special understanding of their relative value, had no direct contact with the company or with the institutional investors (NYSE Rule 113), and had no way of hedging positions of size by shorting comparable companies. And because trading volume was usually modest, it was difficult to satisfy institutions looking for size. If Weeden bought 1,000 or 2,000 shares of Florida Power & Light (FPL) from a client, we would adjust our market in Florida Power Corp. (FDP) in order to balance the purchase of FPL with a short sale of FDP. We studied the relative value of all the utility stocks, would talk to our customers about how they felt and would thus have more confidence in assuming larger positions than the specialist would.

I remember someone from Lazard Freres phoning us one afternoon and saying they had a customer with 1,800 shares of Kansas City Power & Light (KLT). The specialist was making a hundred-share market. We said we'd pay 3/8 off the last sale net (meaning without a commission being charged) for his stock. Lazard came back and sold the block to us, saying that the specialist had no appetite for that kind of size and was pleased that Lazard found a place to park it. At the time, KLT might not trade for a day or so, so it was understandable for the specialist to not want that much inventory. Meanwhile, we went to an interested institutional account and they were pleased to pick up a block at the last sale net.

It was when we began making markets in the more active industrial common stocks that New York became concerned. Those were the stocks where the specialist made his money. That was in the late 1940s. At the time, total daily volume on the NYSE seldom exceeded 1 million shares. We started slowly, quoting markets in General Motors (GM), Standard of New Jersey (J), General Electric (GE) and a few other industrials. We had been encouraged to do so by some of the trust departments who did business with us in corporate bonds, preferreds and utility common stocks. Old Colony Trust in Boston was the most insistent, telling us they had lots of individual trust accounts owning these shares. They would add to them from time to time or sell small amounts for a variety of reasons having nothing to do with whether anyone thought the stock was going to go up or down. Old Colony Trust had no reason to use a broker and liked the convenience and lower cost of dealing with us net of commissions. A similar demand quickly developed with the non-member brokers who knew that our net markets, narrower than the two commissions charged on an exchange, enabled them to be competitive and yet earn all or part of the minimum commission. We found that we could normally attract enough buy and sell interest to be able to balance our positions without having to use the Exchange floor.

It was just this time that I began working in Weeden's New York office during summer breaks from Stanford. I was 18 in the summer of 1948 and remember well how good it felt to be able to go into a bar on West Eighth Street, order a beer and not have to lie about my age.

In 1948, Weeden's business was primarily in municipal bonds. Besides specializing in California names, we did an active business in issues that were quoted in dollar prices rather than basis points. All five of our offices participated — San Francisco, Los Angeles, Chicago, Boston and New York. We would buy in one office and sell in another; one of the tricks was to ship the bonds quickly so as to minimize interest loss caused by any delay in delivering beyond the settlement date. I was put in charge of developing a system for spotting where and when bonds were being delivered and making sure they got to the selling office pronto. We called it the "gadget," and I guess I did a pretty good job because I'm still with Weeden.

My brother Jack went to work for Weeden in our San Francisco office full time after graduating from Stanford in 1950, and Alan began working on the New York municipal desk about the same time. For two summers Alan and I played water polo for the New York Athletic Club. In 1950 we went to St. Louis with the team and placed third in the AAU outdoor meet held in the 50-meter pool at Busch Park.

As I started to say, Weeden began making markets in a few industrial common stocks in the late 1940s. At the time, volume on the NYSE was around 1 million shares a day. Market making in 50 or so utility common stocks still dominated our business during the 1950s, with the industrial stocks remaining secondary and experimental.

In 1952, NYSE volume had risen to 1.5 million shares per day, and would grow to 2,350,000 in 1956. Weeden also did a very good business in arbitraging the rights and "when issued" common shares connected to new issues by utility companies, which were then taking place with great frequency. I can remember our being active in five or more at one time. Our head trader, Billy Lee, was a master at the game and dominated the marketplace away from the Exchange floor.

I should explain this kind of financing, as it doesn't occur too frequently today. A utility company desiring additional capital would offer its shareholders rights to buy additional stock at a discount to the market. They would go to an investment banker, or bankers, to help set a price for the offering and to underwrite, or guarantee that the offering would be completed. Often those underwriting syndicates would include First Boston Corp. and Blyth, which would preclude those firms from participating in the arbitrage between the rights and the common stock. During the offering period, the trading of the rights and common would be transferred from the regular New York specialist to McDonnell & Co., another specialist, who would handle the flow coming from their members. Weeden generally monopolized the off-board flow, which sometimes was quite considerable because of the minimum commission structure on the NYSE. Not only was there a fixed commission per hundred, there was also an absolute minimum of $6 for any transaction, no matter how small it was. Thus, if an investor owned 100 shares and thereby received 100 rights but did not want to exercise them, he would pay a $6 commission selling on the Exchange, even though the value of the 100 rights may only be $20.

Consequently, many shareholders with rights looked to the off-board market, where no commissions were charged. Bank trust departments and custodial accounts were our biggest customers, since we would give them a net bid and separate confirmations for each account. At the same time we would offer the "when issued" shares of common net to the institutions, whose appetite for shares in these newly independent utility companies was considerable.

The American Telephone & Telegraph Co. (AT&T) was also raising money for its expansion needs, and it usually did so through the sale of rights to buy debentures convertible into common stock. Weeden had a field day with this three-way arbitrage. Billy enjoyed a very good reputation with the major institutions and helped us enormously in getting their support as we developed our Third Market activity. I remember our taking stacks of rights certificates every day to the Guaranty Trust Co. (which later merged with Morgan), along with confirmation slips showing our sales of "when issued" debentures, and then borrowing enough money to pay for the rights. Our loans from Guaranty sometimes exceeded $100 million by the end of the deal, establishing us as one of their largest and most profitable Wall Street accounts.

In addition, we had initiated a program of buying stock from employees who had participated in their company's stock purchase plan. Normally these were odd-lot purchases where the employee had no other stock ownership and no broker to go to. We would pay one-quarter off the last sale net with a small service charge. It was a very popular service, especially for the thousands of AT&T employees. The various corporations cooperated informally with us through the office of the treasurer to make it more convenient for the employees. In the case of AT&T, it might mean 100 to 200 transactions a day.

Some days we would accumulate 1,000 to 2,000 shares this way and then offer them to the institutional buyers. Some were astonished as to where we found all the stock. So one might say that as Weeden moved through the 1950s it was providing net markets to a wide range of investors in "Odd Lots, Round Lots and Blocks," which became our slogan when we began to advertise.

Looking back, 1948 was the defining year with respect to my long-term interest in Weeden & Co. I had spent some time in the San Francisco office between high school and when I entered Stanford, and over the years I'd listened to my father talk about the business at the dinner table. His stories always excited me, as much as a young kid can become excited about that sort of thing. Making split-second decisions about whether to buy or sell, the need to change directions suddenly, the uncertainty of what would happen next — it all required lightning-fast reactions, some smarts and complete confidence in one's abilities. It was like a game of water polo, or flying a jet — both of which I later became fairly proficient at. It seemed my cup of tea, and now that we were getting more involved in stocks I became even more excited.

Yet I spent almost eight years doing other things before I joined Weeden full time. Knowing there was a job for me there, I had the luxury of being able to take my time, look at other things and make sure it was what I really wanted.

First there was Stanford to get through. Even there I grew restless my junior year and spent six months on a Norwegian freighter working as a deck boy. I was the only American on board, which was challenging in itself. We sailed to Bombay, Lorenzo Marques in Portuguese East Africa, Trinidad and then to Baltimore (shades of the old man). I had wanted to end up in Europe, and when I found out we wouldn't be sailing there I decided to jump ship in Bombay and make my way overland. I made the jump but was talked into returning to the ship by some older and wiser Americans with whom I was having dinner. Just what I was thinking I'm not sure, because if you look at the map it's a long trip through very questionable and dangerous parts of the world. Such is the confidence and naiveté of youth.

As the *S.S. Janna*, a Liberty ship registered in Dramman, Norway, made its way through the south Atlantic, the Korean War started, and that event sent me in another direction. First I came back to New York

City, worked at Weeden, played water polo for the New York Athletic Club, and then returned to Stanford for my senior year.

I wanted to fly and was accepted into the U.S. Air Force air cadet program. They were slow in calling me up, and I spent six months at Yale Law School before getting my orders to report for training. Then it was four great years of flying the best planes in the world at the time: the F-86 Sabre jet, star of the Korean War, and then the F-86D all-weather interceptor. I was part of the first "dog" squadron assigned to Germany, where our mission was patrolling the Iron Curtain during bad weather and at night. While in Europe I met my first wife, a Swissair stewardess. After I was discharged we traveled for six months through much of the Middle East, living out of a Volkswagen bug. Then it was back to New York and full time at Weeden.

Prior to the publication of the Special Study of the Securities Markets, little was known about the Third Market. In 1955 we were maintaining markets in somewhat more than 100 stocks, divided evenly between industrial and utility names. First Boston, Blyth and American Securities were also making markets in approximately 50 utility common stocks. Others were making markets in industrial stocks for the broker-dealer community.

In Chapter 4 on the Special Study, I summarized its data comparing the Third Market volume with that of the NYSE and the regional exchanges. Even more interesting to us was how we compared to the other firms doing Third Market business.

At the core of Third Market activity were seven market makers doing 95 percent of the volume. While the Special Study did not name the seven, a process of deduction made it clear to us who they were.

There were Blyth & Co. and First Boston Corp., who made markets only in utility common stocks mainly with institutions and some high-net-worth individuals; and American Securities, who also made markets in utility stocks only but divided between institutions and non-member brokers. A.W. Benkert in New York, Stuart Miller in Chicago and J.S. Strauss in San Francisco made markets mainly in industrial common stocks. They served the growing interest of customers of the non-member brokers registered with the NASD.

Weeden straddled the fence and was all things to all people. We made the most markets, divided between utilities and industrials, in

"Odd Lots, Round Lots, and Blocks" available to non-member broker-dealers and institutional investors alike. The result was that Weeden & Co. dominated the data.

- In 1961, of the seven market makers, Weeden was the largest and made markets in 161 listed stocks. A.W. Benkert was next with 115, followed by Blyth and First Boston.
- In the three sample weeks covered by the Special Study, Weeden's transactions totaled 3,446 (48%) out of 7,180 total, and our shares traded were 361,720 (53%) of the 678,079 shares purchased and sold by the seven.
- In 1961, Weeden's average inventory in listed stocks totaled $11,534,000 and its average daily sales were $1,664,000, giving it a turnover rate of once every 6.9 days.
- During the three-week sample, Weeden's percentage of its total activity in NYSE listed stocks effected on the NYSE was 2.9%.
- Weeden's overall daily inventory of $11,534,000 in listed stocks compared to only $7,940,000 total for the other six market makers.
- Of Weeden's 3,446 trades done in the three-week sample, 2,792 comprised less than 100 shares while 38 were 1,000 shares or more.

The most interesting part of these figures was the size of our overnight inventory. It was very high in comparison with the inventory normally held by our competitors: the specialists and the much larger investment banking firms. These levels were not unusual for us, as we had learned to handle a large bond inventory over many years. But they also showed our determination "to get into this business," "to do the trade" and "to satisfy the customer." It was our way of countering the NYSE's efforts to degrade the value of our growing inroads into their marketplace.

We continued to believe it was best to keep a low profile and limit any publicity to the distribution of a list of those stocks in which we were prepared to quote a two-sided market net of commissions. But as the saying goes, the cat was now out of the bag. It was clear to everyone interested, the NYSE in particular, that the Third Market was a force to be reckoned with, despite the past efforts to restrain it.

6

Who Are These Weedens?

The message from Jim Jacques in 1959 had been more than a mere wake-up call for us at Weeden. I for one was angered at the NYSE's action against Municipal Securities as well as the implied threat to our business. My six months in law school gave me some appreciation of the legal issues, and I knew that what they were doing was plain wrong. This kind of arrogant behavior was reinforced by stories Frank had told me about the Multiple Trading Case of 1940, in which the NYSE tried to put the regional exchanges out of business. And I was around in 1948 when Blyth & Co. suddenly and mysteriously ceased trading listed industrial common stocks after announcing their intentions to do just that. Nevertheless, Frank felt at the time that market forces would determine the outcome, and that all we should do was continue to do our business quietly and without fanfare. Unfortunately, my four years of flying fighter planes had not trained me to be passive and unassertive.

Over the next few years, discussions of what to do dominated our family gatherings. Of course, there were differences in approach among the five Weedens, but I have to say no one in the family ever considered stepping back and getting out of the Third Market business. In fact, there was a shared determination to continue doing what we were doing and not be intimidated. If we had to fight for our rights, so be it.

I had always thought of my father and uncle as strong in character and determination but also mild mannered, modest in their aims, certainly not pushy, and quite sensitive to their standing in the industry.

After tracing their upbringing, I came to understand them better.

They were sons of a sea captain and grew up on a three-masted clipper ship that many times made the trip from coast to coast around Cape Horn or through the Strait of Magellan. As youngsters they sailed to all corners of the world, experiencing typhoons and smallpox epidemics, strange people and exotic ports. Their mother was always with them, teaching them their ABCs and keeping them out of trouble. Uncle Norman was actually born at sea, and the event was registered at their next port, Le Havre, France, making him a French citizen if he wished. (Uncle Norman told us with a straight face that he always avoided going to France because he was afraid they would take him and put him in their army for two years.) Norman was the precocious child of the two. When he was 3 and the ship was anchored in the port of Honolulu, the local newspaper wrote an article about him, noting his ability to spell such words as "hippopotamus."

Frank's first real experience at sea was the time they sailed into the middle of a typhoon in the South China Sea. He had been strapped to his bunk while they began weathering the turbulent seas, but his father brought him up on deck while they went through the "eye" so he could experience the strange light and quietude. Then he took Frank below again and strapped him into his bunk while they rode out the other side of the storm.

Another of Frank's childhood experiences was having his tonsils removed without anesthesia. Then there was the extreme poverty in the port of Manzanillo, Mexico, contrasted by the tall, gilded church at the end of the main street. There were visits to the old whaling port of Lahaina on Maui, and the opportunity to climb up into the crater of 10,000-foot Mt. Haleakala.

Life aboard ship was certainly an adventure for these two young boys. And while it must have been lots of fun, it also taught them the disciplines of a sailing ship, which required everything to be in its place and ready for any emergency or sudden shift in the wind. While Frank remembered having the run of the ship, being the captain's son, there were plenty of eyes keeping him in sight just in case he fell overboard. Those times together made Frank and Norman inseparable until Norman passed away in 1970.

Their father, Henry Frank Weeden, had grown up in Wallasey, near Liverpool, England, and began his sailing career as a young cadet on the *S.S. Savoir Faire*. In December 1872 they anchored in San Francisco

Bay, and young Henry, having been away from home now for four years, asked if he could go ashore. When the captain refused, Henry said "to hell with you!" and jumped ship. He was 17 years old.

Henry Frank became an American citizen and worked his way up through the ranks until he commanded his own ship. Returning to Wallasey, he married a childhood sweetheart, Mary Alice Dexter, and introduced her to life at sea. Eventually a third child was due, so they decided to settle down to a more normal life and bought a house in Alameda, California, across the bay from San Francisco.

This occurred sometime before the 1906 San Francisco earthquake. Frank, now 13, remembered having a narrow escape on the morning of the quake when the chimney of their house crashed through the roof and into the bed he normally slept in. He had decided to sleep outside on the porch the night before.

By this time Henry Frank had become captain of the Matson Line flagship the *S.S. Lurline*, which had become the premier ship for passengers traveling between San Francisco and Honolulu. Captain Weeden retired in 1913 after 63 trips between the two ports. In 1917 he returned to the sea as commander of a Navy transport ship during World War I. He was cited for heroism when his ship beat off a surfaced German submarine in a four-hour exchange of cannon fire at night in the mid-Atlantic. He died in 1927 of a heart attack at age 72.

My brother Bill remembers the captain well as a gregarious old gentleman who loved to entertain the neighborhood children with tales of life at sea. When his son Frank moved to St. Charles Street, two blocks away, the captain would often visit his daughter-in-law Mabel, who loved playing cards with him and had no objections when he would smoke a cigar and have a drink away from the disapproving eye of his wife of 40 years.

My mother's parents had similar experiences in their passage to California. Olaf Henrickson started his journeys as a young farm boy from the northern part of Öland, an island off the southeast coast of Sweden, and ended up as a laborer on the docks in San Francisco. Along the way he was shanghaied for a time, returning eventually to San Francisco. He was badly injured when a girder fell on his head, causing him to contract epilepsy in his later years. He worked his way into the job of port captain and spent the rest of his career guiding the incoming sailing ships through the Golden Gate Bridge and to anchor in the bay.

Sophia Nelson started off from the southern part of the same island as a girl of 17. She had recovered from typhoid fever and was sent off alone to find her brother, who was supposedly living in Butte, Montana. When she arrived there she was told he had moved on. She eventually found him in the growing Swedish community in San Francisco. There she also met Olaf, and the two were married around 1875.

The Henricksons lived in San Francisco on Greenwich Street, just west of Van Ness, a wide avenue running north-south and the point where they stopped the progress of the Great Fire from the aftermath of the 1906 earthquake. The couple had two daughters 18 years apart; my mother, Mabel Lillian, was the younger (she did not like the Mabel or Lillian, so she added Clarice when introducing herself). Mabel remembered, as a child of 9, helping her father ladle out soup to the many families who had lost their homes to the earthquake or fires on the other side of Van Ness. She was a tomboy who loved to play marbles with the boys in the vacant lot across the street and skate down California Street with a hockey stick between her legs. Soon after the earthquake, the Henricksons moved to Alameda — not too far, as it turned out, from the Weedens.

They say it's your genes that get you started, and your upbringing and environment do the rest. Looking back at the early upbringing of my parents and grandparents, they appear to have enjoyed some very solid qualities, and gained a good amount of independence and self-reliance. Growing up aboard ship or during the Gold Coast days of San Francisco was a good test of one's mettle, as was leaving your home and traveling halfway across the world. Much of what they became was well honed by the time the Weedens and Henricksons ended up in Alameda. It would be almost 10 years before these two families came to know one another.

Frank and Norman both attended Alameda High. Norman graduated, but Frank slipped away to work in the oil fields around Taft, the fruit orchards south of Fresno and the lumber camps in Humboldt County in northern California. He was a restless youth and in later years prided himself on being a high school dropout. The Weedens, incidentally, had a younger son, Dexter, who also worked at Weeden & Co. until his death in 1928 at age 25 from appendicitis.

My mother also left school early. Her father had to be placed in a Masonic home because of his epilepsy, and this put a strain on the family finances. Her older sister, my aunt Charlotte, worked at Fireman's

Fund Insurance Co. as a cashier, but her income was not enough to make ends meet. So in her junior year at Alameda High, Mabel quit and also went to work at Fireman's Fund, as a file clerk.

It was on the daily commute to San Francisco by ferry boat that my father first spotted Mabel. They met, and though Mother was a very attractive blond with several beaus at the time, Frank persisted. She married him at the tender age of 19.

In 1912, when he was 19, Frank had gotten a job with Louis Sloss & Co., a family investment firm. He soon rose to become office manager. The next year the firm was dissolved, and the four salesmen opened their own investment firm, Blyth Witter, with Frank joining them as their first salesman. The four partners — Charles Blyth, Dean Witter, Lou Shuertleff and George Leib — came to have long and distinguished careers as bankers in the securities industry. Dean Witter's name is still prominently displayed today as part of the Morgan Stanley firm.

Frank told the story of going to Dean when the stock exchanges closed for six months at the beginning of World War I and asking for a leave of absence to work in the lumber camps until business got better. Dean was delighted to accommodate, and also quick to take Frank back when business improved. Frank helped start their municipal bond department, spent a year as an officer in the Navy, and then in 1921 went out on his own to form Bradford Weeden. In 1922, the two Weeden brothers bought out Bradford and started Weeden & Co. with two friends from Alameda.

From what I've been told by my brother Bill, the Frank Weedens were socially active in the 1920s, hobnobbing with the Witters from Piedmont, Herbert Hills (Hills Bros. coffee) and other prominent people around the bay. But as the Depression deepened, they settled into a more modest lifestyle focused on their four sons and the need to keep Weeden & Co. on firm footing. (In reviewing Weeden's annual reports going back to its incorporation, it wasn't until 1952 that annual revenues returned to 1928 levels.)

When I came along in 1930, the two grandfathers had passed away and everyone else, including Uncle Norman and Aunt Charlotte, was living in Alameda.

By then Alameda was one of the many bedroom communities serving Oakland and San Francisco. As an island, its access consisted of two bridges at the east end and the ferry boats that ran back and forth to Market Street in San Francisco. Eventually a tube was built running under the estuary at the west end, connecting to downtown Oakland. Alameda's location made it a back eddy community, away from the growing population corridors.

Alameda's population was something more than 30,000, mostly middle-income, middle-class families living on modest quarter-acre lots. It attracted hardly anyone you could call rich, and the poor were few and far between. The residents were mostly Caucasian, reflecting the earlier waves of immigrants from northern Europe. An Italian community owned the truck farms, and Japanese worked as gardeners and household help. In addition, there were a few Chinese, Blacks and some Hispanics. That was pretty much the environment into which my parents settled, and it remained that way through World War II.

Alameda is flat as a pancake, and is basically a large sandbar. Its highest point is less than 10 feet above high tide. It had a seawall running along the southern edge with steps cut into it leading down to the edge of San Francisco Bay. At low tide the mud flats extended 100 to 200 yards into the bay and contained a treasure trove of exciting things for the young and curious.

In 1926, Frank Weeden had moved his family to a solidly built house of 3,500 square feet on the standard quarter-acre lot. It was only four houses away from the bay on a dead-end street shaded by large elms, chestnuts and sycamores. This quiet cul-de-sac was protected on all sides by friendly neighbors, accessible back yards, and the ebb and flow of the tides against the seawall. It was the center of the world for the four Weeden sons.

It was similar in many ways to life aboard a sailing ship. The Weedens were reasonably well off — live-in servants, a laundry woman, gardeners and others contributing to the daily maintenance of the house — yet there was no pretentiousness in the air. Frank was acutely aware of the difficult times most people were experiencing and fully supported the government's efforts to solve the country's economic problems. Yes, there was a month in the summer spent at the Russian River or at the Mount Diablo Country Club, Frank's visits to Weeden offices in other cities and mother's trips abroad with one or another of the children or her friends. But for the most part St. Charles Street was the center of our lives. Seldom did the family go to San Francisco, participate in cultural events, or visit museums and the like. Fancy restaurants were not our cup of tea, although the original Trader Vic's in Oakland was a popular stopping-off place dating back to the days of Prohibition.

Dinner at home was around the breakfast table. Uncle Norman would come over for a game of dominoes with mom and dad, or hearts when the boys were included. Sunday nights spent in Frank's room listening to Jack Benny, Fred Allen or *One Man's Family* was our family entertainment during the 1930s and '40s.

My parents were very solid, low key and down to earth. They were also very independent, and through their example they encouraged their sons to be the same.

Thus, my father was many things to me and someone I admired throughout his life. Not only was he a good father, he was my swimming coach, later my boss, a respected leader in his industry, an independent thinker, honest to the bone, and a Wall Streeter who thought Roosevelt a great man. He loved youth and preferred their company over that of his own age group. He spent untold hours teaching young children in the neighborhood how to swim, and he created a successful program for making every kindergarten child in Alameda water safe. He also considered himself a ladies' man. He loved to dance and flirt, and had been married 67 years when he passed away at 91.

Uncle Norman was five years younger than Frank. While Frank was outgoing and gregarious, Norman was quieter, more introspective and intellectual. Norman was also quite religious; many of his close friends were members of the Episcopal ministry. In some ways you might say Norman grew up in the shadow of his older brother, yet there was never any indication of tension, jealousy or antagonism between the two. In fact, they seemed to be especially good friends with mutual respect for one another. Frank always told people that Norman was much smarter, and I think everyone agreed. Norman had a much better eye for the value of bonds, which Frank always respected. They understood each other so well that sometimes they made an important decision together by a mere nod of the head.

It was in this atmosphere of a close family, a friendly neighborhood and a climate that was mild but invigorating that the four of us were raised. The area surrounding our house on St. Charles Street was filled with kids of all ages, with each of us having our own gang challenging one another and irritating the older folks with our noise and pranks.

Our elementary, middle and high schools (all public) were within walking distance or a short bike ride. City parks with slides, swings, merry-go-round, baseball diamond and even tennis courts were within a stone's throw. We knew every back yard for five blocks on either side of our house and the easiest back fences for moving quickly from one street to another. After school we played in the streets or explored the mud flats until dinnertime or later. Most of the time our parents seemed indifferent to our whereabouts. This environment encouraged us to be independent and creative. Freedom to do what I wanted is something I've felt from my earliest years. Mowing the lawn and making my bed were the only chores I remember.

Ten years separated the four of us. Bill was the oldest; Alan was four years younger than Bill, Jack came three years after Alan, and I was three years younger than Jack. We all attended Alameda High School, with some 2,200 students, and made swimming our major sport. Alan, Jack and I all were elected student body president in our senior year.

All of us worked during the summer and waited on tables during the school year. Actually, I started my first summer job in 1942 when I was barely 12, working as a dishwasher at Camp Curry in Yosemite Valley Park. (I told them I was 14 years old.) I worked in the valley for five years until 1947, when I spent that summer working at Weeden & Co.'s San Francisco office.

We were all good students, with fairly high IQs, and attended Stanford, following our brother Bill. At Stanford, sports, fraternity life and girls rounded out our "halcyon days on the farm" (the Leland Stanford, Jr. university "farm," that is). The three of us studied economics (the theoretical kind taught in undergraduate school) while Bill went on to medical school, the army and various residencies before settling down to practice in Oakland.

Jack had taken first place in the 100-meter backstroke at the national AAU swimming meet while still in high school. Then he joined the navy for two years. Alan started at Stanford in 1942, left for the navy and ended up as an officer in an underwater demolition unit (frogman) in the Pacific. This caused the three of us to end up at Stanford together, living in the same fraternity house (Zeta Psi) and finally getting to know each other in a way the three years' separation had prevented. Jack and I had been fairly close as kids growing up, and Jack and Alan saw a lot of each other when they were both nationally ranked backstroke swimmers. We also roomed together at the firm's apartment at 14 W. Ninth St. in New York when we were working at Weeden during the summer.

But it was in 1947, after the Senior AAU outdoor swimming meet in Tyler, Texas, that Alan, Jack and I really came to know one another. It was during a three-week trek on the John Muir Trail, which runs some

220 miles along the crest of the Sierra Nevada Range on the eastern edge of California. It starts at Whitney Portal in the south and makes its way north over 13 passes, some more than 13,000 feet high, to the Yosemite Valley. Food had to be carried on your back or caught in the streams and lakes along the way. It was up and down, up and down every day. By the time we reached Yosemite we had a pretty good idea of each other's basic traits. We found ourselves definitely different from each other, but at the same time there were a lot of solid similarities that would prove valuable at Weeden come the 1960s and '70s. None of us were rocket scientists, nor particularly driven individuals, but we were each smart in our own way. We were achievers of sorts, with the confidence that comes from success in athletics, social acceptance and exposure to military service. What I would call the "California spirit" — social equality, exuberance for life and open-mindedness — was something we all carried with us as we slowly moved back to New York City. In many ways it was akin to the experiences and attitudes of our family's prior generations.

The move to New York City and to Weeden & Co. varied in time for each of us. I think it's safe to say that all of us were "laid back" regarding our career paths. We felt Weeden & Co. was always there for any of us who cared to go that route. I believe Alan and Jack had other agendas in mind besides Weeden, but circumstances were such that they both accepted Frank's entreaties to join the firm.

It was 1956 when the three of us finally came together in the New York office. We took our jobs seriously, worked hard and found ourselves in sync on our basic response to the NYSE.

Brothers Frank and Norman Weeden on the clipper *S.S. Marion Chilcott*, 1901

Henry Frank Weeden, clipper ship captain, circa 1900

Frank Weeden, U.S. Navy, 1917

NEW INVESTMENT HOUSE OPENED.

San Francisco.—Another important investment firm has been launched in this city under the name of Weeden & Co. with offices on the fifth floor of the Insurance Exchange Building.

Associated in the new concern are Frank Weeden, until recently of the firm of Bradford, Weeden & Co., and Norman Weeden, his brother. Both are bond men of long experience on the Coast. Their new association together forms the first between brothers in a single concern here.

Frank Weeden began his career here in 1912 with Louis Sloss & Co. and later became a member of the staff of Blyth, Witter & Co. with which house he served until 1917, when he went into the service in the war.

Returning from service, Mr. Weeden reestablished himself in the investment business with Carstens & Earles, from which firm he withdrew upon the formation of Bradford, Weeden & Co.

In the present move Mr. Weeden has sold out all his interests in the Bradford-Weeden house.

Mr. Norman Weeden has had extensive experience with both Blyth-Witter and R. H. Moulton houses.

Associated with the new firm in the venture, among others, are Sherman Asche and Edward Durst, bond salesmen.

The new house will deal in a general line of securities.

FRANK WEEDEN.

NORMAN WEEDEN.
—Photo by Boyé

These brothers have formed the new San Francisco investment house of Weeden & Co.

"New Investment House Opened," reprint of article in *Coast Banker*, February 1922

Weeden & Co. stock certificate, 1927

NEW ISSUE

$3,000,000
Golden Gate Bridge and Highway District

(Embracing all of the City and County of San Francisco, Marin, Sonoma, and
Del Norte Counties and portions of Napa and Mendocino Counties, California)

Series B 4¾% Bonds

Dated July 1, 1933   To be due July 1, 1942 to 1971

Principal and semi-annual interest (January 1 and July 1) to be payable in lawful money of the United States at the Bank of America, N. T. & S. A.,
San Francisco and at the Manufacturers Trust Company, New York City. Coupon bonds in denominations of $1,000, with privilege of registration
as to both principal and interest.

Exempt from all present Federal Income Taxes
Exempt from California Personal Property Tax
Legal Investments for Savings Banks and Trust Funds in California

These bonds in the opinion of counsel are general obligations of the District and are payable, to the
extent that revenues of the District are insufficient therefor, from ad valorem taxes upon all of the
property taxable by the District. The Bridge and Highway District Act specifically provides that
taxes for District purposes shall be levied by county authorities and shall be collected in the time,
form and manner that county or city and county taxes are collected. The Act further provides that
such taxes shall be a lien of the same force and effect as other liens for taxes and their collection may
be enforced by the same means as provided for the enforcement of liens for county taxes.

Circular available on request.

Legality to be approved by Messrs. Orrick, Palmer & Dahlquist, San Francisco, and Messrs. Masslich & Mitchell, New York City

Amount	Maturities	Yield	Amount	Maturities	Yield
$15,000 each year	July 1, 1942 to 1944	4.75%	$30,000 each year	July 1, 1950 to 1951	4.95%
15,000 each year	July 1, 1945 to 1946	4.80	75,000 each year	July 1, 1952 to 1956	5.00
30,000	July 1, 1947	4.80	105,000 each year	July 1, 1957 to 1961	5.00
30,000 each year	July 1, 1948 to 1949	4.85	135,000 each year	July 1, 1962 to 1966	5.00

$240,000 due each year July 1, 1967 to 1971 to yield 5.00%

Blyth & Co., Inc.   Bankamerica Company
Dean Witter & Co.   Weeden & Co.
Incorporated

All statements made herein are believed by us to be correct but are not guaranteed.

Tombstone: $3,000,000 Golden Gate Bridge and Highway District bonds, 1933

Home of Frank and Mabel Weeden at 1236 St. Charles St., Alameda, California, 1926 to 1990.

The Frank Weeden family in the back yard of the family home, late 1940s. Left to right: Alan, Don, Mabel, Jack, Frank, Patty (Bill's wife) and Bill.

Jack, Don and Alan Weeden in Yosemite Valley, 1947

U.S. Air Force fighter pilot First Lieutenant Don Weeden (lower right), West Germany, 1954

7

Rule 394

The report of the Special Study of the Securities Markets was issued in May of 1963 and precipitated a number of events affecting the Third Market. I have already mentioned its possible impact on the decision of the U.S. Supreme Court in the *Silver* case. Its publication also attracted other dealers to the Third Market, some quite substantial participants in the market for over-the-counter stocks. Jefferies & Co. began its business sometime in this period, concentrating on the less-active industrial stocks, acting primarily as agent where they would bring a large buyer and seller together away from the NYSE. Others limited themselves entirely to crossing blocks, committing no capital at all, and came to be known as the Fourth Market.

The NYSE obviously studied the data closely and responded in a number of ways. A study they had made back in 1955 found that 20.4 percent of commercial bank share volume done on the Exchange was done as intermediary for private investors. The Special Study showed a similar percentage was being done in the Third Market. Later in 1963, the NYSE distributed an 11-page memo to banks titled "Making the Best Use of the New York Stock Exchange Market."

Their memo argued that getting a print on the ticker tape of the NYSE was very important, that if everyone used the off-board market there would be no market at all, and that many times, if you are patient enough and opened up to your broker, you could end up getting a better price on the Exchange.

Our response was to print the section from the Special Study on the

Third Market in its entirety and mail it out to everyone we could think of.

It was at about the same time that two of our good customers, First National City Bank and Irving Trust Co., on almost the same day, notified us that they would no longer be using our markets in listed stocks. The powers that be had determined that they had a responsibility to support the "central market" — that is, the NYSE. They told their trading desk, "You can never be sure that you are getting the best price in the Third Market. Besides, we'll never be criticized by doing a trade on the NYSE." (This was true until Abe Pomerantz began questioning their practices in court in the late 1960s.) In private discussions later with those on their trading desks, we were told that the banks were being threatened with the withdrawal of all member-firm deposits, obviously important to their commercial bank profitability, if they persisted in using the Third Market.

Frank talked to Foster Cooper, the head trader at First National, who liked us and was quite uncomfortable with the decision of his bank. Frank and Foster worked out an arrangement that allowed us to continue doing their odd lots by pricing our net execution one-quarter off the next sale on the Exchange exactly the same way the odd-lot specialist operated. Thus, the bank's customer would be saving the entire commission without question.

Weeden's Ben Rundquist had the job of recording every "tick" in those stocks we made markets in, so we could tell our customer what the last sale was before we quoted a market to him. When the market was active, Ben looked like a one-armed paper-hanger trying to keep up. Ben thought he should get paid time and a half during these busy periods, but Frank was unconvinced.

Some days we would do 50 to 100 trades with First National City Bank, all in odd lots. Yet it was several years before First National joined the growing number of banks using our markets in round lots and blocks as well.

Ed Sinclair was our principal industrial stock trader at the time. He had been a trader with Weeden for a number of years, starting out making markets in utility stocks while Billy Lee handled the arbitrage situations as they came along. Ed was the spitting image of Humphrey Bogart, lived on Long Island and for a long time commuted into New York City with his close neighbor and friend, Sandy Weill (now head of Citigroup). Ed was a good-natured, relaxed trader who wanted to do the business and was perfect for taking on the more volatile industrial common stocks that were being slowly added to our list. I can still see Eddie, talking on the phone and hearing someone call out that ABC Bank wanted a 1,000-share market in XYZ. Almost without even looking up, Eddie would raise his right hand and wiggle it back and forth, signifying to the salesman to quote the market a quarter point on either side of the last sale net of any commissions. Ben would call out "last sale XYZ at one-half" and the salesman would relay our market one-quarter bid, offered at three-quarters, 1,000 shares either way. For the trader at the bank desk or the partner at the investment advisory firm, he knew that whatever side of the market he was on he would be saving a good portion of the commission that would be charged by a member broker going to the floor, and maybe all the commission or even more than that depending on what the specialist was willing to do. Eddie made it so easy, so consistently, that it was only because the institution felt it had obligations elsewhere that would cause it not to do the business with us.

As we traded more and more stocks, we added others to our trading desk, but it was Ed Sinclair who made it easy to do business with Weeden.

It was the Special Study that first brought the NYSE's Rule 394 to our attention.

Rule 394 read in its entirety:

"Except as otherwise specifically exempted by the Exchange, members and member organizations must obtain permission of the Exchange before effecting a transaction in a listed stock off an exchange, either as principal or agent."

As then interpreted, Rule 394 prohibited a member of the Exchange from buying or selling nearly all Exchange-listed common stocks in the over-the-counter market, even if an over-the-counter dealer could provide a better price than was available on the Exchange.

Rule 394 had been filed with the SEC in 1957 along with a general revision and renumbering of their rules, at a time when SEC policy was "to express neither approval nor disapproval of rule changes" (Seligman, *The Transformation of Wall Street*, p. 272).

It turns out that Blyth's announcement in 1948 had triggered a change in policy. At that time, member firms' Circular #52 effectively said the same as its replacement, Rule 394, but approval was given quite readily when a utility stock was involved. A 1965 SEC staff study found that from June 1948 to May 1949, "705 (82 percent) requests for approval for off-board trades were granted of 857 applications received," or almost three every trading day. But in 1956, according to testimony by a NYSE staff member, "In view of the present attitude of the governors ... the staff does not approve *any* requests during trading hours" (ibid., p. 389).

Frank's reaction when the Rule 394 issue first came to light was to continue to do our business quietly. "Let's not get in a public fight with the 600-pound gorilla," he said. "Our business is growing nicely. Let's keep our head down in the foxhole as much as we can."

The Special Study had obliquely expressed its concern over Rule 394 by asserting that "restrictions on members doing business away from the primary market ... may sometimes motivate other than best executions from the customers' viewpoint." ... "Among the subjects that appear to need further and continuous attention ... are ... factors contributing to or detracting from the public's ready access to all markets and its assurance of obtaining the best execution of any particular transactions" (ibid., p. 390).

That was where the issue rested until May 1964, when Chase Manhattan Bank applied for and received listing on the NYSE. At the time, and ever since the 1929 crash, almost all bank stocks were traded in the over-the-counter market. Prior to the crash, most of the leading bank stocks were actively traded on the NYSE and had been leaders in the speculative frenzy during the late 1920s. It was when they also led the market downward, causing widespread public concern about their deposits and large-scale withdrawals, that many felt bank stocks should be delisted and removed from the glare of publicity. Thirty years later, Chase Manhattan Bank, sensing renewed public interest and desirous of increasing its capitalization through a public offering, accepted the NYSE invitation to relist.

This move to the NYSE would have elicited no more attention than other over-the-counter stocks moving to the Big Board, except for the reaction of M.A. Schapiro & Co., the leading bank stock trading and underwriting firm. Their business was solely in bank stocks, and their customers were evenly divided between institutions and the broker-dealer community, primarily members of the NYSE.

As soon as Chase listed, under Rule 394, Merrill Lynch and all other member firms who had a long-standing relationship with M.A. Schapiro were prevented from using its market in Chase. Needless to say, Morris Schapiro, a strong, tough, well-respected and successful member of the investment community, was outraged, feeling this was a classic case of "a conspiracy in restraint of trade" prohibited under the Sherman Act. And he was right.

When the NYSE refused M.A. Schapiro's request that Chase be placed on the exempt list (meaning that NYSE firms could still deal with Schapiro off-board), Morris made it known that he intended to file suit against the NYSE. He was immediately in touch with the Justice Department's Antitrust Division through his law firm of Cadwallader, Wickersham & Taft and their partner George Reycraft, who had been part of the Antitrust Division before entering private practice. Morris also contacted Weeden, whom he recognized as the leading Third Market maker.

Morris soon took out a full-page ad in the *New York Times* and the *Wall Street Journal* describing this injustice, and then circulated a proposed brief he had readied for filing against the NYSE. (He never did bring his complaint to the courts.)

Morris was anxious to have Weeden join with him in the lawsuit, and it was only after much internal debate that we declined. We told him that while we had a strong interest in seeing Rule 394 removed, we felt that our joining with him was not quite right because we could not claim that a business relationship was being "taken away from us." Our Third Market activity up to now did not include any trading with NYSE members, except for a few isolated situations. Frank also felt that it would cause a bad reaction from some of our friends on the Street, and Alan pointed out that we were trying to get into the underwriting business, and we were bidding jointly on municipal bond issues with many member firms. We all agreed that litigation was not the way to challenge the establishment. We ought to just quietly keep trying to offer a competitive service and a lower price, and let it go at that.

Frank's caution was probably right at the time, but it was hard for me to remain quiet. In 1964 I was 34 years old and not used to being pushed around by anyone — except my older brothers, of course. *New York Times* economic policy reporter Eileen Shanahan had just reported, on October 13, 1964, on the "cordial meeting" held "privately" between the SEC commissioners and the top officials of the NYSE at which "Funston seared the Third Market," accusing us of "dumping" securities into the market and selling stock short. I felt someone had to reply. Inasmuch as Weeden had become the unofficial spokesman for the Third Market, that responsibility fell on our shoulders. Frank again felt that such counter-punching only drew further attention to their accusations and could well be counterproductive at this stage in the game. "And besides," he told me, "such accusations only highlight the NYSE's concern about our growing inroads into their core business. The less said, the better." Nevertheless, the article rankled me, and 40 years later I can still see the photo of one of their members with the caption "Opponent of the Third Market," stern, establishment and righteous.

Meanwhile, Morris' threat triggered the SEC into trying to work out a solution acceptable to him. We participated in many meetings with a number of the SEC staff while Frank developed a friendly relationship with Manuel Cohen, who had been appointed chairman of the SEC by President Johnson in the summer of 1964. Frank felt confident that Manny understood the important economic role we were playing in forcing change on the NYSE, and that he would do the right thing.

Let's take a moment to reflect on the SEC under Manuel Cohen. According to Joel Seligman, "Manny," as everyone knew him, came up from 22 years in the ranks and shared the Commission's "less than enthusiastic devotion to the antitrust law's economic theory of competition" (*The Transformation of Wall Street*, p. 350). Manny's conservative views saw the NYSE as "the envy of the world, far preferable to the more fragmented securities markets then common in Europe" (ibid., p. 351).

Manny was a "consensus builder" and "an advocate of cooperative regulation" (ibid., p. 360). "New rules" must have the "cooperation of the industry" (p. 357); "a concern that a purely antitrust approach to the structure of the securities might remove an SEC responsibility to federal courts less familiar with securities regulation" (p. 358). "In July 1965, in a letter to Senate Banking Committee Chairman Willis Robertson, Chairman Cohen suggested that the exchanges be accorded a full antitrust immunity in areas subject to SEC review" (p. 386).

Later in his term, Chairman Cohen would become a votary of securities industry competition and regulatory activism (ibid., p. 360). But when Rule 394 was before the Commission, he was no friend of competition, the Third Market or Weeden & Co.

When Morris Schapiro visited the SEC and told them of his intentions to file suit against the NYSE, the SEC ordered a comprehensive staff investigation of Rule 394. Over the next six months, Gene Rotberg, then chief counsel of the SEC's Office of Policy Planning, directed an inquiry that took approximately 2,000 pages of transcript, including extensive documentary materials from the NYSE. In September 1965, a 211-page staff report on Rule 394 was circulated within the Commission. It was endorsed by SEC General Counsel Philip Loomis and Division of Trading and Markets Director Irving Pollack.

After considering all the arguments put forward by the NYSE, the report predicted that 394 would be held illegal under the *Silver* case's application of the antitrust laws.

It went on to recommend two solutions: 1) allow a member firm to deal with a Third Market dealer off-board when the price offered was better than the specialist's, or 2) charge only one commission on a member order done with a Third Market dealer on the floor of the Exchange. In November, the NYSE rejected both solutions in a private meeting with the commissioners. The staff wanted to publish their report for public comment, but the five commissioners refused, and it wasn't until six years later that Morris was successful in his suit to have it published under the Freedom of Information Act. (In *The Transformation of Wall Street*, Joel Seligman comments that "The SEC's response to its staff report represented the rock bottom low point of the Cohen commission" (p. 393)).

Some will say that Chairman Cohen, in his desire to be a "consensus builder" and advocate of "cooperative regulation," could not stand up to his conservative colleagues on the Commission plus an adamant and unyielding NYSE. Chairman Cohen was characterized by those closest to him as having a "limitless faith in his ability to talk anybody into anything" (ibid., p. 355). Unfortunately, while my father, Frank, along with the rest of us at Weeden, was one of those, the NYSE was not. After some 10 additional months of negotiation with the SEC, the NYSE proposed Rule 394(b), in which the language was softer and the process seemingly more favorable to an interaction between all parties: the Third Market dealer, member broker and the floor. However, bottom line, the NYSE still kept tight control of such trades in the hands of the floor governors, whose interests were to minimize such activity.

Throughout this time, Frank believed that he had an excellent relationship with Manny Cohen. Manny was anxious to do whatever was possible to solve this problem equitably, but he insisted that 394(b) was a solution that everyone should be willing to accept and persuaded Frank to go along. Some of us at Weeden thought it no real change at all, but unless we were prepared to join Schapiro in a lawsuit, we had to live with it.

We not only lived with it, but tried our damnedest to make it work. In the year following its publication in October 1966, Weeden completed 55 trades under the Rule, less than 1 percent of our Third Market volume for the period. The next year, the volume under Rule 394(b) declined to insignificance. (As a footnote, Rule 390, which replaced 394(b), was modified periodically over the years, but was only abolished in 2001, 35 years later.)

In 1966, Weeden's Third Market business was still growing at a faster rate than volume on the NYSE. This was due primarily to increased trading activity by the institutions in larger and larger sizes and their growing recognition of our value as an alternate liquidity source.

At this point in time, the issues of fixed commissions, give-ups and institutional membership had not been raised. All we talked about was Rule 394, fragmentation, unequal regulation and non-disclosure.

Should we have joined Morris Schapiro in challenging the NYSE in court? Who knows! Litigation was not our style. We were doing all right. Understanding and respect for our way of doing business was growing. We decided not to alter our game plan, although changes within the management structure of Weeden would alter many things within the next two years.

8

A Time of Transition

When I came to Weeden full time in October 1956, Alan and Jack had been with the firm for more than five years. Alan had readily settled into our municipal bond department and became head of it about the time I arrived. He attracted additional traders to our New York office, Bill Simon and Bob Tighe from Eastman Dillon Union Securities, and concentrated on the underwriting of new issues. Almost all municipal bond underwritings were competitively bid. It took a good sense of the market and the relative value of the issue to bid high enough to win but low enough to attract buyers. Our active trading in the secondary market provided Alan with a good perspective on the market's current level, and Weeden was looked to by other members of the syndicate for direction on pricing. Eventually, we joined with the other firms active in the secondary market, such as Salomon Brothers and Morgan Guaranty Trust Co., forming what became known as the "Guerilla Group," comprising several of the leading trading houses. The group was knowledgeable, aggressive and flexible and took much of the new-issue activity away from the larger but more cumbersome syndicates led by such firms as First National City Bank, Chase Manhattan Bank and Bank of America.

Jack worked out of San Francisco at first and then came to New York. He enjoyed the money, clearing and operational end of the business, and Frank had him overseeing all of that activity when I arrived. A bit of nepotism, you might say, but both Alan and Jack were clearly good at what they did. Alan became highly respected on the Street and was critical to Weeden's becoming known as a leading national bond dealer and eventually a major bracket firm in all municipal bond underwritings. Jack became our computer expert and was later influential in establishing continuous net clearing throughout the industry.

Frank ran the business and set strategy, determined bonuses, and hired and fired. Unfortunately, firing was not his cup of tea, which led to some critical jobs remaining in the hands of old and loyal employees who were not up to the changing ways on Wall Street.

The board was composed of Frank, my uncle Norman and three long-time employees working in our West Coast offices. While the three had been with the firm for more than 20 years — one since our founding in 1922 — none represented our rapidly growing Third Market activity and our national presence in the bond market.

This situation began to create some tension between the two generations of Weedens, egged on by the more aggressive employees on the New York municipal desk.

Issues such as use of capital, stock ownership, bonus allocations, long-term strategy and composition of the board found the three of us many times in strong disagreement with Frank. As our mother, Mabel, would lament, family gatherings at Thanksgiving and Christmas always seemed to deteriorate into squabbles across the dinner table on how to run Weeden & Co.

In frustration, the three of us took to meeting at the Downtown Athletic Club for dinner to plan a united front in our confrontations with Frank. Alan, as the eldest, took on the task of relaying our ideas to Frank, one which he did not find pleasant at all. Not that we three didn't have differences of opinion among ourselves. One issue we disagreed on was Alan's desire to have the three of us present Frank an ultimatum to relinquish control of the firm, with Alan becoming president and CEO. I'm not sure exactly when this idea first surfaced (probably the early 1960s), nor why I was reluctant to go along with it then. Perhaps it was my judgment that it would not be well received by those on the stock side of Weeden, or, perhaps, I had illusions of ultimately running the firm myself. Anyway, nothing along those lines occurred until 1967.

By 1967 the business emanating from the New York office, both in bonds and stocks, constituted well over 50 percent of our revenues. Frank was 75 and all but retired, spending most of his time at home in Alameda, building swimming pools and teaching kindergarten kids to be water safe. He had installed a teletype machine in his closet at home and read all that was going on around the Weeden circuit, but it was time to leave the running to others. This time I agreed that we should press to have the baton of leadership passed on to the younger generation. After all, we were not getting any younger. Alan was 43, Jack 40 and I was 37. We enlisted the support of Norman, and Frank agreed to make Alan president and CEO, Jack executive vice president and me a vice president. The three of us agreed among ourselves to run the firm as a team (Frank jokingly referred to "the Troika"), and Alan assured me that he was not interested in running the firm for more than five years.

So it went, until Jack contracted a severe case of hepatitis and had to give up running the day-to-day operations. This caused a confrontation between Alan and me as to which of us should assume that additional responsibility. I was then in charge of our stock business. Of course, I felt I was more suitable; but Alan felt that if I had both jobs, I would be viewed as running the firm. That would not be understood or acceptable to the bond people, the Street in general or to Alan personally, since he was the elder brother and better known and respected. By this time our Third Market activity was beginning to dominate and I had convinced myself that I would be better at running the firm, knowing this end of the business as well as having had experience on the bond desk. Alan wouldn't hear of it. Frank still felt more comfortable with Alan as CEO, feeling he was less disruptive in his style and demeanor. So Alan took over operations and I was named chairman of the board in April 1970 as a way of assuaging my ego.

9

From Passive to Active

Rule 394(b) was a non-starter — a disaster, in fact. The NYSE won that round hands down. We now realized we were in a tough game and that we could no longer remain passive. Still, our business was growing nicely. In 1966, Third Market dollar volume equated to 2.9 percent of the NYSE volume, up from 2 percent in 1961 when the Special Study first collected data.

Shortly after Rule 394(b) was promulgated, Frank was asked to speak before an American Management Association Briefing Session held at the New York Hilton. His subject was "The Third Market: Past, Present and Future," which we made into a little pamphlet and mailed to a lot of people.

In the July 1967 issue of *Institutional Investor* Magazine, Frank was featured in their lead article. Gil Kaplan had started the magazine that year; it quickly became the forum for exposing industry issues and trends through its articles and conferences, and it helped accelerate the push for change. The article on Frank provided added exposure to the Third Market and the leading role played by Weeden.

Then in November 1968, Weeden was asked to give testimony before an SEC hearing on stock exchange commission rates. Since I was head of stock trading, the job fell to me.

The SEC hearing occurred less than a week after I lost my race for the congressional seat from the 19th District in New York.

In 1965, during evenings and on weekends, I had worked for the John Lindsay mayoral campaign as his coordinator in the 67th Assembly District, which ran south of 14th Street to Houston and East of the Bowery. After his election I remained active in the district. In 1968 the Republicans had no one from the regulars willing to run for Congress, so, with the family's agreement, I accepted Republican chief Vince Albano's appointment to the role on the condition I would be willing to spend some of my own money for the cause. Stock I owned in National Semiconductor had recently shot up nicely, and, with the help of my brothers, I spent about $150,000 along with contributions from members of the Wall Street community. In 1962 I had joined the board of National Semiconductor, and Peter Sprague, the chairman and a long-time friend, was my campaign manager. My firm was very good about letting me take time off to campaign, and I tried to stay in touch with what was going on at Weeden.

The 19th district encompassed the Lower East Side, Chinatown, Wall Street and the West Side through Greenwich Village, Chelsea, Clinton and up to 79th Street. It was adjacent to the "Silk Stocking District," which ran up the east side of Manhattan, and was the district that produced John Lindsay and later Ed Koch. The 19th was the "No Stocking District." It was largely Democratic, liberal and Jewish. As a Republican living on Park Avenue and working on Wall Street running against the six-term incumbent, Leonard Farbstein, my chances were minimal. But as somebody quipped, "The odds were no worse than taking on the NYSE."

Running for public office is an experience I'll never forget. If nothing else, it is a test of physical stamina and mental agility. It also forces you to clearly spell out how you view the world and how you stand on issues important to your constituency. There is no hiding. I was fortunate, because my odds of winning were so long that I could say what I really believed. I came out strongly against the Vietnam War and favored some legalization of drugs. (I've included my final advertisement run in the *Village Voice* summarizing my position for the record.) I found campaigning hard work but very stimulating. I had a ball, although I never got involved in politics again.

Back to the SEC hearings. My testimony was an opportunity to comment publicly on issues affecting our Third Market business and to point out the value of our participation in the market. I told the Commission that Weeden had $19 million in capital, of which well more than half was used to finance overnight inventories in NYSE-listed stocks. These inventories averaged more than $29 million throughout the year 1968. As a comparison, this was almost three times the overnight inventory carried by <u>all</u> the specialists on the two floors of the Pacific Coast Stock Exchange.

Our Third Market sales in the 230 stocks in which we now made a market totaled $1.6 billion for the first nine months of 1968. This meant we turned our inventory an average of every 5.3 working days. The average trade size was 254 shares.

I went on to say that our capital plus that of other Third Market dealers contributed more than $100 million to satisfy the needs of the growing institutional interest in the market. Rather than fragmenting the market, it helped provide greater depth and liquidity.

We pointed out that Rule 394(b) continued the separation of our market from that of the NYSE and was the principal reason for what the NYSE referred to as "fragmentation." Rule 394(b) was almost equally unworkable as its predecessor, Rule 394, despite the efforts of Third Market dealers to adapt to its cumbersome process. We denounced Rule 394(b) as blatant hypocrisy on the part of the NYSE and called for its elimination as being in the public interest.

Those hearings appeared to go nowhere, even though the Justice Department had filed a 65-page document pointing out the various antitrust practices being condoned by the Commission.

The ineffective result of those hearings, plus the cozy and secretive way in which the Commission had handled the Rule 394 debate, convinced us that the Commission had not yet seen the big picture and something had to be done. At Weeden, we debated among ourselves what to do, if anything. While still less than 5 percent of the total, the Third Market was slowly but surely capturing a larger percentage of the trading volume and was becoming an increasingly important factor.

I was all for speaking out. Jack supported me, while Alan was understandably reluctant to rock the boat with our strong relations with the bond community. Frank was spending more and more time teaching kids how to swim and was leaving it to his "boys" to make those decisions.

While I lost my race for Congress, the experience I gained speaking in public and debating a wide variety of issues was invaluable for my self-confidence (although some have said that a lack of self-confidence had never been my problem). Also, our work with the Justice Department and involvement at the SEC during the Special Study and 394(b) negotiations gave Weeden a certain leadership role. And besides, we were still almost 40 percent of the Third Market, even with new, powerful firms coming on the scene and doing the same thing.

Other factors played a role in our decision to speak out. We understood very clearly how the bond market developed and subsequently moved from the auction market to the over-the-counter market. Also, we felt we knew what the institutions wanted from the marketplace.

And we had a good understanding of how new technology was changing the way the business was done. This knowledge came easily to Weeden's management, both from necessity and interest. Frank was the leader and inspiration. Frank's first job on the Street, going back to 1912, was as office manager for Louis Sloss & Co. in San Francisco. He always enjoyed tinkering with systems, making them more efficient. His upbringing on a sailing ship had taught him the importance of detail. Contrary to most heads of Wall Street firms, Frank spent much of his time wandering through the "cage," as the back office (now operations) was then called, checking to see how people were handling the paperwork, delivering the bonds and getting stock certificates into transfer, and whether our cash was being used efficiently. He was well liked by the employees, who all called him by his first name. They understood his desire for efficiency and worked eagerly to improve it.

Jack fell easily into Frank's footsteps and took the talent even further. It was Jack who reorganized our stock transfer and dividend departments, set up our extensive relationship with the banks, designed the stock borrowing arrangement with Merrill Lynch — which incidentally provided that firm with up to $30 million of stock loan business daily — and saved Weeden a ton of interest expense by reducing late deliveries. Jack was one of the first on the Street to introduce IBM punch cards into the clearing process. Weeden's ability to turn a profit was dependent upon our doing these things better than anyone else. As trading volume in equities began to accelerate and the industry moved toward its eventual paperwork crisis in 1968, our efficient handling of securities became even more important.

Because of my participation on the board of National Semiconductor, first monthly, then quarterly, I became privy to what was going on in that dynamic new industry. What I saw coming down the pike convinced me that the way Wall Street operated would change — would have to change — and that it would make for lower costs, greater efficiency and higher volume.

So, in the latter part of 1969, we sat down to write the Securities and Exchange Commission a letter. Once the decision was made, all three brothers contributed. I would lay out what I thought the issues were and discuss them with Alan and Jack. Alan did the writing and I signed it. Rereading our letter to the SEC 33 years after its submission, it still rings loud and clear. It runs for more than 15 pages, and I have included a reprint of it in the Appendices.

We pulled no punches.

"An overwhelming increase in institutional business in common stock was acting upon archaic and inflexible rules maintained by the industry's principal stock exchange and causing the rise of a Third Market, the advent of member-firm block positioners and demands for public ownership of member firms to meet the increased capital needs of the Street."

"The increase in institutional block business has drastically reduced the effectiveness of the specialist, not so much because the specialist lacks capital resources, but because he has lost contact with the market. Because NYSE rules preclude the specialist from dealing directly with the public, he has found it impossible to obtain direct exposure to the full sweep of institutional inquiry."

"Consequently, he is flying blind and is, understandably, unwilling to risk his capital on large positions. Into this vacuum has come first the Third Market, and more recently the member-firm block positioners."

"The NYSE persistence in perpetuating the monopolistic position of its specialists in fostering its members' isolation from other marketplaces, and particularly in maintaining a commission structure for block business that greatly exceeds the cost of executing and processing that business, has resulted in tortuous distortions in the securities industry."

We continued by spelling out our thinking on how to better structure the listed market.

"The central marketplace today is no longer a geographical concept. It is a communications concept" (emphasis added).

"With today's electronic miracles available to the industry, all market makers wherever located could be combined into a central, interrelated market for fast and efficient access by investors to all of its segments. The true central marketplace demands access to all available pools of positioning capital for maximum liquidity."

"There is no reason why all inquiry in listed stocks cannot be centered in an up-to-date version of the central marketplace, involving computers and electronic display panels such as envisioned in the NASDAQ system. *Such a system could be enhanced by a "public" ticker tape capable of reporting trades in all marketplaces, including all exchanges on a real-time basis"* (emphasis added).

Then we responded to the NYSE accusations.

"The NYSE, in trying to preserve its concept of the central marketplace, has made a concerted effort through public utterances and letters to regulatory agencies to discredit the Third Market by charging that it is unregulated, as compared to the NYSE, lacks adequate standards for reporting to the public, and assumes no responsibility."

"As a major Third Market maker we are not averse to the daily reporting of our trades in some manner to the public if the public is interested or if the Commission feels such reporting serves a regulatory purpose."

"Our firm is not averse to any regulation of the Third Market by the Commission or the NASD if it appears that such regulation is necessary to curb questionable practices or to protect the integrity of the market."

"But keep in mind our firm does not 'enjoy a monopoly franchise in which there is a continuous conflict between our role as an agent for public orders on our book and our activity as a dealer for our own account.' "

"We are convinced that free and open competition is the best regulatory force available and that such competition imposes a level of responsibility far higher than minimum standards formally stated."

We ended on a sober note.

"The combined system for trading listed stocks which we envision should be more efficient and less expensive than the present system. A lot of fat in the present system would be eliminated. Marginal producers and well-established firms, including ours, might find the going so rough that merger or liquidation becomes their only course. It is understandable that this specter causes some firms to seek a return to the past. It is less understandable or defensible that the NYSE lends them support through its policies and actions. The system the Exchange seeks to perpetuate is moribund. The forces acting on the marketplace for listed stocks are irreversible and will ultimately prevail.

"We urge the Commission to resist the temptation to compromise in favor of the status quo."

And so, the gauntlet was thrown down not just to the NYSE, but to the SEC as well. A path that we had not sought lay before us, as a firm and for me personally. For the next eight years, most of my time was spent explaining our position in Washington and around the country, in speeches, hearing rooms and industry conferences.

This took me away from the daily business of Weeden and from the trading desk. The latter was probably a very good thing for Weeden, since I was not a particularly good trader. I had little sense of the market — rather, I had little interest in the short-term ups and downs and what caused them. Some say my head was in the clouds and my feet were barely on the ground. I would be the last to argue with this. There was a larger purpose out there, and I was willing to be its advocate.

And besides, there were immensely competent people at Weeden to make markets, cover the institutions, run the trading desk and coordinate our respective offices, which now numbered seven with the addition of Houston and an outpost in London, England.

10

At The Center

In trying to make sense out of the maelstrom of activity that began swirling around the issue of market structure and to properly assess the role of Weeden & Co., it is best to start with a few statistics.

According to a NYSE research report dated February 9, 1971, Third Market competition in NYSE stocks, measured by dollar value, had increased from 3.4 percent in 1965 to 5.5 percent in 1969 and to 8.5 percent in the third quarter of 1970. This was despite the NYSE's success in preventing member firms from using the Third Market.

If measured by share volume, the Third Market had grown from 2.7 percent in 1965 to 6.7 percent in the third quarter of 1970.

Even these numbers failed to show the extent of Third Market activity, which was concentrated in less than 300 of the 1,700-odd stocks listed on the NYSE.

For instance, in 1970, Weeden, describing itself as "specialists in competition" in a full-page ad in the *Wall Street Journal* and the *New York Times*, listed the 50 stocks selected by the SEC and compared their volume with that of the NYSE. In the third quarter of 1970, our sales volume equaled 10.55 percent of the NYSE volume. In some stocks, like Procter & Gamble, Pacific Gas & Electric and Houston Lighting & Power, our volume was more than 30 percent that of the NYSE. In a number of stocks, Weeden's buying and selling exceeded that of the specialist.

In the same research report, regional exchange volume in NYSE-listed stocks reached 14.2 percent measured by dollar volume.

As the NYSE report concluded,

"Undoubtedly the increasing institutionalization of the market has been a major factor in this diversion of trading. During 1969, 56 percent of all public share volume on the NYSE was by institutions and intermediaries and 44 percent individual. Only three years before, the pattern was exactly reversed." (When one includes institutional volume on the Third Market and the regionals, the spread becomes much wider.)

As we noted in our letter to the SEC in November 1969,

"The hard truth is that the economic interests of the institutional investor are better served by a negotiated market than by an auction market. The institutional investor prefers to control his own order; he wants direct access to the market makers. Under normal conditions he would rather avoid paying an unnecessary commission to a broker inter-positioned between himself and the market maker."

Despite the surge in institutionally directed volume, Third Market participation by the institutions was uneven and limited by practices that had developed when there was only one price — the next sale on the NYSE plus or minus a *fixed minimum commission*. Trust departments would tend to favor brokers who carried large deposits with the commercial side of the bank. Investment advisors were happy to direct their commission business solely through the introducing broker. Mutual funds found commissions a way of adding additional incentive for brokers to sell their funds, over and above the customary load. State pension funds favored their in-state brokers.

The introduction of an alternative price and a lower commission — or no commission at all in the case of Third Market trades — threw these arrangements into a cocked hat. Seeking a better price for their clients was against their economic interests and was firmly resisted.

The mutual fund industry was the most flagrant in ignoring its fiduciary responsibility. Most of Weeden's early business came from those groups with their own internal sales forces: Hamilton Funds in Denver, United Funds out of Kansas City and Investors Diversified Services (IDS) located in Minneapolis. The larger funds like Fidelity and the Affiliated Funds had enough business to give out to satisfy the brokers, research providers and the Third Market. The rest of the mutual fund industry was resistant — even antagonistic — to our call. This showed up in the

Special Study data, which indicated that mutual fund use of the Third Market was only 6 percent in 1961, compared to more than 15 percent done by other institutions.

Not surprising, the opposite was true for the regional stock exchanges, where the give-up (a practice by NYSE members sharing their commissions with other members who did nothing to execute the trade) and four-way tickets were popular means of directing commission dollars to non-member brokers who also sold mutual funds. The insensitivity of most funds to their fiduciary responsibility extended to the practice of setting up broker subsidiaries which would buy from Weeden and then put the trade into the fund plus a regular commission. Some funds wanted to simplify the process by doing the trade themselves and then have us confirm the trade to their broker subsidiary. This was too much for us, and we declined to do it. We thought all inter-positioning was not proper, but we had no method, nor responsibility, for policing it. We were quite frank with the SEC during informal discussions about what was going on, but we declined their request to volunteer to be their witness in court. On the other hand, if they subpoenaed us, we would have to testify. We were never subpoenaed.

Many banks had a policy to pay back in commissions an amount equal to a certain percentage of any deposits kept in the bank. This was done with commissions generated from trust and pension funds under their fiduciary control.

In a series of lawsuits brought by Abe Pomerantz against the banks, the existence of the Third Market was pointed out and the practice of paying out a higher price than necessary was exposed and documented. This soon caused the practice to stop, or at least go into hiding. There were always some banks — Morgan Guaranty Trust comes immediately to mind — that stood up to broker pressure and did their business where the price was best.

It was frustrating for us trying to attract business from what should be an eager customer — but also a challenge for me to find a way around this resistance.

When I first came onto the stock side of Weeden, they put me onto some of the out-of-the-way banks in Ohio and Pennsylvania where I could practice my sales pitch without causing too much damage.

Akron was on my list of stops. After calling on the bank there, I visited Goodyear and Firestone to see whether they went into the open market to buy their own stock. They didn't, but both companies had a pension plan managed by several New York banks, including Chase Manhattan. They became interested in my description of how they could save money by buying through Weeden and asked me whether we did business with them. I said that I did not know but they could probably tell by looking at the bank's confirmation tickets.

In the case of Chase, they must have looked and found no trades with Weeden and called Jim O'Brien, the vice president at Chase in charge of pension funds. I don't know what was said, but it got back to Chase's head trader, Tommy Cahill, that someone (me) was going around saying that Chase wasn't getting the best price for its pension funds. Well, you can imagine the hot seat I was in, because we did do some business with Chase and had a good relationship with the traders there. I had trouble convincing our people that I had done no wrong, so I had our head trader, Billy Lee, call Chase and arrange a meeting between me, Cahill and O'Brien so I could tell them what I did say. Thank goodness that meeting worked out all right and the firm let me continue to make my calls. Our business with Chase grew nicely, and I've always wondered whether my trip to Akron had something to do with it.

An exception to the practice of most state funds was found in Minnesota. In the 1970 Report of the State of Minnesota Board of Investment, the executive secretary, Robert Blixt, goes to some length in describing their use of the Third Market dealers, none of whom had offices in the state.

> "The off-board or 'Third Market' has proved to be very helpful, especially in obtaining stocks that show comparatively low trading activity on the major exchanges. Our experience during the past *eight years* (emphasis added) indicates that savings on these transactions may approximate three-eighths to one-half point per share, or $375 to $500 per thousand shares."

I have included one page of that 1970 report as an illustration of the business being done with the Third Market, and with Weeden in particular. As an aside, we were told at the time that the local brokerage community had made such a stink about the amount of business going out of state that Merrill Lynch was asked on each order to see if a better price could be found on the floor of the NYSE. Merrill was quite surprised at the result and ceased to object to their political friends in St. Paul about the practice.

Adding to these developments was the condition of the market itself. The period of 1967 to '69, known as the "go-go" years, had seen annual trading volume rise significantly along with a surge in the Dow. This was largely due to activity by the institutions. But 1969 saw a reversal in both volume and market level, causing widespread concern and red ink on Wall Street. In 1969 alone, the Dow Jones average dropped 15.2 percent. Leon Kendall, president of the Association of Stock Exchange Firms, outlined the grim facts in his "State of the Securities Industry" speech on September 9, 1970:

> "While share volume was off 3.8 percent in 1969 from the previous year, commissions earned were off 23 percent. For the first eight months of 1970, there was a 1.5 percent decline in NYSE volume and another 18 percent decline in the price of shares, causing a 40 percent drop in sales volume from the peak in 1968."

Lee went on to say that workforces had already been cut 20 percent, capital equipment expenditures had been curtailed and, in the past 18 months, mergers, consolidation and other causes had taken 80 member firms from the NYSE rolls.

> "Net, our industry has lost more firms in the last 18 months than we lost during the entire Depression from 1929 to the low for our industry in 1940.
>
> *"Today, without a doubt, higher commissions are the number-one priority on everyone's agenda* (emphasis added). There is no way this industry can survive without higher prices for the service it sells the public."

It was in this atmosphere that the NYSE was being forced to grapple with increasing pressure to allow institutional membership, to expand the volume discount and to provide discounts to non-member brokers. Their problem was that, in each case, any action would in the short run have further eroded the profitability of its upstairs members.

Weeden & Co. was not immune to these trends in market and volume. In a prospectus dated October 1970, Weeden showed trading profits declining from $16.5 million in 1968 to $8.9 million in 1969, causing us to lose money for the first time since 1942. Both bond and stock trading contributed to the loss. On the other hand, our trading volume in stocks continued to increase, going from 36.3 million shares in 1967 to

41 million shares in 1968 and then jumping to 55 million shares in 1969. By 1969, stock trading had outgrown our bond business. Because of this fact, plus the growing public confrontation between us and the NYSE, Weeden became known primarily as a Third Market firm.

Thus, for the NYSE, the period of 1968 to 1970 was a difficult one. Along with the bad market, lower volume, disgruntled and unprofitable members, and increased competition from the Third Market and the regionals, it had to contend with an aggressive Justice Department, a less-friendly SEC and the 1968–70 paperwork crisis that caused mid-week closings of the Exchange, public ire and a growing interest by Congress to get involved.

Although the SEC hearings on commission rates were inconclusive, the problems raised by a fixed-commission structure — give-ups and institutional membership — did not go away.

At Weeden, we generally felt pretty good about what was happening, despite the setback on Rule 394. But we were not complacent.

In 1970, Fred Siesel joined Weeden as my executive assistant. Fred had previously been with the 1963 Special Study of the Securities Markets and a staff member of the American Stock Exchange. He provided useful insight into the ways of Washington and the issues within the exchange community. Almost more important were his sense of humor and analytical mind. Fred was very smart, with a quick mind and almost eidetic memory. He had also established good personal relationships with many of his colleagues at the SEC and AMEX, which were maintained and nurtured while at Weeden.

Fred and I worked together from 1970 until 1978, and I cannot say enough about his contributions. I was the speech maker, member of various committees, the front man, while Fred collected the data, developed strategy, honed the speeches and was together with me when we visited Congress or met with industry leaders. After leaving Weeden in 1978, Fred spent the next 22 years with the NYSE in charge of their Automated Bond System (ABS).

11

Other Initiatives

I don't want to leave the impression that we were idle at Weeden since losing the battle over Rule 394. Although that effort would continue for 10 more years, we were developing initiatives of our own. One involved using technology to better communicate with our customers, the institutions and other investors.

We had watched while companies like Ultronics, Bunker Ramo and Quotron (formerly Scantlin Electronics) were introducing new and better ways to collect and disseminate market information to the public. We supported this trend, because it de-emphasized the ticker tape as the preferred source of information and over time forced the NYSE to discard its arbitrary rules on who could and could not receive last-sale information.

(As an aside, in 1976 Milt Moore and George Levine, the new management at Quotron, asked my father to purchase a large block of stock being offered by Dow Jones. That purchase, for something less than $100,000, was the seed capital of the Weeden Foundation, now worth in excess of $30 million.)

Then in 1968, Alan Kay conceived of a way to gather information from brokers on blocks of stock for sale, or being looked for, and to communicate that information via computer screens to institutional investors interested in this information. AutEx, as he named his new company, would replace, or at least supplement, the telephone calls made by salesmen at each brokerage house to each institution separately. The institutions, on the other hand, would save a lot of incoming calls and the manual, time-consuming process of taking down long lists of names that they had no immediate interest in. For many brokers without nationwide coverage it was a terrific service, as it allowed them to compete for institutional orders without the attendant costs of personnel and additional offices.

We embraced the idea, and when Kay raised a second round of funding for AutEx we were a significant investor. Not only did we believe this was the way the industry was heading, but we also wanted to protect ourselves from being excluded because of our non-member status. This decision proved prescient when the NYSE developed a competing system called the Block Automation System (BAS), which was available for use by member brokers only. BAS had the full weight of the NYSE behind it, with considerable pressure exerted on the member brokers and institutional investor community to use it rather than AutEx. Fortunately, its design turned out to have an Achilles' heel: It operated on the premise that the center of the market was the specialist, and that BAS was merely a vehicle to assist brokers in showing large orders to the specialist before routing them to other institutions. Jimmy Murray at IDS said, "Hey, I'm the center of the market. Show your orders to me first." It wasn't too long before AutEx became the dominant system, and the NYSE, after spending millions of dollars, quietly deep-sixed BAS.

In 1975, Kay sold AutEx to Itel Corp. and Weeden realized a handsome profit.

Another technology initiative came along in 1969 called Instinet. This was a far more radical system, taking the emerging technology to the point where brokers would not be needed at all in the execution of institutional orders. It allowed institutions to display their buy and sell interest anonymously to all Instinet subscribers. Instinet would then charge a modest fee whenever there was an execution. It came at a time when there was growing criticism, even lawsuits, because the institutions were not taking advantage of better prices in the Third Market.

Obviously, the brokerage community was not happy with Instinet. In his 1970 "State of the Securities Industry" speech, Lee Kendall also cited the "growing concern over AutEx and Instinet" along with "public ownership" and "institutional membership."

At my urging, Weeden also made an investment in Instinet. It was the first of many (at decreasing valuations) we would make over the next eight years. This investment was not supported by our salesmen, who felt it threatened their livelihood. My rationale for the investment was as follows: "If such technology pervades our industry, at least Weeden will have a piece of the action." Somehow this argument was not persuasive. When Weeden began putting bids and offers anonymously into the system, our salesmen would invariably call the institutions with an Instinet terminal and tell them that it was our bid or offer and they should come to us directly. But we had to do it for the same reason BAS failed: All the institutional users considered themselves the center of the market and they only responded, never initiated. The result was that nothing entered the system unless we put it there. In addition, the institutional traders had close personal relationships with many of the salesmen who covered them and had little interest, and no incentive, in bypassing them. Also, many felt that this kind of system was a threat to their jobs, as it could eventually be modified to eliminate the need by portfolio managers to use a trading desk. Even the threat of lawsuits didn't change matters. While 30 or 40 of the larger institutions subscribed in order to say they were willing to use it when it had something to offer, most of the Instinet terminals sat in the corner of the trading room and were never turned on.

As a postscript, Weeden continued to pour money into Instinet upon my insistence (bordering on a temper tantrum on one occasion) and consistent support from my brother Jack. Weeden at one time owned more than 90 percent of Instinet, and still owned 70 percent at the time of our merger with Moseley, Hallgarten and Estabrook in 1979. It was Bill Lupien, in 1983, who took over the reins of Instinet from Jerry Pustilnik and catapulted it into what it is today by transforming it into the de facto limit order book, or repository, for over-the-counter stocks.

But I'm getting way ahead of my story about Weeden's several initiatives during that period when the NYSE was stonewalling the SEC and everyone else on market structure issues. I use the word "stonewalling" as the only apt description of the NYSE's strategy to slow the process of opening up their market to competition and toward a central marketplace. Before discussing these efforts in detail, I want to describe Weeden's developing relationship with the Cincinnati Stock Exchange.

In 1969, we approached the Cincinnati Stock Exchange Board of Governors with the idea that Weeden become the odd-lot dealer on their floor in those stocks in which we made a Third Market and which were also listed on their exchange — as I remember, it was a total of

112 issues. At the time, Cincinnati's volume was averaging 1,700 shares a day (yes, 1,700), mostly small trades in Cincinnati Gas & Electric and Cincinnati Telephone. Cincinnati thought it was a great idea that would help their local firms and might also attract business from their larger, nationally based firms who would be willing to use Weeden's markets when they had large orders unattractive to the NYSE specialists.

A proposal for a rule change to accommodate us was submitted to the SEC and received the approval of the staff. It was published for written comment with the expectation that no one was interested in what the Cincinnati exchange was doing. Not so. Bob Birnbaum, executive vice president of the American Stock Exchange — Ralph Saul was president — wrote a strong letter to the SEC criticizing the idea of a non-member, Third Market dealer assuming such a role without appropriate regulatory restrictions and oversight. Bob called for public hearings, a rather formal and time-consuming procedure on this "important" matter, and was successful in delaying the rule change for a year. Frankly, I was surprised that Bob or Ralph would take such a position, having been key members of the Special Study and long-time members of the SEC staff, both of which supported competition among marketplaces. Because no AMEX stocks were traded on the Cincinnati exchange, or traded by Weeden (or anyone in the Third Market, for that matter), I have always believed that Bob (Ralph) was put up to it by Big Brother at 11 Wall St.

Finally, in April of 1970, the rule was approved and Cincinnati became the first regional stock exchange on which New York members could deal with Weeden without suffering the intimidation of the New York floor. (In 1971, Weeden became a member of the Detroit, Philadelphia (PBW) and Boston stock exchanges, and in 1972 we joined the Pacific Coast Stock Exchange).

Third Market volume surged from 5.5 percent of NYSE volume in 1969 to 8.3 percent in the third quarter of 1970, while regional volume climbed from 12.1 percent to 14.2 percent.

Another initiative was our decision to go public. In 1969, Donaldson, Lufkin & Jenrette (DLJ) had surprised the Exchange community by registering with the SEC to become a corporation and issue shares to the public. Up until then, the NYSE had prohibited public ownership of its members on the ostensible argument that member-firm ownership should be in the hands of persons active in the business. The restriction had to do more with their concern over institutional membership and the undermining of the fixed-commission structure.

Weeden & Co., Inc. had been a public corporation ever since 1927, when it had sold an issue of convertible preferred to relatives, friends and some clients. We raised additional capital in 1946. This had always precluded Weeden from joining the Exchange, even if it would have been in its interest to do so. First Boston Corp., a spin-out of shares from the First National Bank of Boston, and later the Mellon Bank, also came under the same prohibition.

Whether DLJ pushed the issue on the NYSE or the NYSE encouraged it, in June of that year they agreed to accept public corporations with certain conditions that were meant to preclude non-securities firms (institutions) from joining. First Boston was the underwriter for DLJ and brought them to market early in 1970.

In October 1970, Weeden sold 300,000 shares of common stock through an underwriting managed by Bache & Co., raising $4,275,000 net of fees. The list of underwriters is interesting, since it included no other major stock exchange firm and few of the middle-bracket firms. Harry Jacobs, then president of Bache, was a good friend of my brother Alan and was willing to take on the ire of the NYSE community.

Interesting also was the fact that in our last full year of operations, Weeden had lost almost $3 million, our first loss since 1942. On the other hand, during the six months ending June 30, 1970, we had a complete reversal and were quite profitable. It was the continuing growth in our Third Market revenues over the previous five years that was attractive to our new investors, who realized that dealer firms will have a loss now and then. In our annual report for 1970 we said:

> "We have often in the past warned our stockholders that the large inventories we carry expose the firm to major losses when markets move substantially against us. The average price of the 220 stocks in which we deal dropped 19 percent in 1969, while the Bond Buyer Yield Index, the most widely used measure of municipal bond yields, indicated a 21 percent average drop in tax-exempt bond prices during the year. In both areas our trading profits were greatly diminished by reductions in the value of our inventories."

As stated earlier, our total Third Market business was growing handsomely on an absolute basis and also as a percentage of total NYSE volume. Total average inventory carried by the firm was normally between three and four times capital. Our stock inventory averaged 610,000 shares in 1967, 758,000 shares in 1968 and 706,000 shares in 1969; it rose to 804,000 and 978,000 shares in the two six-month periods of 1969–70. Average turnover ranged between 3.2 and 4.6 days.

Weeden sold another 300,000 shares in June 1971, again through Bache, raising $8,745,000 net of fees. The underwriting group this time included a number of the better-known regional and New York-based member firms, indicating some softening in member firms' attitude toward Weeden.

These two underwritings, plus several good years, brought our net capital up well over $30 million and set the stage for us to consider other secondary markets in which we could establish ourselves.

12

The NYSE on the Offensive

Meanwhile, the NYSE was not idle. While they began to deal with the pressure to unfix commissions, allow institutional membership and provide discounts to non-members, they were faced with the reality of the growing Third Market. It was slowly but surely eating away at their core business, namely the high-volume industrial common stocks. Unless something was done about it, our penetration of their market would continue to grow. Those members who had studied the history of markets understood as clearly as Weeden did what happens to auction markets when institutional trading begins to dominate.

Soon after the Special Study report came out, Keith Funston, president of the NYSE, led a contingent of the more-powerful members of the Exchange down to the SEC for a private meeting concerning the Third Market. It was reported in the *New York Times* that Funston described the Third Market as one which "harbors market manipulators, deceives investors and circumvents government regulations."

Some might observe that this was a surprising accusation from this otherwise congenial man known mainly for marketing the concept "every American a shareholder." Funston, whose only data on the Third Market was the recently published Special Study report, could not have been referring to Blyth & Co. or First Boston Corp., with whom his own Exchange members had an excellent relationship and who regularly participated in their secondary distributions of utility stocks. Nor could he be concerned with the likes of New York Hanseatic and A.W. Benkert, who made markets in odd lots and small round lots to small non-exchange broker-dealers. Our suspicion was that Weeden's net markets to the institutions in popular industrial names was the target of his comments.

In 1964, the issue before the SEC was how the Third Market should be regulated. The NYSE wanted us to bear the same restrictions which had been imposed on their specialists over time because of a past history of misuse and their conflict of interest with the public book. The SEC recognized the difference, and sensibly did nothing more than take the recommendation of the Special Study to "identify the number and size of over-the-counter firms that deal in listed stocks and to regularly report the volume of Third Market transactions" (Special Study of the Securities Markets, Part 2, Chapter 7, Section D, p. 911).

Funston's rather uncharacteristic remarks reported in the *Times* by Eileen Shanahan turned out to be only the tip of the iceberg as to what was being said in private by NYSE members and staff to the institutions, regulators and even corporate officials of listed companies. "Pirates," "the dark market," "fragmenters" and "un-American" (believe it or not) were some of the phrases being used to describe our business.

Clearly, the NYSE was concerned. Their successful parrying of Morris Schapiro's (and the Justice Department's) effort to remove Rule 394 during the next two years did nothing to reduce their concern. A little-known fact that Weeden had been asked by the SEC to comment privately to the commissioners on their proposed Rule 10b-10 (which would have the NYSE eliminate give-ups) must have been unsettling. This occurred in March 1967 and must have signaled to them a growing respect at the SEC for our opinion.

Then came the bombshell: a 67-page comment on the proposed Rule 10b-10 from the Antitrust Division of the Justice Department. Their comments went well beyond why give-ups should go, raising the larger issues of existing rules that violated antitrust laws, caused fragmentation in the market and prevented the proper development of competitive forces. Someone was obviously whispering in their ear, and having some effect.

The fact is, we had continued our dialogue with the Antitrust Division ever since our first contact in 1962. This effort was led by Bob Beshar, who came to know Donald Baker very well and established a long personal friendship. In 1968 Don became head of policy planning for the Antitrust Division; he later became assistant attorney general in charge of the division.

According to SEC Chairman Manuel Cohen's belief, voiced after his retirement in 1969, it was the Justice Department's intervention on Rule 10b-10 that triggered the calling of a public hearing on stock exchange commission rates in 1968 (Seligman, *The Transformation of Wall Street*, p. 404). It also was partially instrumental in helping Chairman Cohen's efforts to obtain Congressional authorization for an Institutional Investor Study to begin in 1969. Thus, the stage was being set for a series of public hearings that would give a full-blown airing of all major issues confronting the industry.

This is probably as good a time as any to ask why Weeden was getting involved in these issues, especially the elimination of fixed commissions. Weren't fixed commissions the thing that made our net markets so attractive? Wouldn't Weeden lose its advantage with the institutions, especially, and find its Third Market business dwindling? All good questions, and all were hotly debated within Weeden and among the family members. I argued that our strength came from our willingness to make markets, take positions, assume risks, operate efficiently, work for narrower margins than others, establish strong relationships with our customers and handle their inquiries with integrity. Our daily contact with the institutions would allow us a better understanding of the forces playing on the market than the specialists, who lacked that contact and were not used to taking large risks. Because we were not in the underwriting business, nor that of providing research, we would not be viewed as a competitor by the member firms who shunned risk-taking and who would become good customers of ours given the opportunity. And besides, the genie was out of the bottle and we would be asked to comment on all the issues being raised.

As I mentioned in an earlier chapter, I testified for Weeden at the SEC hearings on commission rate structure. Our main pitch was the removal of restrictions on member firms' ability to access our markets, but when asked about a volume discount and concessions to non-member brokers, we had to be consistent. We said we believed both were appropriate — even necessary. Although we felt that both would tend to reduce our competitive position and could result in reduced business, we could hardly argue against them. After all, they were what the Third Market was all about. We then couldn't resist the needle. We went on to observe that "in this period of unparalleled prosperity" (my testimony) it was only because of the Third Market that the NYSE was showing any response to the public clamor for reduced commissions.

The NYSE's response to these hearings was an escalation of their determination to see us go away. In 1969 or 1970, they reached out to an old friend and distinguished ex-chairman of the Federal Reserve Board to help find a suitable solution to the issues of market structure that excluded us. With the completion of the hearings on commission rates and the beginning of the two-year Institutional Investor Study, William McChesney Martin agreed to study the issues thoroughly, and objectively, and report back in a reasonable period of time. He engaged a young man named Donald Beer, a Yale graduate and member of the gold-medal eight-oar crew team at the 1956 Summer Olympics in Melbourne, to help him during what turned out to be the next 14 months. As I remember, we at Weeden, along with the rest of the financial world, waited with bated breath for his report.

In retrospect, it's hard to believe that anyone expected anything but a biased report supporting the continuation of the NYSE as the primary, if not sole, market center for trading of securities listed on the NYSE. Martin's relationship with the NYSE had been impeccable. He had worked on the floor as early as 1933. In 1939, as the first paid president of the NYSE at the young age of 33, Martin had initiated a rule that would prohibit New York members from dealing in NYSE-listed stocks as principal on all regional exchanges. At the time, the regionals collectively accounted for less than 5 percent of the total business in NYSE-listed stocks. This rule, if allowed by the SEC, would have put the regionals out of business. Under Martin's leadership, the NYSE conducted a bruising battle with the SEC over a two-year period and finally lost out when the SEC ordered them to rescind the rule.

To say that the Martin Report was a dud would be an understatement. It probably raised more adverse comment than anything else going on in the industry for years. Criticism came from a wide range of academics, national magazines and the editorial pages of *Barron's*, the *New York Times* and the *Wall Street Journal*. The general reaction was so bad that Charles Morin, representing the committee for the Martin Report, said while testifying before the Subcommittee on Securities of the Committee on Banking, Housing and Urban Affairs, chaired by New Jersey Senator Harrison Williams:

"Let me now respectfully suggest that all of us in the securities industry not become emotionally enmeshed in the issues before us. We believe that there has been too much talk of monopoly and the 'monopolists.' We believe there has been too much purple language in the street like describing the NYSE as 'the rabbit guarding the lettuce' or 'burn the Martin Report in effigy.' We don't think that this contributes to the dialogue in vitally important issues."

The central issue, of course, was what kind of central marketplace should we have? Martin called for all trades in listed stocks to be traded only on an exchange, and even leaving open whether NYSE-listed stocks would still be allowed to trade on the regionals. Institutional membership should not be allowed, and the move toward unfixing of commissions should be done very deliberately, if at all.

Blatantly, Martin called for the elimination of the Third Market. The NYSE hastily embraced the Martin Report, but then, over time, began to distance itself from its recommendations as being too self-serving and running counter to what everyone else was calling for.

Our reaction was clearly one of concern. This was a calculated strategy on the part of our 600-pound adversary, whom we had come to respect for its ability to get its way. Coupled with President Nixon's appointment of William Casey to the chairmanship of the SEC, it looked as though their game plan was well thought out and had a good chance of success. On the other hand, the criticism was widespread and we felt there was good support for us.

The one very positive thing was the wording in the Martin Report — "ELIMINATION of the Third Market." It was a poor choice of words, a red flag, and we did our best to capitalize on it.

Meanwhile, the NYSE had attacked the Third Market in what we felt was our own back yard. The issue was the trading of listed stocks on the NASD's new trading system called National Association of Securities Dealers Automated Quotations (NASDAQ), which was to begin operating early in 1971.

To set the stage, on December 16, 1968, the NASD, by full membership vote, overwhelmingly adopted bylaws to implement the NASDAQ system and provided that listed securities traded in the Third Market could be included. At the time, I had requested confirmation that no discrimination would be practiced "by the NASD in making available the NASDAQ system to listed stocks which enjoy an active over-the-counter market." I received a prompt reply from the president stating that "no security will be excluded from consideration in the system because it is also listed on a stock exchange."

Then, early in October of 1970, the presidents of both the NYSE and AMEX wrote the SEC and the NASD urging that listed securities be eliminated from NASDAQ. On or before October 20, the president of the NASD, Gordon Macklin, met privately with SEC Chairman Hamer Budge and discussed with him the exclusion of markets in listed securities from the NASDAQ system. On October 20, by telephone vote, the executive committee of the NASD "met" and reversed their two-year policy of inclusion. All six members of the executive committee were associated with firms who were members of the NYSE.

On October 22, Gordon Teach, chairman of the NASD board, prepared and hand-delivered a request for comments from the full Commission on the elimination of Third Market securities from NASDAQ. The same day, Teach said he was "informed" that the commissioners had unanimously approved this "boycott."

On October 23, the full board of governors was solicited by telephone and by mail to ratify this act. There was no information as to the reason for the change except the letters from the two exchanges requesting the reversal, Teach's letter to the Commission, and a cover letter "expressing his opinion" that the Commission would approve the boycott.

A meeting on October 27 requested by me and my brother Jack with Teach, Macklin and Lloyd Derrickson, chief counsel for the NASD, was unproductive, as was a meeting with Chairman Budge later that morning. The NASDAQ system went into operation in early 1971 — without listed stocks.

I have to say it was a real downer for us — and coming just after we had gone public in anticipation of further growth through, among other things, our markets being shown on NASDAQ.

I have always thought this act was a blatant and arrogant misuse of power by the NYSE and AMEX in a raw conspiracy with the SEC chairman to stifle competition. Because our colleague, J.R. Smith, was at the time a member of the NASD Board of Governors, we found out about it in a timely fashion. It was Bob Beshar's sharp pen that put them all on notice that we would not stand by and let them push us around. While I was not happy with Gordon Macklin and his role in this, I always understood that his responsibility was to carry out the orders of his six-man executive committee chaired by Gordon Teach, all of whom were also members of the NYSE.

It was Gordon Macklin and Lloyd Derrickson who quickly sought a compromise with Weeden that would avoid legal action that could have delayed the introduction of the full NASDAQ system. From our suggestion, they engineered the pilot project early in 1971 that reinstated listed stocks on NASDAQ. Gordon and I were soon on the same track again, and I followed his career with the NASD and then as chairman of Hambrecht & Quist with admiration. Besides leading the NASD into its great period of unparalleled growth and broad acceptance, Gordon is a very nice guy with a wonderful sense of humor.

13

394 Revisited

I have already noted that Rule 394 had lost the interest of the SEC. This was made clear in a speech by its recently appointed chairman, William Casey, on May 5, 1971, in which he outlined the many issues and problems competing for the Commission's attention. Casey stressed his personal concern for the small investor while failing to mention the unresolved problem of Rule 394. At this point in time we had pretty much given up on the SEC on this issue and were aggressively joining regional exchanges and calling on Congress.

Nevertheless, on June 30, I wrote an eight-page letter to Chairman Casey stressing the fact that the existence of Rule 394 harmed the small investor more than anyone. I began by quoting from a recent article by Seymour Smidt, who had been the associate director of the SEC's Institutional Investor Study.

"Individual investors are the main victims of inadequate market making by specialists since they have no effective alternatives."

"The present inadequacies of the NYSE specialist system can be traced, in very large part, to regulations and practices that serve to create barriers to competition."

I then drew his attention to the data being collected since the introduction of listed stocks on NASDAQ in mid-1971, which confirmed that small investors were being harmed by Rule 394. After that, I spent a good bit of space going over the whole history of Rule 394 and the Commission's prior involvement. At this point it might be interesting to review the dialogue between Roger Foster, the hearing officer at the SEC Rate Structure Investigations of National Securities Exchanges, and Gustave Levy, chairman of the NYSE, back in 1968, as an illustration of the ineptitude of the SEC in dealing with "one of the major subject matters of the rate structure hearings" — and our frustration.

The Commission staff's opening comments at these hearings emphasized that "statements concerning the fragmentation of the auction market ... will have to be supported by *fact* and *reasoned argument*" (emphasis added). Levy, chairman of the Exchange, was the only person to testify in support of Rule 394. He sought to justify the Rule by stating repeatedly that it was "essential to the maintenance of a central market" and that there was no need to go elsewhere for a better price.

Foster, with obvious impatience, asked Levy, "If a member firm can always do as well or better on the floor of the Exchange as on the Third Market, why was Rule 394 necessary at all?" Levy replied: "It is the bulwark of the (New York) stock exchange and it is necessary. There is enough proliferation and we don't want any more."

Foster then put the issue squarely to Levy, saying, "It seems to me the legal issue we are confronted with is, is there a justification for an exemption from the antitrust laws which would normally allow your members a choice as to where they thought they could do the best job for their customers. And the burden, it would seem to me, would be on the Exchange to show not that your members are stupid and need to be prevented from doing a bad job, but that somehow or other it would hurt the auction market if they were permitted to go off-board when in their judgment they thought they could do better for their customer there."

Levy replied, "We had to put a stop to it. That is all."

Levy's testimony is the total extent of the Exchange's public defense of Rule 394.

As our letter to Casey progressed, we became measurably caught up with the rightness of our arguments and turned to chastising the Commission for its unwillingness to enforce "best execution."

First, we dismissed NYSE's claim that when an investor selects a member broker, he knowingly directs — or at least agrees — that his broker will only execute on the Exchange and will not go to the Third Market, even if a better price is obtainable off-board. We quickly pointed out that the member broker will take that same customer's order to a regional exchange without his permission whenever it suits the "broker's private purpose" — and does so frequently.

And with one final burst of high-blown rhetoric, we told the new chairman what he should do.

> "If this flimsy argument is the Exchange's final position, then the Commission should require it to engage in a broad advertising campaign to make the public aware of Rule 394. If it is appropriate for the Surgeon General of the United States to require cigarette manufacturers to put a health warning on each package of cigarettes, the Food and Drug Administration to require drug companies to inform physicians whenever their products have been judged less than effective, and the Federal Trade Commission to compel advertisers to document their product claims, so, too, the Securities and Exchange Commission ought to demand that every NYSE-member firm warn its customers that transactions handled by them may not be at the best available price because of Exchange rules. Otherwise, to my layman's mind, the Commission and the Exchange are sanctioning a fraud on the investing public."

Bob Beshar deserves credit for the above, as well as for other speeches and articles by me during this period. His efforts with the Justice Department were considerable. We had been friends since Yale Law School, and both of us had married European women and started our families in New York City at about the same time. He was always available for advice and counsel (even when he was serving as assistant to the undersecretary of the Commerce Department at the tail end of the Nixon administration).

At Weeden we fully understood the strategy of the NYSE. While they spoke of the two pillars holding up the Exchange — fixed commissions and Rule 394 — there was one fundamental difference: fixed commissions were important to the profitability of the upstairs firms, while Rule 394 was vital to the preservation of the floor. In the former case, "fight the critics, delay change, prolong the inevitable," but in the case of Rule 394, "stonewall, stonewall, stonewall 'til the cows come home." As it turned out, they were successful in holding the line on 394, which only disappeared in 2001, almost 37 years after Morris Schapiro first raised the issue.

Incidentally, the new chairman graciously acknowledged the receipt of my letter.

14

Speaking Out: SEC Hearings on Market Structure

As 1971 unfolded, everyone was beginning to talk about a central marketplace. Both houses of Congress were studying market structure, and the SEC was about to hold hearings. A consolidated tape was favored as the first step. It would seem this would be good news for Weeden. Unfortunately, not so, as Rule 394 was now relegated to the back burner, with the Martin Report on the front burner.

As the upcoming hearings would show, most of the industry were still against the idea of competing dealer markets. Of the 37 exchange firms that testified before the SEC, not one said, "Boy it would be great to have an alternate market to that specialist who often uses my inquiry for his own benefit, who many times isn't there when I need him, and who often embarrasses me before my client." Not one. They were all talking about fragmentation, net prices and the complications of having more than one place to check. Their collective opinion was "Let's get back to how it was, back on the Exchange floor, back to when the market was protected against outside intrusion and price-cutting."

During this period I became quite active in speaking out, not only about the Third Market, but also on the larger issue of market structure. I spoke before a variety of groups including academia, investors and people from our industry wherever they would have me. Much of the content of these speeches was repetitive, and a few titles should be sufficient to give their flavor.

In November 1970, I spoke about the "Central Market vs. The Single Market" before the National Investor Relations Institute. Then in March 1971, at a luncheon with brokers and financial analysts from Minneapolis, I spoke about "Keeping the Power Spread Around." And then "Competition: Key to Market Structure" before the Western Finance Association gathering in Vancouver, B.C. I was even asked to appear before the Securities Industry Association at their annual get-together at the Greenbrier. And I went into the lion's den itself when the NYSE asked me to spell out my ideas before its membership, gathered in the richly paneled Board of Governors Room.

Probably the most interesting statement, in terms of timing, was my article that appeared in the *New York Times* on August 1, 1971 under the rubric "Point of View." It reflected Weeden's thinking on the eve of the release of the long-awaited Martin Report.

In rereading it, I liked it, especially for its tone. It reflected not so much the confrontational aspects between the NYSE and Weeden, but rather Weeden's sincere belief that the public would be better served by a broadly based market beyond that which the NYSE could provide.

First, I hoped that William McChesney Martin's report would help guide us toward a broad national securities market. I reiterated our support for the reporting of all trades and recommended a spinoff of the ticker tape into the public domain. I thought equal regulation of all markets a reasonable goal, but pointed out the different needs of a monopoly environment vs. a highly competitive one. I thought that equal regulation was a red herring, as it had never been suggested by the NYSE to apply to its members' over-the-counter activities in the bond markets and in OTC stocks. I pointed out that the NYSE auction market involved a dealer on one side of the transaction more than 40 percent of the time.

I reiterated that a market system should try to maximize the availability of liquidity provided by well-capitalized dealers through easy and equal access to the center of the market. Commission rates should be unfixed so they could better relate to the costs and services involved. And lastly, I felt the national securities market should take advantage of the efficiencies, cost reductions and information distribution capability afforded by new computer technology.

Whatever I or others thought about Martin's report, events were converging to bring the whole issue of market structure front and center.

In 1970, Congress had authorized the SEC to conduct a study of institutional activity in the markets. The Institutional Investor Study, as it came to be called, differed from the 1961–63 Special Study of the Securities Markets in that the staff's independence was significantly restricted. The report was to reflect the views of the Commission, which, at the time, was chaired by Hamer Budge. As we found out in October 1970, Budge was no friend of the Third Market. The study also had an advisory committee that was dominated numerically by NYSE, NASD and institutional investor executives who were given the opportunity to "spell out in the final report any irreconcilable differences they may have with its findings, conclusions and recommendations" (Seligman, *The Transformation of Wall Street*, p. 415). The Third Market was not represented on that committee.

Nevertheless, I, Fred Siesel and my brother Jack were anxious that our views on market structure and the needs of the institutions were in front of the staff and represented in their report. We trudged down to Washington many times, sometimes just hanging around waiting for the opportunity to chat with anyone who would listen.

We found Don Farrar, who headed up the study, and Seymour Smidt, associate director, to be good people, properly motivated and very good at designing questionnaires, collecting data and analyzing it in various ways. But after spending a fair amount of time with them, we were left with the impression that they never fully understood the nature of an institutionally driven market and how it differed from what the NYSE offered.

The final report was half a loaf in that it failed to come down hard on the value of competing market makers, the need for dealer capital to provide liquidity and the need to eliminate existing barriers to competition. Bottom line, Rule 394 was hardly mentioned, while they emphasized the need for auction principles of trading.

Fortunately, the cover letter to the study, written for the Commission by Phil Loomis, strongly endorsed a central marketplace in which "all qualified broker-dealers and existing market institutions would participate."

It was gratifying to see, after the publication of the Institutional Investor Study and the release of the Martin Report, that both Sy Smidt and Don Farrar strongly criticized Martin's solution. Farrar's article in *Financial Analyst Journal* titled "The Martin Report: A Great Leap Backward" was pleasing to read.

At about the same time, I became involved with a committee spawned from a speech by Andrew Melton, who was then a partner at Smith Barney and president of the Investment Bankers Association (IBA). In his remarks before their New York group on October 28, 1970, he cited "the seriously fragmented state of our secondary markets" and called them "our main problem areas."

Andy went on to "urge the formation of a securities industry commission to review thoroughly all aspects of the secondary markets and develop a practical plan for a new or revised structure that would better serve the public interest."

Such a commission was promptly formed, consisting of staff and member representatives from all the major stock exchanges. They began to meet regularly in the various stock exchange board rooms around the country. They soon realized that there could be no solution without the involvement of the Third Market, and reluctantly asked Gordon Macklin, president of the NASD, to suggest someone to represent this point of view. I was the obvious choice, but one that was not well received by many on the committee. Gordon explained that there really wasn't anyone else, and so I attended those meetings with the understanding between Gordon and me that I would behave myself and be as quiet as possible. I did the best I could.

These meetings usually attracted 20 or so people around the conference table, with lawyers and staff members sitting against the wall. I was always placed down at the end of the table, where I kept myself busy, and my mouth quiet, by smoking the cigarettes that were available in great quantity and included all the popular brands. I had never smoked until then, and I soon grew addicted. It took me almost 17 years to kick the habit.

The committee continued to meet over the course of the next year, but then it ended in a bizarre way one evening shortly after completion of the SEC hearings on market structure. Chairman William Casey hosted a dinner to which our committee members were invited. It was in his large and beautiful home on Massachusetts Avenue in Washington. After many cocktails and a sumptuous dinner held at a monstrous circular table, we all retired into the smoking room for brandy and cigars. After much discussion, Casey turned to me and said, "Well, Don, what do you say to all this?" I said, "I like your choice of cigars, but I'm sorry to say that these meetings haven't changed my position. Eliminating the Third Market would not be right, nor would it be in the public interest."

William Casey had been appointed chairman of the SEC in March of 1971. In October 1971, two months after the Martin Report was made public, Casey called for hearings on market structure.

From the beginning, his appointment had us very worried. We knew him to be well situated in the group around President Nixon. He came from Long Island and was a loyal Republican player and law partner to former Republican National Committee Chairman Leonard Hall. Also, the fact that Bernard "Bunny" Lasker was Nixon's main fund-raiser, as well as chairman of the NYSE, made Casey's appointment appear part of a well-thought-out scheme.

A *Business Week* article on October 16, 1971, just prior to the market structure hearing called by the new SEC chairman, said just what we feared.

"The brokerage establishment prefers to retain and strengthen its basic monopoly."

"Wall Street is convinced that Casey intends to give the Big Board precisely what it wants."

"He (Casey) now appears to favor harnessing the industry along lines that would preserve the NYSE's private club nature and restrict, if not eliminate, competition within the industry altogether."

The article quoted Stephen Peck, a specialist and vice chairman of the NYSE Board of Governors, seeing Casey as "tough and decisive."

The hearings on market structure drew considerable attention from the press and testimony from the Street.

Besides the regulars — including all the exchanges, and the Securities Industry Association — there appeared a plethora of the leading member firms from across the country who opined on what they thought "good for the public."

Most everyone's testimony, including mine, was very predictable and shed little new light on the issue. Some speakers were sufficiently surprising or colorful to bear reprinting.

For instance, Cliff Michel, representing Loeb Rhodes, "firmly believed that this is and must be a *regulated* (his emphasis) industry ... intensely regulated by the government, and that the commission rates charged by members of the industry should be fixed and regulated under intensive and streamlined government supervision."

Cliff went on to say,

"Everyone agrees that competition is a good thing. All of us know that it is the essential animating principle in the dynamic economy that characterizes this nation.

"But competition is a complex and subtle concept. Competition in the securities markets is not the same thing as competition in the automobile business or the grocery business."

Whatever Cliff meant by "complex and subtle," it translated into a strong antipathy toward Weeden.

"At the present time any Third Marketeer can position long or short any listed stock, and can undo his position at any time against the primary market without any oversight or reporting, and without any obligation to make a continuous market in the stock he has positioned."

To Cliff, our competition created

" ... the real danger of destroying investor confidence in the integrity and fairness of the market."

He was right, but he had the shoe on the wrong foot.

Ralph Saul testified for First Boston Corp., a former Third Market firm since the early 1930s but since May 1971 a member of the NYSE.

"A unified exchange market can be built upon a reorganized NYSE or upon a new central market system as recommended by the Martin Report. The important point is there be a single exchange market where all public orders for widely traded equity securities should flow. We cannot favor 'competition' among exchange markets if this competition results in an exchange market structure which may not be in the best interest of the public."

Ralph must have had some uneasiness about his remarks, for in a footnote immediately following he took pains to explain First Boston's recent application to join three regional exchanges in order to trade blocks of stock for valued customers, "although we fail to see how this step has anything to do with 'competition.'"

We were naturally disappointed in Ralph's testimony and only hoped that his former colleagues at the SEC were, too. I wanted to press him on his views for restructuring the government and corporate bond markets according to the Martin Report, but I was not asking the questions.

More refreshing and "from the heart" was the testimony of I.W. "Tubby" Burnham. Here was an old-timer, a well-respected leader of the exchange community, sincerely expressing his frustrations, concerns and anger over the changes taking place.

Tubby minced no words, and in his testimony one can see how vehement was his antagonism toward us and his opposition to what was being discussed at these hearings:

"I am appalled by the overwhelming number of investigations going on, by the credence given to every economics professor who speaks up."

"There is absolutely no need for more than one market for a listed U.S. stock."

"It is impossible to know what the Third Market really is. We can be a buyer on the NYSE and because the Third Market is unregulated, we can pay a higher price than the Third Market because on the latter, a short seller can offer on a downtick and frequently does. Why does the SEC permit this? Is the object to destroy the regulated exchanges by unregulated competition?"

"Even though we are members of most of the regional exchanges … I see no reason for regionals except the time differential of the Pacific Coast."

"With respect to access of member firms to the Third Market, I find it hard to request access to a market which in my opinion should not even exist."

"The only possible reason why we would want access to the Third Market would be to execute our orders wherever the best market may be. However, if we were so permitted I don't think the listed market would last very long. It is, therefore, not in the public interest for a Third or Second market to exist, and we have no desire for access to it."

Needless to say, Mr. Burnham had no liking for me personally, as Chris Welles clearly pointed out in his book *The Last Days of the Club* (E.P. Dutton, 1975). I have always been sorry about that, as he did stand for many good things and it would have been most interesting to hear his "colorful" opinions on other matters. My loss.

After I had testified there were some questions from the staff about how I viewed certain procedures on the Exchange floor such as "priority, precedence, and parity" which were meant to be in the public interest. I said that most people have no idea what they are or how they work, but I might be able to shed some light on them using as an example my neighborhood bakery, which instituted the same rules as the NYSE for taking care of its customers.

"Auction Bakeries requires its customers to take a number in the order in which they come in. This establishes priority.

"Customer Number 1 wants to buy three loaves of bread. Auction Bakeries sells him just one loaf. Once the sale is made, all customers throw away their tickets. Priority is gone.

"The rules of precedence take over. The precedence rules are based on order size, and therefore all customers line up on the basis of how much bread they want to buy. Old Customer Number 7, who wants 15 loaves, is now first, followed by old Customer Number 5, who wants 10 loaves. Old Customer Number 1, who still wants two loaves, is now seventh. If Auction is now willing to sell 15 loaves, new Customer Number 1 gets them all. Number 1 would also get everything if Auction decides to sell 11 loaves. However, if Auction decides to sell 10 loaves, new Customers 1 and 2, who each want 10 loaves, are on parity.

"To resolve parity, these customers toss a coin to determine who gets the 10 loaves. This is called matching. If the two customers agree, and no other customer objects, they may split the sale and each take five loaves. If Auction had decided to sell only five loaves, all customers who wanted five loaves would be on parity and they would match until a winner is established.

"As far-fetched as Auction Bakery's business methods appear, this is exactly how the three P's operate on the New York Stock Exchange floor."

Probably the most influential input at these hearings was a letter originally addressed to Congressman John Moss, chairman of the Subcommittee on Commerce and Finance of the Committee on Interstate and Foreign Commerce of the U.S. House of Representatives. In it, James Lorie, a professor of finance at the University of Chicago Graduate School of Business, excoriated the whole concept behind Martin's proposal for a central market. He pointed out that Martin would "increase the monopoly power of the NYSE and defend the public interest through self-regulation by the Exchange. This is a little like having the rabbits guard the lettuce."

The letter was barely two pages long but was signed by 19 of the "21 especially well-qualified academicians." Lorie failed to reach one of the 21, and one declined to sign despite his agreement with the statement.

The signers:
William J. Baumol, Princeton University
Fischer Black, University of Chicago
Paul H. Cootner, Stanford University
Harold Demsetz, University of Chicago and UCLA
Donald E. Farrar, University of Pennsylvania
Lawrence Fisher, University of Chicago
Milton Friedman, University of Chicago
Michael C. Jensen, University of Rochester
John Lintner, Harvard University
James H. Lorie, University of Chicago
Burton G. Malkiel, Princeton University
Morris Mendelson, University of Pennsylvania
Franco Modigliani, MIT
Alexander A. Robichek, Stanford University
Paul A. Samuelson, MIT
Myron S. Scholes, MIT
William F. Sharpe, Stanford University
Seymour Smidt, Cornell University
George J. Stigler, University of Chicago

It was the kind of letter Bill Casey had to respect.

Jim Lorie had walked into my office at 25 Broad St. one morning, introduced himself and described his support of competition over regulation and open systems over closed ones. He had read what I was saying and asked how he could help. The result was the above-mentioned letter in which the co-signers ranged from Milton Friedman on the right to Paul Samuelson on the left.

Jim and I became good friends, especially during the National Market Advisory Board (NMAB) meetings held from 1975 to '77. Among other things he did for me was introduce me to a student of his, Victor Niederhoffer, philosophically a libertarian but also a five-time national squash champion. (Jim and Victor teamed up in doubles competition and did very well, as long as Jim remained well back in the right-hand corner of the doubles court.) Victor belonged to the Harvard Club in New York City and I played at the Racquet and Tennis Club. We would start a match with his giving me 10 points in a 15-point game. If I won, he would give me only 8 points the next game; if he won, he'd give me 12 points next time. I don't think it ever got to 14, but it seldom got below 8. I would emerge from the challenge as exhausted as I can ever remember and wondered at times whether Victor would become the NYSE's secret weapon to put Don Weeden out of commission.

The Commission's white paper on market structure had not yet been released when Casey had asked me, "What do you say to all this, Don?" At the time I was not sure whether he was giving me one last chance to cooperate or whether he was looking for a compromise on our part that would meet the desires of the exchange community. The problem was there was no compromise available to us short of capitulation. And Casey knew it. He also knew that we had been successful in convincing powerful people in Congress, in the Justice Department, the Treasury Department and even the Council of Economic Advisers that the Third Market was very important, not only as a competitive force making the market better, but also useful in pushing the NYSE toward the unfixing of commissions and the creation of a National Market System.

Whatever Casey's initial intentions were, he came down on the right side of this issue.

Finally, in February 1972, the Commission spoke. They began by saying that they had completed a series of hearings and special studies extending over a period of three and a half years, and that

"This policy statement is based on the data and testimony accumulated in this entire process of hearings and studies."

They pointed out certain changes which had occurred in the equity markets. Of particular interest was the growing institutionalization of the market.

"The auction market and the specialist system have not been able to absorb this pressure without the assistance of other markets."

After citing

"The remarkable ability of block positioners and other market makers, including some specialists, to handle the large offerings and bids which come from the institutions"

it quickly stated that their

"Policies are designed to maintain depth and liquidity by concentrating trading in a central market *system* (emphasis added) in which competing market makers will generate the best prices, in which comprehensive disclosure will show how and where to obtain the best execution, to which all qualified broker-dealers will have access."

The Commission continued:

"This (central market system) represented something of a shift in the historical position of the Commission, which ... tended to favor competitive but separate markets. This shift resulted from technological developments which made it possible to tie markets together so that one could foster competition within a central market ... and from the need to strengthen the existing market structure, including market making capacity."

The Commission went on to say that, among other things, a central market system would entail

- Elimination of artificial impediments, created by exchange rules or otherwise, to dealing in the best available market
- Integration of Third Market firms into the central market system by including them in the disclosure system

We were elated. Despite language that called for new regulation and reporting requirements for Third Market firms that might be onerous or restrictive and would add some costs to our business, we couldn't have been more pleased with the outcome.

Martin's vision seemed dead — with the Commission "clear-headed and determined," 394 was about to disappear. It was almost too good to be true.

And so it was.

Specialist off the floor

FRANK WEEDEN, a lanky Californian of sixty-six, is an off-the-floor specialist whose firm makes markets in a wide variety of municipal bonds and stocks listed on the New York Stock Exchange. Currently Weeden makes markets in seventy-seven of the most active industrials and fifty-four rails and utilities; he does most of his business with large financial institutions. A fund that wanted to sell 10,000 shares of General Motors, for example, might fear that offering the lot on the floor would disturb the market; Weeden, however, takes it all at one price, perhaps only a half-point under the market. He charges no commissions, instead makes his income on the spread between the prices at which he can find buyers and sellers. Weeden sells from an inventory of between $10 million and $15 million that, he hopes, anticipates the appetites of the institutions. His typical deals involve middle-sized blocks of shares, largely bought and sold by banks and mutual funds. In 1959 his volume came to almost $700 million.

Frank Weeden in article on ten powerful men on Wall Street, *Fortune* Magazine, February 1960

*[373 US 341]
*HAROLD J. SILVER, Doing Business as Municipal Securities
Company, et al., Petitioners,

v

NEW YORK STOCK EXCHANGE

373 US 341, 10 L ed 2d 389, 83 S Ct 1246, reh den
375 US 870, 11 L ed 2d 99, 84 S Ct 26

[No. 150]

Argued February 25 and 26, 1963.   Decided May 20, 1963.

SUMMARY

The New York Stock Exchange directed certain of its member firms to
discontinue private wire connections with two nonmember over-the-counter
securities broker-dealers, without assigning any reason therefor or giving
the nonmembers notice or an opportunity to be heard. The broker-dealers
brought suit against the Exchange in the United States District Court for
the Southern District of New York, alleging that the Exchange had violated
§§ 1 and 2 of the Sherman Act (15 USC §§ 1, 2) by this action. The
District Court held that the antitrust laws applied to the Exchange, and
it granted summary judgment and a permanent injunction against its
interfering with private wires between its member firms and the nonmember
broker-dealers. (196 F Supp 209.) The Court of Appeals for the Second
Circuit reversed on the grounds that the Exchange was exempt from the
restrictions of the Sherman Act. (302 F2d 714.)

On certiorari, the Supreme Court of the United States reversed. In an
opinion by GOLDBERG, J., expressing the views of six members of the
Court, it was held that (1) absent any justification, the Exchange's
conduct constituted a group boycott which was a per se violation of § 1
of the Sherman Act; (2) the Securities Exchange Act does not totally
exempt exchanges from the antitrust laws, but particular instances of
exchange self-regulation which fall within the scope and purposes of the
statute may be regarded as justified in answer to the assertion of an antitrust claim; and (3) the Exchange's violation of the antitrust laws in the
instant case was not justified, because the nonmember broker-dealers were
not given notice and an opportunity to be heard.

CLARK, J., concurred in the result on the ground that the antitrust
laws apply generally to securities exchanges.

STEWART, J., joined by HARLAN, J., dissented on the ground that the
Securities Exchange Act removes antitrust liability for any action taken
in good faith to effectuate an exchange's statutory duty of self-regulation.

Page from *Silver, dba Municipal Securities Co., et al. v. New York Stock Exchange*,
U.S. Supreme Court decision, May 20, 1963

Eugene Rotberg, associate director, and Irving Pollack, director of market regulation, U.S. Securities and Exchange Commission, *Fortune* Magazine, January 1967

To the members of the New York Stock Exchange;

One year ago, the New York Stock Exchange implemented Rule 394 (b). This rule authorizes a member firm to go off the Exchange floor to the over-the-counter market for listed securities (Third Market) to execute a public order whenever it will result in a more favorable price for its customer.

To many members firms, Rule 394 (b) appears sufficiently complicated in its concept and cumbersome in its operation as to be unworkable in practice. Although it is obvious that the advent of the rule ushered in no great surge of business done under its provisions, it may be illuminating to review our experience with the rule during its first year of existence.

We are a registered market-maker, qualified to accept inquiries under this rule in over 200 listed stocks.

During the past year, 108 inquiries were received by us from 45 different member firms. These inquiries concerned transactions ranging from 500 shares to 40,000 shares. We responded with a competitive bid or offer to 105 of these inquiries. In 96 cases our bid or offer was for the entire number of shares involved.

With respect to our 105 responses:

50 were an improvement over the price on the floor and resulted in off-board transactions with us.

15 were an improvement over the price on the floor but were disallowed by the Exchange for technical reasons.

12 were an improvement over the price on the floor but were subsequently bettered by the floor in response to our competitive bid or offer.

16 were an improvement over the price on the floor but no trade occurred on or off the Exchange because the order was limited in price or for other reasons.

12 were not an improvement over the price on the floor.

The size of our actual purchases and sales ranged from 800 shares to 10,000 shares involving dollar values from $26,000 to $485,000.

The 189,700 shares involved in the above transactions represent less than one percent of the 50,000,000 listed shares purchased and sold by us as principal during the 12 months Rule 394 (b) has been operative. It represents an infinitesimal part of the shares traded on the New York Stock Exchange during the comparable period. Yet it also represents proof that the use of Rule 394 (b) can provide benefits to a member firm and its customer.

It is gratifying to have had a start in this business, and it is hoped that member firms will increase their use of 394 (b) during its second year of operation.

WEEDEN & CO.
INCORPORATED

NEW YORK CHICAGO BOSTON SAN FRANCISCO LOS ANGELES HOUSTON LONDON

This ad appeared in the Wall Street Journal November 27, 1967.

don weeden the first republicrat

PARTY LABELS JUST DON'T MEAN A THING TODAY. THE PROBLEMS FACING THIS COUNTRY MUST BE LOOKED AT FROM A PERSONAL POINT OF VIEW— ONE MAN, FREE FROM PARTY RESTRICTIONS, FREE FROM POLITICAL DEALS, FREE TO ACT AS HIS CONSCIENCE TELLS HIM AND NOT AS A CLUB BOSS ORDERS HIM; FREE TO TALK WITH AND LISTEN TO THE PEOPLE.

Don Weeden's first state of the district message

AFTER 12 YEARS OF INEFFECTIVE AND INDIFFERENT CONGRESSIONAL LEADERSHIP, IT'S TIME TO REPLACE THE OLD ORDER WITH SOMETHING BETTER. WITH SOMETHING NEW AND VITAL AND POWERFUL. WITH CHANGE.

after Chicago, what?

FIGHT FOR CHANGE WHENEVER THAT FIGHT CAN BE FOUGHT. MY FIGHT OFFERS YOU A CLEAR AND DISTINCT CHOICE BETWEEN THE OLD AND THE NEW, BETWEEN YESTERDAY AND TOMORROW, BETWEEN THE STATUS QUO AND MEANINGFUL CHANGE.

now is the time for all good democrats to vote for a republican

THE N. Y. TIMES ENDORSED HIM OVER THE INCUMBENT. HE'S REFUSED TO SUPPORT THE NIXON-AGNEW TICKET. BEFORE THE DEMOCRATIC CONVENTION, HE PUBLICLY SUPPORTED SENATOR EUGENE McCARTHY FOR THE PRESIDENCY. HE'S SHOWN HIS INDEPENDENCE AND HE WILL REMAIN AN INDEPENDENT MAN.

Let's get out

SYSTEMATICALLY, ORDERLY, RESPONSIBLY—BUT OUT. WE MUST CHANGE OUR POLICIES IN VIETNAM AND WE MUST CHANGE THEM QUICKLY. WE MUST STOP THE BOMBING . . . BECAUSE EVERY BOMB WE DROP OVER NORTH VIETNAM FALLS ON HARLEM AND WATTS.

You don't have to be JEWISH to support ISRAEL

YOU ONLY HAVE TO BE A THINKING, FEELING HUMAN BEING. I STRONGLY BELIEVE THAT THE UNITED STATES HAS A FIRM AND IRREVOCABLE COMMITMENT TO PROTECT ISRAEL, BY WHATEVER MEANS NECESSARY, FROM ANY ARAB EFFORT TO PUSH HER PEOPLE INTO THE SEA.

...and the WAR goes on

IT'S AS IF EUGENE McCARTHY NEVER SAID A WORD AGAINST THE WAR. IT'S AS IF ROBERT KENNEDY NEVER SAID A WORD AGAINST THE WAR. THERE WAS HOPE, REAL HOPE, JUST A FEW MONTHS AGO. BUT THERE DOESN'T SEEM TO BE ANY NOW.

Cops and Robbers

CRIME IN THE CITY IS ONLY A REFLECTION OF LIFE IN THE CITY, FOR TOO MANY PEOPLE, THAT REFLECTION IS UGLY AND DEPRESSING. BUT IT DOESN'T HAVE TO BE THAT WAY. IT CAN BE CHANGED. IT MUST BE CHANGED.

Maybe we should call it the Leonard Farbstein Memorial Lower Manhattan Expressway

THE LOWER MANHATTAN EXPRESSWAY WILL BE A TOTAL AND COMPLETE DISASTER. AND THE RESPONSIBILITY FOR THIS DISASTER BELONGS TO LEONARD FARBSTEIN. BECAUSE ONLY HE HAS HAD THE POWER TO STOP IT. BUT HE DIDN'T.

IF YOU HAVE BEEN READING THESE ADS OVER THE LAST FEW WEEKS
AND LIKED WHAT YOU READ,
DON WEEDEN'S NAME APPEARS ON THE BALLOT
IN COLUMN A ROW 34.
VOTE FOR HIM.
IF YOU LIVE IN THE 19TH DISTRICT — THE LOWER EAST SIDE,
MOST OF THE VILLAGE, CHELSEA, THE UPPER WEST SIDE —
YOU CAN VOTE FOR HIM.
IF YOU DON'T LIVE IN THE DISTRICT, PERHAPS YOU KNOW SOMEBODY WHO DOES.
IN ANY EVENT, THANK YOU FOR READING.

don weeden
for congress

Advertisement: "Don Weeden for Congress," 19th District of New York, *Village Voice*, 1968

Weeden & Co.
specialists in competition

The Securities and Exchange Commission reports exchange and over-the-counter volume in 50 selected common stocks listed on the New York Stock Exchange. Volume figures for the third quarter of 1970 (latest report) based on this report are as follows:

Share Volume *

Security	Weeden & Co.	NYSE	Weeden Volume as a % of NYSE	Security	Weeden & Co.	NYSE	Weeden Volume as a % of NYSE
American Can Company	70,248	561,400	12.51	Monsanto Company	117,211	1,175,000	9.98
American Cyanamid Co.	78,545	1,701,800	4.62	Occidental Petroleum Corp.	103,185	7,855,400	1.31
American Tel. & Tel. Co.	207,928	4,842,500	4.29	Pacific Gas & Electric Co.	340,784	960,100	35.49
American Electric Power Co.	129,289	2,057,700	6.28	Procter & Gamble Co.	316,912	958,500	33.06
Bethlehem Steel Corp.	41,167	1,251,900	3.29	RCA Corporation	78,976	2,487,700	3.17
Caterpillar Tractor Co.	291,289	1,217,500	23.93	Royal Dutch Petroleum Co.	111,011	1,394,400	7.96
Chase Manhattan Corp.	58,180	883,700	6.58	Scott Paper Co.	57,475	1,987,700	2.89
Chrysler Corporation	356,484	4,619,700	7.72	Sears, Roebuck & Co.	199,640	1,717,200	11.63
Continental Oil Co.	165,784	3,556,900	4.66	Southern California Edison Co.	148,420	935,800	15.86
Delta Air Lines, Inc.	91,990	1,425,300	6.45	Southern Co. (The)	142,443	1,282,700	11.10
Dow Chemical Co. (The)	29,455	950,800	3.10	Sperry Rand Corporation	59,812	3,241,700	1.85
Eastman Kodak Co.	284,428	3,432,600	8.29	Standard Oil Company of Calif.	208,410	2,402,000	8.68
Federated Dept. Stores, Inc.	115,628	1,220,100	9.48	Standard Oil Company (Indiana)	196,138	1,111,400	17.65
Firestone Tire & Rubber Co.	90,674	1,182,400	7.67	Standard Oil Company (New Jersey)	376,677	3,907,500	9.64
Ford Motor Co.	231,429	2,039,600	11.35	Texaco Inc.	543,715	4,258,000	12.77
General Electric Co.	158,849	2,114,200	7.51	Travelers Corp. (The)	276,337	1,194,200	23.14
General Motors Co.	308,026	3,290,800	9.36	UAL, Inc.	83,480	1,491,300	5.60
General Tel. & Electronics Corp.	170,465	2,868,700	5.94	Union Carbide Corp.	73,342	1,596,600	4.59
Gillette Co. (The)	119,835	1,410,500	8.50	U. S. Steel Corp.	105,541	1,202,800	8.77
Goodyear Tire & Rubber Co.	536,219	2,508,400	21.38	Virginia Electric & Power Co.	153,790	1,513,000	10.16
Gulf Oil Corporation	501,992	3,776,300	13.29	Western Bancorporation	73,048	692,800	10.54
Houston Lighting & Power Co.	179,292	588,300	30.48	Westinghouse Electric Corp.	90,562	2,300,900	3.94
Int'l Nickel Co. of Canada, Ltd.	158,416	1,625,000	9.75				
International Paper Co.	190,947	1,398,100	13.66				
International Tel. & Tel. Corp.	121,641	4,169,400	2.92				
Litton Industries, Inc.	61,658	3,513,700	1.75				
Middle South Utilities, Inc.	201,083	903,400	22.26				
Mobil Oil Corp.	222,721	2,044,100	10.90				

Average Weeden Percent 10.55

*Included in Share Volume

	Weeden	NYSE
Round Lots:	Sales Only (none through the NYSE)	Volume figure includes all sales plus principal purchases by specialists, block positioners and other member firms.
Odd Lots:	Sales Included	Volume figure includes only round lot transactions by odd lot specialist.

Schedule 8

STATE OF MINNESOTA
STATE BOARD OF INVESTMENT
COMMON STOCK PURCHASES NEGOTIATED OR ORDERED ON THE BASIS OF
LOWEST AVAILABLE PRICE
January 1 - December 31, 1969

Total Shares	Issue and Vendor	Total Shares	Issue and Vendor	Total Shares	Issue and Vendor
CONSUMER-ORIENTED STOCKS		**Telephone-Telegraph**		**Retail Trade**	
UTILITIES		5500	American Tel. & Tel.	27500	Dayton-Hudson Corp.
Electric			1000 First Boston		500 A.G. Becker
9000	American Electric Pwr.		4500 Weeden		1000 Allison-Williams
	4000 J.S. Strauss	5000	General Tel. & Elec.		1000 Bache & Co.
	5000 Weeden		2000 American Securities		1000 Blair & Co.
6600	Central & S.W.		3000 First Boston		1000 Blyth
	3100 First Boston	20000	United Utilities		500 Burnham & Co.
	3500 Weeden		5000 American Securities		500 Caldwell Phillips
9000	Cincinnati Gas & Elec.		5000 First Boston		1000 Clark Dodge
	9000 Weeden		10000 Weeden		500 Courts & Co.
6000	Commonwealth Edison				1500 Dain Kalman
	6000 Weeden	**FINANCIAL SERVICES**			1000 Dean Witter
6000	Consumers Power	**Banks**			500 Dominick
	3000 First Boston	3000	Conill		500 Drexel Harriman
	3000 Weeden		3000 Keefe Bruyette		1000 Eastman Dillon
3000	Florida Pwr. & Light	6500	First Bank System		500 E.F. Hutton
	3000 Weeden		1500 Blyth		250 Faulkner Dawkins
10500	Houston Lgt. & Pwr.		5000 Dain Kalman		1000 F.I. duPont
	3500 American Securities	3500	First Nat'l City Corp.		2500 Goldman Sachs
	4000 First Boston		3500 Keefe Bruyette		1000 Hornblower Weeks
	3000 Weeden	1500	J.P. Morgan		500 J. Barth
2000	Louisville Gas & Elec.		1500 Blyth		1000 Kidder Peabody
	2000 First Boston	2000	National City Cleveland		500 Lehman Bros.
5000	Middle So. Utilities		2000 Blyth		250 Loewi & Co.
	5000 Weeden	24000	Sec. Pacific Nat'l Bank		250 Model Roland
5000	Minn. Pwr. & Light				1000 N.Y. Hanseatic
					1000 Paine Webber

31100 5000 Weeden
Northern States Pwr.
5900 American Securities
25200 Minn. Mutual Life

22000 Pacific Gas & Electric
6000 American Securities
2000 J.S. Strauss
14000 Weeden

15800 Public Serv. Indiana
3800 First Boston
12000 Weeden

9000 Southern Calif. Edison
4000 American Securities
5000 Weeden

16500 Southern Company
3000 American Securities
13500 Weeden

18100 Texas Utilities
2500 Blyth
2500 First Boston
100 J.S. Strauss
13000 Weeden

34700 Virginia Elec. & Pwr.
7500 American Securities
22000 First Boston
5200 Weeden

Gas

53400 Northern Illinois Gas
10000 Dean Witter
100 F.I. duPont
200 Estabrook
100 Walston
43000 Weeden

23500 Keefe Bruyette
500 Merrill Lynch
4000 Valley National Bank
4000 Keefe Bruyette
5000 Wells Fargo
5000 Bear Stearns

Insurance

4700 N.W. National Life Ins.
700 Dain Kalman
1000 Eastman Dillon
1000 F.I. duPont
500 Merrill Lynch
500 Piper Jaffray
1000 Smith Barney

17500 Safeco Corp.
11000 Blyth
1000 Eastman Dillon
5000 F.I. duPont
500 Merrill Lynch

16800 St. Paul Companies
12500 Blyth
2000 Dain Kalman
800 F.I. duPont
1000 First Boston
500 Merrill Lynch

CONSUMERS GOODS
Food-Beverage

3000 General Foods
2000 American Securities
1000 Weeden

3000 Piper Jaffray
250 Reynolds & Co.
1000 Smith Barney
250 Sutro
1000 White Weld
250 Wm. Blair & Co.
500 Woodard-Elwood

2000 Federated Dept. Stores
2000 Weeden

RESEARCH STOCKS

Office Equipment

1000 Internat'l Bus. Mach.
1000 J.S. Strauss

Photography

1000 Eastman Kodak
1000 Weeden

NATURAL RESOURCES

Petroleum

6000 Continental Oil
1000 J.S. Strauss
5000 Weeden

2000 Mobil Oil
2000 Weeden

9000 Std. Oil Indiana
4000 N.Y. Hanseatic
4000 Smith Barney
1000 Weeden

This spring the market had more than a touch of fall in it.

At Weeden & Co. we had our share of the cold weather. May of 1970 was all too reminiscent of May of 1962. From April 10th to May 26th the Dow Jones Industrial average sold off 161 points or 20%. During this same period of time, Weeden & Co. helped our customers sell 7,300,000 shares, buying over 6,000,000 shares for our own account, and helped them buy 7,400,000 shares. An average daily volume for Weeden & Co. of over 450,000 shares. Unfortunately, many of the shares we sold were at a price less than that which we paid for them.

We doubt our customers were aware of our loss — and there is no reason they should be. They look for "best execution" from Weeden whether they are buyers or sellers, bull market or bear, calm or panic. And that's what they got in May. We don't think they'll forget it.

Our customers really have only this one reason for dealing with us — best execution. We don't sell anything else, just good old fashioned price. So if you are at all interested in achieving best execution in the spring or in the fall, be assured, you can't be sure unless you check Weeden.

New York/Chicago/Boston/San Francisco/Los Angeles/Houston/London

Weeden & Co. INC.
The 48 year old upstart.

"Beyond his prodigious qualifications, the unique thing about Bill Martin is how very desperately Wall Street needs him."

William McChesney Martin, *Institutional Investor* Magazine, 1971

The 10 most active stocks of 1971.

On the Weeden Market, that is. To demonstrate the scope of Weeden & Co. as a market maker, we're listing the 10 securities—of the 250 NYSE-listed stocks in which we maintain markets—that had the greatest share volume on the Weeden Market during 1971. As a frame of reference, we also list the volume of the same 10 securities on the NYSE.

Security	1971 Share Volume*		Weeden Market
	Weeden	NYSE	As % of NYSE
Gulf Oil Corp.	4,522,600	19,852,400	22.8
International Nickel	4,425,500	14,189,700	31.2
Texaco Inc.	3,869,600	21,157,900	18.3
Standard Oil of New Jersey	3,364,900	14,177,500	23.7
General Motors	3,253,500	15,676,700	20.8
Middle South Utilities	2,817,200	5,609,200	50.2
Southern Company	2,769,800	11,290,400	24.5
American Tel. & Tel	2,765,600	32,231,900	8.6
Caterpillar Tractor	2,591,000	7,909,200	32.8
Mobil Oil Corp.	2,432,600	8,573,600	28.4

There's also another way to look at Weeden & Co. as a market maker. Listed below are 10 leading securities on the Weeden Market showing their volume as a percent of NYSE volume for 1971.

Security	1971 Share Volume*		Weeden Market
	Weeden	NYSE	As % of NYSE
General Mills	1,788,300	3,451,600	51.8
Middle South Utilities	2,817,200	5,609,200	50.2
Procter & Gamble	2,071,600	4,995,700	41.5
Northwest Bancorporation	221,900	564,000	39.3
Commonwealth Edison	1,189,900	3,321,900	35.8
Northern Indiana Public Service	677,300	1,986,300	34.1
Northern Illinois Gas	504,600	1,513,300	33.3
Caterpillar Tractor	2,591,000	7,909,200	32.8
Illinois Power Co.	696,800	-2,140,900	32.5
J. C. Penney	1,735,500	5,351,000	32.4

*NYSE volume as reported by The New York Times—1/9/72. Both Weeden & NYSE volumes represent round-lot sales plus round-lot principal purchases by the market.

Institutions and brokers transact over a million shares a day on the Weeden Market. They deal with us for one overriding reason—best execution. To make sure you're getting best execution, you or your broker should check us locally or at (212) 344-2300 before you buy or sell any of the stocks in which Weeden maintains markets.

Weeden & Co.
specialists in competition

New York · Boston · Chicago · Houston · Los Angeles · Philadelphia · San Francisco · London

NEW ISSUE

This announcement is neither an offer to sell nor a
solicitation of offers to buy any of these
securities. The offering is made only by the prospectus.

WEEDEN & CO.

300,000 Shares Common Stock (No Par Value)
Price $15.50 per Share

Copies of the prospectus may be obtained from such of the undersigned and other
securities dealers as may lawfully offer these securities in this State.

Bache & Co.
Incorporated

Equitable Securities, Morton & Co.   CBWL-Hayden, Stone Inc.
Incorporated

Thomson & McKinnon Auchincloss Inc.   Wood, Walker & Co.

Bateman Eichler, Hill Richards   The Ohio Company
Incorporated

Sutro & Co.   First California Company
Incorporated   Incorporated

Roberts, Scott & Co., Inc.   J. S. Strauss & Co.

October 14, 1970

15

Enter Jim Needham

Jim Needham was elected chairman of the NYSE Board of Directors in August 1972. (Note: That year, the NYSE changed from a "board of governors" to a "board of directors.") In *The Last Days of the Club*, Chris Welles described Jim as a "short, stout, pugnacious former accountant and SEC Commissioner recruited to do battle against the reformers" (p. 293).

One of the "reformers" happened to be Bob Haack, who held the job that Jim was being recruited for. In 1967, Bob had replaced Keith Funston as president of the NYSE, having come from the NASD, where he had also served as president. Bob was a tough, honest, tell-it-like-it-is Dutchman who was a known administrator and understood the markets.

Bob came to understand that the problems confronting the NYSE — fragmentation, give-ups, pressure for institutional membership, the Third Market — were due primarily to a fixed minimum commission structure that was increasingly unrelated to the costs of doing business with the growing institutional business.

In October 1970, Bob took the opportunity in a major speech before the prestigious Economic Club of New York to point these facts out without getting clearance from the NYSE leadership. Bunny Lasker, chairman of the NYSE Board of Governors, was furious, and tersely stated to the public that "The policy of the NYSE is made by the board and not by the president." Clearly the power structure didn't want to be lectured about the need to change. They wanted someone to fight against change. They had hired William Martin to set the stage and now reached out for Jim to lead the charge. As Don Regan, head of Merrill Lynch and the one who proposed Jim to the NYSE board, said, "We got him to lead the Exchange to bigger and better markets" (*Institutional Investor*, March 1973, p. 50).

Our reaction to Jim was wait and see. Bob Haack had been right. Fixed commissions had to go or else the NYSE would continue to lose market share.

Unfortunately, this "need to change" came at a time when volume was down and profits to the upstairs brokers had all but disappeared.

Martin had outlined the solution but somehow it wasn't getting across to the boys in Washington. Comfortable in the belief that Martin's solution had been rejected, we wondered how the NYSE would proceed.

Enter Needham.

It wasn't long before Jim went on the offensive. In a speech on January 11, 1973, to the Bond Club of New York, he announced that the NYSE was going to seek Congress' support for the elimination of the Third Market. Jim didn't mince his words. "Third Market firms must be given the choice *now* of joining an Exchange or going into some other business."

Actually, the speech was more than that. It was an extraordinary display of arrogance and misuse of the phrase "public interest." It was something you might expect to be said orally to one's friends in Congress quietly, outside the public eye. But to say what was said in a public speech, which was then reprinted in a full-page layout in the *Wall Street Journal* and *New York Times*, was unbelievable. Personally, I felt this kind of language coming from the chairman of the Exchange played into our hands and strengthened our credibility in Washington.

As Fred Siesel and I moved from one set of staff to another in the SEC, the Senate and the House, we found that Jim's language was offensive and counterproductive. Typical was the reaction of one congressional source, who complained that Needham kept promising to radically change the existing structure of the securities markets but this new marketplace looked very much like the old. "Every time Needham gives a speech he talks about restraints, closed groups, controls, exclusives" (*Institutional Investor*, March 1973, p. 50).

About this time I received the first of a series of letters from someone calling himself a Chevy dealer who was complaining about what was going on in his industry. These obviously tongue-in-cheek letters were a great way to illustrate the position being taken by the NYSE on market issues, and at least the first letter deserves to be reprinted in full.

We all thought they were very funny and made sure a few people in Washington received copies. Believe it or not, we never did find out who the sender was.

Dear Mr. Weeden:

I'm writing to ask your personal help in two areas. Neither involves money. Here's the story.

I represent Chevy dealers, and, as you know, we buy and sell new and used Chevrolet cars. There are also Ford dealers who buy and sell Ford cars, and these are the two major markets for cars in the United States. There are, of course, smaller regional markets conducted by American Motors, Chrysler, Volvo, Volkswagen, Toyota, etc., but Chevy and Ford are the two basic markets.

In recent times, however, a Third Market has come into existence. We have found Ford dealers trading in used Chevy cars. These dealers take Chevy cars into their inventory as trade-ins, and also sell them in direct competition with authorized Chevrolet dealers.

Now we don't mind competition, Mr. Weeden, but these Ford dealers are competing selectively. I mean they don't always take every Chevy car that's offered to them. They can pick and choose the cars they want to take in trade. If they don't want to take a lemon, they don't take it. We Chevy dealers are in there with the lemons all the time. And if a large institutional, or fleet, customer wanted to sell a large number of Chevy cars, these Ford dealers can easily close their lots and go on vacation.

Furthermore, these Ford dealers trading in used Chevy cars don't tell anybody but the customer the price they give him for his old Chevy trade-in. And while they advertise and quote prices for used Chevys on their lots, these prices, we have found, are often negotiated, especially when a fleet customer is involved.

What's more, conducting business in this manner does not allow any-one to know just how many Chevy cars are bought and sold by these Ford dealers. This secrecy, we suggest, may not be kosher. These deals may or may not be on the up-and-up. We have reason to believe, Mr. Weeden, that many buyers of Chevy cars are going to Ford dealers specifically so they can hide the details of their transac-tions. The large institutional, or fleet, customer, it appears, is doing this in increasing numbers, and is contributing to the fragmentation of the Chevy market which has done so much for America over the years. Remember, what's good for General Motors is good for America.

We believe strongly that if Ford dealers want to buy or sell used Chevys, they ought to become Chevy dealers. It's as simple as that. This also goes for sneaky regional dealers who sell or buy used Chevys. Anyone who meets our qualifications, incidentally, may become a Chevy dealer, so we can't be called a "closed club" in any sense of the word.

Now there has been some talk, as you know, of having one central market for buying and selling cars. We are in agreement with this concept. We feel an issuing car manufacturer such as General Motors should have the right to say which dealers can buy or sell its cars. Investors who wish to buy a used Chevy would have to buy it from an authorized Chevy dealer. Similarly, if the man on the street — or his Aunt Jane — wanted to sell his or her old Chevy, he or she would have to sell it to a Chevy dealer, as per the wishes of General Motors. Ford dealers could continue buying and selling Ford cars exclusively, that is unless the Ford Motor Company decided to have its cars traded by Chevy specialists.

That's the story, Mr. Weeden. Now here's where I need help. First, would you write your congressman on our behalf, and second, do you think you could convince your friend, Mr. Needham, of the wis-dom of this approach.

Sincerely,

In his January 1973 speech, Jim contrasted the Third Market, or non-Exchange market, with the NYSE, which did business in a "fish bowl." Among other things, he warned of a domino effect in which more and more investors would lose confidence in auction markets if institutions reduced their trading there.

Soon after, Jim invited me to a private lunch on the sixth floor of 11 Wall St. I decided to test his sense of humor by bringing a fish bowl stuffed with a ticker tape and a set of dominos. He actually got a big kick out of it, and I understand it remained prominently displayed in his office at the Exchange until he left.

I came to like Jim personally. I always knew where he stood on issues, as he did with me. We were both strong-headed with little mincing of words during the many committee meetings we both attended and in front of the press. One confrontation, better a discussion, was a little unusual and deserves recounting as best I can.

We had both attended an evening at the Waldorf in its grand ball-room celebrating the National Hockey League All-Stars. I was the guest of Lehman Brothers at their front-row table while Jim was at the next table. When dinner broke up, we met as we were walking out. One of us said, "How about an after-dinner drink at the Bull and the Bear?" We were among the first to arrive and took our place at the bar. Jim ordered some exotic cognac and I ordered Black Label scotch and soda. My guess is it was no later than 10:30 when we got our first setup.

As I mentioned, neither one of us minced our words, but the evening was such we were both making an effort to listen to the other's point of view.

The Bull and the Bear quickly filled up with people stacked two or three deep at the bar, but strangely enough there remained a space on either side of us. No one came to say hello or introduce themselves, although most in the crowd were Wall Street types and certainly knew Jim. It was as though a ring had formed around us, which politely kept its distance while Jim and I struggled to find understanding — maybe even accommodation.

The evening wore on and slowly the crowd around us dispersed. Like two fighters we stood toe to toe, ordering round after round, oblivious to the fact that we were having too much to drink. Beyond a certain point, what we said to each other, at each other, I have no recollection. I do remember that at one point they ran out of Courvoisier and Jim turned his attention to correcting the situation. Finally the bar closed, and they ushered us out into Jim's limousine. They rolled me out at Weeden's apartment on East 65th Street. It must have been well into the early morning.

Shortly after, Brad Cook, who had become chairman of the SEC in 1973, replacing Casey, gave a speech at the New York Financial Writers' Association. I wasn't sure where he stood on these issues, as he had not been a commissioner during the Casey era. This would be the first public indication of what the new SEC white paper on market structure would look like. I remember being there with Fred Siesel. We were not disappointed in what we heard: a consolidated tape, composite quotation system, removal of Rule 394(b) and a strong emphasis on priority to and protection of public limit orders systemwide. This was the first time the Commission was absolutely clear on this issue.

Jim was not deterred and continued his strategy of bad-mouthing the Third Market, slowing all progress toward a central marketplace and lobbying for our elimination.

As one looks back, Jim was winning the battle even though it looked as though he had lost. After conceding, under pressure from everyone, that the Third Market could not be excluded from the ultimate design, he shifted to a strategy of opposing all progress until the full design was in place. That strategy failed as well, so again, they shifted to one of stretch out, delay and control. Thus the Consolidated Tape System (CTS) did not come online until June 1975, the Composite Quotation System (CQS) only in 1977 and the Intermarket Trading System (ITS) in June 1978. A central limit order book (CLOB) was dropped along the way, as was the removal of 394(b). One could say that our side won most of the battles, but the NYSE won the war.

Nevertheless, somewhere along the line the NYSE power structure concluded that Jim was too aggressive, too controversial and not quite the image they had of themselves, and he was replaced by Mil Batten, ex-CEO of J.C. Penney and a well-respected member of the establishment. He was someone who understood the ways of competition and was ready to redirect the Exchange toward modernization, cost-cutting and customer service. It was a change that proved immensely successful, as we came to realize.

I missed Jim, and after his departure we had occasion to get together and reminisce.

16

Spreading Out: My Introduction to Congress

On Sunday, August 15, 1971, in a move that was as decisive as it was unanticipated, President Nixon took the United States off the gold standard. The markets reacted with an upward vigor seldom seen on Wall Street. On Monday, August 16, the popular Dow Jones Industrial Average (DJIA) had risen 32.93 points, closing at 888.95. It was the highest one-day increase ever at that time. This increase of 8 percent did not include General Motors (GM), one of the 30 stocks making up the Dow, because it (along with Ford (F)) had not opened due to an imbalance in orders.

Like everyone else, we wondered at this unprecedented situation, and speculated when General Motors and Ford would open, and at what price. As market makers in both stocks, we were in constant touch with the floor brokers and talking to the institutions. As a matter of habit, we deferred in quoting a market ourselves until the stocks were "opened" on the NYSE. But as the day went on and the market closed, we began to consider opening these stocks ourselves. But how?

We decided to talk to the Philadelphia Baltimore Washington (PBW) Stock Exchange about doing it on their floor. We had recently become a member, acting as a backup specialist. They had a number of institutional members and thought, as we did, that to open the stocks before the NYSE did would make a statement about the strength and the value of their exchange. As they say, "One print is worth a thousand words."

The next day, the markets were still in turmoil over this abrupt change in economic policy. General Motors and Ford remained closed on the NYSE. Finally, around noon, several buy orders in GM were assembled on the PBW exchange, with Weeden supplying the sell side out of inventory. The PBW announced the fact that GM had opened on their exchange and small amounts were trading around the new level.

Shortly thereafter, GM opened on the NYSE close to the price printing on the PBW. The volume in GM was enormous compared to our 20,000 shares, but the damage was done. The fact that a NYSE-listed opened somewhere else was noted in the weekly magazines and newspapers across the country.

Meanwhile, both the Senate and the House had recently authorized studies of the securities markets as a fallout from the 1968–70 paperwork crisis that closed the NYSE on Wednesdays and caused the failure of a number of brokerage firms. Senator Harrison Williams, senior senator from New Jersey and chairman of the Subcommittee on Securities of the Committee on Banking, Housing and Urban Affairs, called a hearing on various securities industry matters for the end of September, and in the course of those hearings raised the issue of GM's opening on the PBW exchange.

Just prior, I had spent 10 days hiking in the High Sierra with my 11-year-old son and friends after Labor Day. I returned home with two weeks' worth of beard, and my wife encouraged me to keep it a few more days. Beards were not as commonplace in 1971 as they are today. In fact, Wall Street considered them an emblem of the radical left, and nary a one could be seen south of Fulton Street.

With this very much in mind, I traveled to Washington on the day of the hearing and quietly situated myself in the far corner of the back row. When it came time for Elkins Wetherill, president of the PBW exchange, to appear, he was asked to describe in detail what happened. "Elkie" was a handsome, well-thought-of Philadelphia blue blood, and perfect for the job of president, but, unfortunately, not that familiar with the language and mysteries of the marketplace. As he sought help from his colleagues, Steve Paradise, Senator Williams' administrative assistant, whispered in Williams' ear while pointing in my direction. Senator Williams then graciously asked me to come before the committee and relate blow by blow what happened. I had never before met any senator and was naturally nervous and uncomfortable. After being sworn in, I first mumbled an explanation of why I was there in this "hirsute" condition but, surprisingly, no one seemed to care. I finished describing our role in the trades and retired to the back of the hearing room. I decided at that moment that if I could appear in front of a group of senators with my beard, I might as well keep it for a bit longer. I still have that beard 32 years later (despite my mother's constant entreaties to "get rid of it").

Both houses of Congress were "determined to make the most searching re-examination of the competitive, statutory, and economic issues facing the securities markets, the securities industry and public investors since the 1930s." In consequence, their studies were conducted by an independent group of lawyers, academicians and specialists familiar with securities industry matters. The Senate subcommittee engaged David Ratner as chief counsel and Alton Harris as one of the assistant counsels. David had been the last executive assistant to SEC Chairman Manuel Cohen in 1969 and was eminently qualified for the job. The House study group was equally well qualified and included William Painter, Harvey Rowen and Roy Schotland.

Compared to the phalanxes of NYSE staff, floor members, upstairs brokers, lawyers, industry association representatives and lobbyists arguing for the implementation of the Martin Report, few were telling our side of the story. While other Third Market firms appeared at the formal hearings, Fred Siesel and I seemed to be the only ones pounding the corridors and educating staff. We felt we were on our own, so we spent as much time "in their face" as possible. One meeting that Fred and I had with Congressman Bob Eckhardt was illustrative of how the cards were stacked. We got there a few minutes before the 45 minutes allocated to us. The door to his chambers opened and out streamed about eight people, headed up by Lee Kendall of the Association of Stock Exchange Firms. After the usual courtesies, Fred and I went in, told our story and answered some very insightful and straight-to-the-point questions from the Congressman. We were rather pleased as the allocated 45 minutes stretched into something over an hour. But as we left, standing there ready to enter the room were another eight or so men led by Don Calvin, vice president of the NYSE.

The same was happening when we visited David and Al in the Senate building. Other issues, of course, were on their table, such as the way the industry handled the clearing, settlement and delivery of securities transactions; the regulatory structure of the industry; and issues involving municipal securities. But on top of everyone's list was market structure, and we were determined that our voice would be heard.

Not only did we visit everyone who would see us, we were cranking out studies to counteract the volumes of unsubstantiated accusations emanating from the NYSE, the Securities Industry Association and individual member firms.

For instance, we pointed out that Weeden's Third Market volume exceeded that of all the specialists on the AMEX. We countered the NYSE claim that we were causing increased fragmentation by showing that it was occurring due to increased AMEX volume and give-ups on the regional exchanges.

At the time the NYSE was insisting on two separate last sale tapes, we were documenting for the SEC and Congress that Third Market plus regional stock exchange volume equaled 43.5 percent of NYSE volume and was considerably higher in certain stocks. These studies were all done in 1971 at a time when both houses of Congress were actively studying the stock markets.

Another influential study was made in conjunction with the 30-stock trial in NYSE-listed stocks that was instituted in April '71 on the new NASDAQ system. This trial was the result of Weeden's fight to reverse the infamous deal between the SEC, the NYSE and the AMEX "by the banks of the Potomac" that initially prevented listed stocks from being quoted on the NASDAQ. Fred pointed out that spreads quoted on the NYSE narrowed by 12 percent in those 30 stocks after they began trading on the NASDAQ.

17

Meanwhile, Back at the Firm

The year 1972 began a period of growth for Weeden that continued through 1977, when the firm suffered a dramatic turn in its fortunes that led to its need to merge with another firm or face bankruptcy.

At the beginning of 1972, we had more than $30 million in capital, placing us among the top 25 Wall Street firms. Alan was president and CEO, and I remained as chairman, nominally in charge of our stock trading department. Earnings in 1971 had reached an all-time high of $5,796,000, or $3.72 per share.

Despite our continued growth in personnel and offices, we still thought of Weeden & Co. as a family firm. A good example of the family-like environment that existed throughout Weeden was the annual Christmas party — I should say "parties," as each office made theirs into a rollicking event with widespread participation by all employees. Frank made a point of visiting each office — and party — while he was active, which meant until he was well over 80. This was much to the consternation of his wife, who, under rules established early on in the life of the firm, was excluded from attending. No spouses. Only employees. The rationale was that the party's purpose was for employees to intermingle with one another in a social atmosphere and get to know each other better.

Some observed that this "getting to know one another a little better" was sometimes taken more seriously than appropriate and led to relationships that complicated the workplace atmosphere and were the basis of many rumors.

These parties cannot take full blame for what one would describe as "extracurricular activities" among employees. That such relationships existed was alluded to in some of the party skits, sometimes in very specific terms. No one was excluded from the role of target or the butt of an inside joke.

While every office had its party, always with some Weeden in attendance, New York, with its far larger employee count, always was "*the party*" and attracted key personnel from the other offices.

The entertainment was home grown. Skits were the medium, with generous prizes given to the best. Every department participated. Preparation started weeks, even months earlier, with elaborate plots and dialogue usually involving everyone in the department. Dividends, stock transfers, accounting, money desk, stock trading, the cage — all participated. Jack normally served as master of ceremonies. I was usually a participant. Alan was a bit aloof, but sometimes participated in some department's skit or song.

A description of Weeden from our Winter 1972 "Hot Line," a quarterly publication produced by the employees, gives one a feeling of the firm. At the time Weeden had 550 employees total, of which 340 were located in the New York office. Brian Lea, our vice president of corporate planning, had joined Weeden in 1954 when the New York office had only 20 employees and the company 40 overall. In 1972, the firm's 50th anniversary, we still thought of ourselves as a family firm. I think it was the next Christmas party when I sang about what it took to become chairman of the company to the tune of Gilbert & Sullivan's famous song "When I Was a Lad" from *HMS Pinafore*. I finished with the line "If you choose your parents very carefully, you too can be chairman of the company." It was just this atmosphere that was both the strength and the weakness of management. Ten years after our collapse, a reunion was organized in New York and attended by more than 200 ex-employees. Frank had recently passed away, Jack and Alan were retired. The mood was bittersweet.

In 1972, it was felt that we should review how the firm was to be run. Naturally I thought I should be the one to do it, but I had mixed feelings about pressing for it, as I was deeply involved in issues involving market structure, which had me hustling around the country, especially to Washington. The Martin Report was on the table, Casey had just come to the SEC and Needham was gearing up to run us out of town.

I also sensed a reluctance on Alan's part to turn over the mantle to his younger brother, who was spending less and less time in the trading room and was stirring up a fair bit of antagonism among the influential members of Wall Street. We were embarking on a hefty expansion of our trading activities in fixed income issues and it was not a good time to change horses. While I never talked to Frank, it became clear as the year started that he had similar reservations. Also, John Krause had joined our firm in June of 1970 in the municipal bond sales department. John was an attractive, dynamic salesman, an ex-Marine captain and former captain of the football team at Washington University in St. Louis. Frank was immediately attracted to him and began to see him as the one who could run the firm. This idea was floated by Frank and Alan, and I met with John for a long cards-on-the-table discussion. It was important to him that he have my support as well as that of the other two.

At the time, I was in Hanover, New Hampshire helping Pete McCloskey in his New Hampshire primary race against President Nixon. Pete had long argued for getting out of Vietnam, as I had. He had been a class ahead of me at Stanford and had served with distinction as a Marine officer in Korea.

After my meeting with John I supported him becoming executive vice president. His responsibilities would include firmwide sales plus being in charge of stock trading, a position that clearly signaled his being the heir apparent when Alan stepped down. This change occurred in May. The expansion plans that had begun in 1971 under John's direction in corporate bonds, tax-exempt notes and government bonds now accelerated. The 1971 results showed the bond department contributing more revenue than the stock department and made us a serious player in corporate and U.S. government bonds for the first time. Overall revenue doubled from 1971 to 1975, all coming from the fixed income area, and then it grew another 26 percent in 1976. Net profits took a roller-coaster ride during this time. The numbers below reflect earnings per share for our fiscal year ending September 30.

1971	*1972*	*1973*	*1974*	*1975*	*1976*
+$3.72	+$1.65	-$1.50	-$4.15	+$3.20	+$4.28

It was a time of significant hires and the opening of six new offices. As our business expanded, the use of capital expanded also. By the end of 1976, our capital was being leveraged at historic highs, a leading factor contributing to our troubles in 1977.

Alan, meanwhile, had started his long-announced and well-prepared trip around the world. He and his three children, Leslie (18), Robert (22) and Donald (23), set off in late spring of 1976 on a 15-month journey to explore many of the largely untouched nature spots on all continents except Europe. They hiked up into the Brooks Range in northern Alaska; kayaked the fiords in Patagonia, Chile; climbed Mount Kilimanjaro; bird-watched in the Celebes; and hiked among the old-growth forests on the isle of Tasmania. It was a once-in-a-lifetime experience for all of them and was written up later in *Fortune* Magazine.

After a bad year in 1974, revenue gains and bottom-line earnings for 1975 and 1976 finally justified our decision to aggressively grow the business. As we went into 1977, Alan was on sabbatical, Jack was setting up Dexter Securities and overseeing our WHAM trading system on the Cincinnati exchange, and I was busy with various industry committees and traveling around the country. Increasingly, the firm had come to rely on John Krause for leadership, direction and the daily oversight of our business.

At this time, one could fairly say that Weeden had one of the finest collections of traders and salesmen active on the Street. Ed Moos ran our government bond department, with Jim Erickson in corporates, Wayne Jahns in municipals and Mike Mallen in municipal dollar bonds. Don Campbell and Josh Gardener headed up listed stock trading, with Dudley Eppel in the OTC department. Individual stock traders including Jason Lumley, Terry Thayne, Lou Ferrari, Don Ghegan and Steve Gladstone maintained our reputation as the leading Third Market house. But they were merely the tip of the iceberg. Working out of our offices scattered across the country were many outstanding traders, salesmen, managers and back-office support people. The real tragedy of 1978 was the loss of this team. For most of its existence, Weeden had been able to attract talent because of the environment offered and maintained by the family. Our attitude toward the business and toward the employees was the glue that brought the best to Weeden and kept their loyalty. Frank and Norman were modest, unpretentious but experienced traders willing to take risks, well versed in the details of the trade, who truly enjoyed the business and all the people with whom they worked. Raised in California, they practiced informality, equality, openness and fairness. They encouraged stock ownership, established one of the first profit-sharing trusts on Wall Street, and insisted that everyone be called by their first name.

Yes, there was nepotism, although Frank didn't think of it that way. He was always as tough on his three sons as he was on others, even bending over backwards to avoid the accusation. It always seemed to me that any nepotism was more than balanced by my modest salary, minimal bonus and smaller participation in stock options.

Reading over the company magazine published quarterly throughout this period, one can only conclude that we had a helluva good time. Our motto: "Work hard, play hard." For much of that period we were still small enough to know one another. The Christmas parties and skits presented by the respective departments demonstrated a companywide knowledge of everyone's weaknesses, foibles and quirks.

There was also fierce competition among divisions, always expressed during bonus discussions as well as on the basketball court at the Downtown Athletic Club. Fortunately, this atmosphere was maintained within our division during our time at Moseley, Hallgarten, Estabrook & Weeden (MHEW) and has fully blossomed again since our re-establishment as Weeden & Co.

18

The Consolidated Tape

A consolidated tape, reporting all transactions in NYSE-listed stocks, became operational in June 1975. This was a month after the Securities Acts Amendments of 1975 were passed by both houses of Congress and signed into law by President Ford. The process of reaching agreement on the structure, ownership and operational control of a consolidated tape informally began in September 1971, when representatives from the American, Boston, Midwest, New York, Pacific and PBW stock exchanges convened a working committee to define a central marketplace.

After several meetings, the working committee agreed to focus on the more narrow issue of a consolidated tape and established a sub-committee to explore and report on the technical requirements for such a tape. The committee included for the first time a representative from the NASD (me), as well as an SEC presence to monitor and oversee its progress.

I was present at that first meeting, and all subsequent meetings on technical and policy issues, and ended up representing the NASD on the Consolidated Tape Association (CTA) committee, which became the governing body of the new tape.

One of the mysteries of the consolidated tape is how and why the NYSE and the AMEX ever conceded sharing their ticker tape with their competitors. After all, their ticker tapes, instituted in the late 1800s, were probably one of the most successful marketing tools ever created and probably did more than anything else to make New York the dominant center of equity trading in the country.

The idea of advertising actual trades on a continuous and real-time basis drew investors, speculators and listings like bears are drawn to honey. At the time there were quite a number of stock exchanges throughout the country — almost every major city had one — each listing and trading the stocks of local corporations, many of which slowly grew to have a national distribution and following. Most of the exchange floors used crude methods for distributing information to the public, usually clerks posting the latest prices on blackboards with messengers running to brokers' offices located off the floor with the latest price changes. When the NYSE introduced the ticker tape, combined with their use of the newly laid transatlantic cable connecting them with the far more active London Stock Exchange, it leapt ahead of all its competitors in listings and volume.

So — what happened?

We have to go back to Keith Funston's private visit to the SEC in October 1964. At that meeting, as reported in the *New York Times*, Funston made the point that "the public is entitled to information on Third Market transactions *as complete* (emphasis added) as that made available each day by the Exchange." It was a theme repeated time and time again by the NYSE staff and members to anyone who would listen. And at the time, everyone listened to the NYSE.

It was their belief that "bad things" were going on in this unpublished market that were very harmful to the public, especially the small investor. If the SEC would require them to report what they were doing, it would expose these shenanigans and they would stop.

This thinking was so strong that even as late as 1972, in heated debate on the CTA committee, the NYSE held out for the identification of transactions by market centers until a full central marketplace was established.

We saw the tape differently. Besides providing market information, it was a marketing tool no different than having front shelf space at a supermarket. To be part of it, especially with identification, was the best of all worlds.

Funston, of course, was not calling for a consolidated tape in 1964. Looking through my files, the first mention of one appears in my letter to the SEC in November 1969, in which I said, when speaking of a central marketplace:

"Such a system could be enhanced by a 'public' ticker tape capable of reporting trades in all marketplaces, including all exchanges, on a real-time basis."

By this time we were talking with everyone — Justice, Congress, SEC staff — and they were listening. We also began participating at the *Institutional Investor* conferences, which had begun in 1968. These conferences, sponsored by *Institutional Investor* Magazine, usually had me somewhere in their program as a speaker or panelist. We were never paid, but Gil Kaplan, founder of the publication, would have a nice present for all the participants, usually an Italian briefcase of some exotic design. I remember one speaker, a well-known economist, receiving his and turning it over and around very carefully. "Feels nice. Looks very elegant. Hmmm! Italian. Never last."

This might be a good time to mention the important role played by *Institutional Investor* Magazine and its founder and long-time publisher, Gil Kaplan.

Gil was a young man working somewhere in the depths of the American Stock Exchange when in early 1967 he began putting together his idea for a new magazine "with ambitious dreams of chronicling, analyzing and perhaps even influencing the changes that seemed destined to sweep the financial world" (Gil's words).

Back in 1967, institutional investing was in its infancy, but Gil clearly saw the future and built his magazine into an institution itself. Twenty years later, Gil boasted a staff of 300, $50 million a year in revenues and a monthly distribution of 136,000 issues. But *Institutional Investor* did much more than chronicle and analyze. Through its lead articles on timely subjects; its willingness to expose controversy; its in-depth profiles of industry leaders; its gossipy "Wall Street Letter," published weekly; its conferences focused on traders, money managers and research; and its private gatherings of the well-heeled movers and doers, it more than reached its goal to "influence the change that it saw as inevitable."

The list of the magazine's editors and writers is too long to do justice to all those who made it happen: Peter Landau, Cary Reich, Heidi Fiske, Chris Welles, Fred Bleakley and last, but not least from my perspective, Solveig Jansson, who let me tell it as I saw it in "The Way It Was." Published in 1988 and featuring the remembrances of 88 key players, "The Way It Was" was a special publication from *Institutional Investor* that served as an oral history and retrospective on the previous 20 years in the financial and securities industries.

I attended all the traders' conferences and spoke at many, but one of the most memorable evenings I had as a participant was at *Institutional Investor's* first European Investor Conference, held in London at the Savoy Hotel in late November of 1969. The climax of the three-day event was an American Thanksgiving Day dinner given in the Grand Ballroom with 500 of the most sophisticated bankers from all over Europe.

As I approached my assigned table, all I saw was a sea of glass: 14 wine glasses of all sizes and shapes at each place setting ready to receive the red and white wines from America that went best with each of the seven courses being served. There was hardly room for the food itself. You can imagine how this impressed the audience, who at the time barely recognized the names Mondavi or Jordan. It was fantastic. It was Gil at his best — that is until the magazine's 15th anniversary celebration in 1982, when he rented Lincoln Center and personally conducted Mahler's "Resurrection" Symphony before an overflow audience of bankers, money managers and other dignitaries from all over the world.

The crowning touch to this never-to-be-equaled display of American wine production to the European elite was the voice of the well-known wine merchant Sam Aaron, who owned the famous Sherry-Lehmann wine shop on Madison Avenue in New York. Aaron described each and every bottle with the gruff nasal accent of one born and bred in Brooklyn, barely understandable even to those of us from other parts of the U.S. Pure Gil.

Not wanting to end on this high note, I should also mention the conference in New York that I did not attend, as I was in Washington on more serious matters. After the conference I received a call from Ed Bunce, head trader for the DuPont Pension Fund and good friend, who complimented me on the entertainment provided by Weeden from the Empire Suite located on the 44th floor of the Hilton Hotel for some 300-odd institutional customers and competitors from the Street. It seems that across the way, on the 43rd floor of the Equitable building, two employees had remained after work and were enjoying themselves on top of a desk located near the windows. As the sun touched the horizon, the soft lights of the adjoining building spotlighted the event to the enjoyment of our 300 guests. For a time the couple was oblivious to the attention until one of them happened to glance up and over to the 300 pairs of eyes watching the spectacle. As Ed described the scene, shock was quickly followed by a large grin and a wave of the hand. Ed remarked with a laugh, as he hung up, that he thought Weeden had gone a bit far this time.

I almost forget what this chapter was all about. Oh yes.

Somewhere down the line, while everyone began focusing on a consolidated tape as the first step toward a central marketplace, the NYSE realized they had trapped themselves — "hoist by their own petard," so to speak — and the only solution was first to stonewall the process, then delay the process and finally, at least, to own and control the process.

The first effort to stonewall was to announce to the CTA committee by letter that the only system the NYSE would agree to was one where their last sales would remain on their tape, while regional and Third Market trades in NYSE listings would appear on the AMEX tape. The idea was so ludicrous as to do nothing but elicit the ire of the SEC.

Another tactic was to say "no tape until all unequal regulation issues were settled." The foot-dragging, as Al Sommer, former SEC Commissioner, described NYSE's stance, was countered in a proposed SEC Rule, 17a-15, which called for a tape to be provided by vendors and controlled by a neutral body. NYSE's response was to question the power of the SEC to do this. Congressman John Moss quickly retorted that he was very upset by the industry's slow progress on the tape and warned ominously that "it might be necessary to have a COMSAT-type operation to bring the (tape) into being."

Having failed to accomplish a postponement, NYSE's strategy now shifted to one of ownership and control. Those of us on the CTA committee were more amenable to these conditions, as long as the initial rules governing how the Securities Industry Automation Corporation (SIAC), owned by the NYSE and AMEX, administered the tape (fairly) and distributed the revenues (favorably) were tied down to our satisfaction. In this respect I believe I contributed more than my share of insistence that it be done right. I was battling a tough group at the NYSE and SIAC: Lee Amaya, Chris Keith, Bob Hall and Frank Palamara. But in the end, with growing pressure from the SEC and the Securities Acts Amendments looming, we (the regionals and NASD) got a tape that met our needs.

I had quite honestly forgotten the role I played until late in the 1990s, when out of the blue Arnie Staloff from the PBW Stock Exchange, their representative during the tape negotiations, called me and said that if ever I wanted to go to Deer Valley, Utah and ski, to please be his guest at his condo at the foot of the ski lift. He then reminded me how critical was my fighting for a tape revenue distribution scheme based on transactions, as opposed to volume, which was desired by the NYSE. He explained that that decision was what saved the regional exchanges from financial disaster during the 1970s and '80s by directing significant revenue to them. I hadn't realized this fully until he called. My wife, Pat, and I plus friends enjoyed a wonderful week the next March in Deer Valley.

Similar confrontational conditions existed on those committees dealing with the establishment of the Composite Quotation System and the Intermarket Trading System. But this story is not for the purpose of documenting my participation in every twist and turn in the struggle with the NYSE to move toward a National Market System.

The consolidated tape took more than four years before it was fully operational, and the Composite Quotation System was not yet up and running when Weeden began to have its problems in 1977 and I took over as CEO. If the consolidated tape fight was like World War II, the Composite Quotation System was World War I vintage: trench warfare, lots of meetings, little movement and tough slogging every inch of the way.

The struggle over an Intermarket Trading System (ITS) was a cakewalk in comparison. Here, the NYSE and the regionals came down on the same side — almost. First of all, both were against any kind of a CLOB, hard or soft, as something they felt threatened the existence of exchanges. They were also concerned with upstairs market making and joined together to keep the NASD (Third Market) out of the ITS, arguing that the technology couldn't handle multiple market makers except at forbidding cost. They also prevented Cincinnati from using its new electronic routing system to connect with the ITS. The NYSE dominated those meetings and had veto power over all changes. The system, as designed by the NYSE, gave the regionals more direct and inexpensive access to the New York floor but still kept them in a role of a secondary market. Nevertheless, the direct access to New York's floor was too good to resist. I remember well arguing, pleading, begging the regional exchanges to use this moment, when the SEC and Congress were receptive, to take a tough stance for creating "a fair field of competition."

In order to satisfy Congress' and the SEC's desire to have a central repository for public orders, the NYSE announced its intention to develop the Market Center Limit Order File (MCLOF) and later the Limit Order Information System (LOIS). Both initiatives were quietly dropped as the SEC under Harold Williams lost its determination to push for a National Market System.

Those were frustrating days for me, as I felt the ITS, as designed, would only lock the regionals into a secondary role in the listed market. Looking back from the perspective of 2002, the ITS still stands as a barrier to the full development of competition in the listed market. But more on that a little later.

19

Congressional Hearings on Market Structure

As I mentioned in an earlier chapter, from the very first moment in 1971 that Congress began studying "the securities industry, the securities markets and their impact on the public investor," we were there in their midst — by telephone, visiting their offices, inviting them to ours, and inundating them with our speeches, articles and gobs of data on our Third Market activity. We helped them understand the way markets work, the benefits of competition, the possibilities of the new technology and the dangers of monopoly. Our influence over their thinking and the resultant language in the two study reports is frankly impressive — and surprising, considering the political resources of the NYSE and its nationwide network of member brokers that were stacked against us.

From 1971 on, the subcommittees in both houses of Congress concerned with securities matters remained in the hands of the same chairmen, namely Senator Harrison Williams, Democrat from New Jersey, and Congressman John Moss from Sacramento, California. They pretty much ran the show, with certain exceptions on highly controversial issues when the Republican minority would get involved. From 1973 through the middle of 1975, several bills were enacted in both houses, causing some confusion even to those of us who were following the process very closely.

During this early period, we were talking to the newly assembled staff members recruited from the outside — primarily lawyers and academicians who were familiar with the securities industry in a general way, although less familiar with the workings of the market. William Painter, David Ratner, Harvey Rowen and Alton Harris were all smart, professional and objective as they absorbed input from every source available. They had been picked by the Democrats, who were in the majority in both the Senate and the House and who had a majority therefore on all committees and subcommittees. And while everything that goes on in Washington is political, it did not appear to affect their judgment.

Our approach was no different than it had been with the Justice Department and the SEC: "tell it like it is" — honestly, objectively and thoroughly. The fact that we saw no need for fixed commissions, that we felt the industry would survive without them, and that the small investor should have protection and priority convinced them that we had the public interest in mind.

Thus, the studies published in 1972 said all the right things. I led the Weeden team, but was ably assisted throughout by Fred Siesel, and from time to time by my brother Jack and Bob Beshar.

The process of developing and passing legislation took some four years, and during that time it was subjected to diversion, delays and determined resistance on the part of the NYSE. The first step resulted in two completed studies, one from each house of Congress. In both, the need for competitive markets, the removal of Rule 394(b) and some new form of a centralized market system rang out loud and clear. These studies were published in 1972 and thus had an influence on the SEC's vision of a central marketplace. These studies were followed by sub-committee hearings in both houses.

In preparing for the initial public hearings, the study team from the House side was concerned that the testimony might well overwhelm and confuse the committee members who obviously had not been deeply involved to date. I suggested to them that instead of having each point of view presented individually, it might be helpful to the committee to hear from all of us at the same time — in a panel forum, where the technical details of how markets work, the role of specialists vs. Third Marketeers, the need for equal regulation, etc., could be argued amongst the protagonists who would be better able to cross-examine one another.

William Painter and Harvey Rowen, along with Charlie Curtis, who was part of the regular staff of the House committee, readily bought the idea. The result was a panel consisting of the best specialists from the major exchanges (Steve Peck, Frank Graham, Dave Heller and Bill Lupien), a NASD market maker (Robert Doyle), Instinet (Jerry Pustilnik) and the Third Market (Weeden), plus Seymour Smidt from the Institutional Investor Study. For two days we went round and round on such issues as: Does the new rule (394(b)) work efficiently? What do we mean by "equal regulation"? Should we hold up the consolidated tape until we solve all issues involving a central marketplace?

The combination of prepared statements, inclusions, and the question-and-answer period took up 242 pages in the House record. In all modesty, our side seemed to win this round hands down. Questions from the staff and from the committee were almost entirely directed toward the Exchange members. My role was primarily to inject a clarification, counter a misleading statement, demolish red herrings, correct inaccuracies or give a different explanation on how markets work.

There were some wonderful interchanges. One in particular I remember was between Frank Graham, specialist on the AMEX, and Congressman Bob Eckhardt from Houston, Texas. The Congressman wanted to know how the public participated in a predetermined institutional cross. Frank, who was well known for his rapid-fire talking, explained how the broker, with both sides of the trade in agreement on price, would come into the crowd and offer stock in between the market and then make a bid at the same price, thus concluding the trade. Eckhardt wasn't sure he understood, and Frank, at an even faster pace, repeated that the broker offered at one-half and then took it. Eckhardt was about to ask Frank to go through it just one more time but then seemed to realize that the millisecond between "offer" and "take it" answered his question about opportunity for the public to participate.

William Painter, head of the study team, at one point asked me to explain how 394(b) works, and I replied, "I think it would be appropriate for me to defer to Mr. Peck." Steve Peck's response was "That would be the first time."

Another illustration of what I would term "frustration" is shown in the following interchange between Frank Graham and me.

Mr. Graham. It seems Mr. Weeden wants both sides of the coin and all parts of the cake. I don't think that is really in the public interest. As I said before, dealer activity takes care of itself. Mr. Weeden, you did make one statement that your price, 96 out of 105 times, was better. Did you mean your bid price or net price to the customer?

Mr. Weeden. In all Rule 394 cases the person coming to us is a member of the New York Stock Exchange and he would be charging the same commission to his customer whether he dealt with us or —

Mr. Graham. Then you are saying that your bid price was.

Mr. Weeden. — was better than the bid price on the floor of the Exchange, whether it was a public order or specialist bid, and the offering was a better net price than an offering on the floor.

Mr. Graham. Better than net price or better actual offer? In other words, I want to make sure we are talking about the same thing.

Mr. Weeden. To use one of your examples, if the stock is being offered on the floor at 82, our net price to the broker was better than the 82 being offered on the floor.

Mr. Graham. Your net price.

Mr. Weeden. Yes.

Mr. Graham. Your net price as against his price on the floor plus commission?

Mr. Weeden. Yes, sir.

Mr. Graham. I think that is an important distinction.

Mr. Weeden. Wait a minute, Frank. You as a specialist offer at 82 net, right?

Mr. Graham. I trade net because I don't charge a commission.

Mr. Weeden. And we trade net because we don't charge a commission. The customer is your customer and our customer, Merrill Lynch, and he comes in and asks for an offering of 1,200 shares of Texas Utility. We offer it at 81 3/4, and the best offering on the floor of the exchange is 82. That is what I meant by in 96 out of 105 cases, our offering net was better than what was available on the floor of the New York Stock Exchange.

Mr. Graham. To make sure we have the same thought, your offering price was a better market price than the price that existed on the floor, right?

Mr. Weeden. Yes, sir.

Mr. Graham. I just wanted to make sure of that.

One should understand that I knew each of these men well, liked them personally and had great respect for their abilities. These clips are not chosen because of any disdain or effort to belittle; rather, I include them to point out some moments of humor and the manner in which our interaction helped to clarify otherwise complex issues.

The one I like best is the following interchange between Will Weinstein, a block trader at Oppenheimer & Co., and Harvey Rowen, counsel to the subcommittee and study team member. Incidentally, I was always envious of Will's being able, at a tender age, to retire to Sun Valley, Idaho. That changed too when he was recruited by newly formed Montgomery Securities in San Francisco to set up their trading operation.

Mr. Weinstein. I don't see how you've accomplished anything by suddenly allowing people to see what they are missing. I think what you have to deal with first is a way to insure that they are not missing it. If you want me to be more specific.

Mr. Rowen. Yes, please be specific.

Mr. Weinstein. I would like to be, but I don't feel competent in this area.

A major discussion ensued between subcommittee chairman John Moss and the various New York representatives, Peck, Weinstein and Graham (AMEX), on whether all regulatory issues should be resolved before a consolidated tape is created and whether equal regulation is ever achievable or even desirable. Again, the panel forum helped keep the discussion on track, with Moss concluding, "If we try to remove all of those differences, Mr. Peck, we will be here on Judgment Day still trying to accomplish a change."

The panel produced some other interesting observations; for instance:

Mr. Weinstein. "I think there is a total consensus, unless I misread anybody here on the panel, that Rule 394 has got to go."

Mr. Moss. "I would only observe, Mr. Weeden, that I doubt very much that Rule 394 could ever have cleared the Congress of the United States. There are very few areas where I am prepared to make any observation, but I think in the case of Rule 394 it is something that should not have been. The quicker it is removed, the better I think the entire industry will be. I sense that comes pretty close to approaching the consensus of the committee as we have moved along on Rule 394.

I couldn't have said this any better:

Mr. Graham. I will give you a for instance as to how I view this thing (central marketplace). I think today and in the very near future we and others who will have the capability can get an input device into a central computer, which would give the Midwest Stock Exchange the ability not only to enter dealer interests in the stock, in the absence of public interest, but to enter public orders from the Midwest that would be stored in this central computer.

I can envision, for instance, in a market being 68½, if you will, where the first bid into the system might be a 68 bid out of New York, the second bid might be a 68 out of the Pacific companies and a third bid might be a 68 bid for a couple of hundred shares from the Midwest exchange, all to the central system.

Then the way this would operate, in effect, wherever an order came in to activate this bid, the bid would be taken in the order it was recorded in the system.

The public would be protected in all markets, and through the markets you would provide the various access of other members and dealers in those markets to trade across and through the markets on an equitable basis.

But the primary thing here is protection of public orders in every market, where Mr. Weinstein says knowing what is going to happen before it happens and not the fact that it did happen, as we see today.

This is the way you can protect that. You can protect your public order, which is my major concern, protection of that public order in the system through a sophisticated computer system. There is no problem with it.

———

Mr. Weeden. I am getting confused about this question of regulation and fair competition. I would like to ask a couple of questions of the panel members.

Will, when you are handling an order, and you deal with Weeden & Co., do you feel that you deal there because there is less regulation in our marketplace?

Mr. Weinstein. I would only deal with Weeden & Co. when Weeden & Co. is the best market.

Mr. Weeden. May I ask a question of Dave (Heller). Dave, when

Merrill Lynch handles a transaction on the Midwest Stock Exchange, is that done because there is less regulation?

Mr. Heller. I think not. I think that they handle the transaction done on the Midwest Stock Exchange or the Pacific Coast Stock Exchange because it is the best bidder or an equally good bid with any other marketplace. Conversely, as we do business we do not do business with you because there is less regulation. We do business because at that given moment of time you are the best bid or best offering available.

Mr. Weeden. Bill (Lupien), when somebody deals on your market, the Pacific Coast Stock Exchange, might it be because your clearing facility is more convenient, because they have a man on the floor of that exchange so they can save their floor brokerage? Might it be because they don't have a man in New York so they can save clearing? Might it be any one of those, as well as having an equal price or better price?

Mr. Lupien. Of course, Don, without question I say all of those things are involved. I can't see that some disparity in regulation is necessarily driving the business to the Pacific Coast Stock Exchange. As a matter of fact, there is quite a bit of regulation that prevents us from being as competitive as we would like to be, even though we may be the best market.

Mr. Weinstein. May I answer your question?

Mr. Weeden. Yes.

Mr. Weinstein. I would like to ask this: Are you not a member of the New York Stock Exchange because there is too much regulation of the New York Stock Exchange?

Mr. Weeden. Weeden & Co. became a publicly held corporation in 1927 and was precluded from being a member of the New York Stock Exchange for some 30 or 40 years. That is the first reason why we are not.

Secondly, we would like to be able to make a market in all of those securities in which we think we have the capability of making a market. We would like to offer the institutions a net price without commissions if they wish to deal in that way.

We believe the exchange is an archaic system involving a great many inefficiencies and a great many costs that are not necessary in this particular age of communications and electronic technology that we have. These are the reasons why we are not a member of the New York Stock Exchange.

――――――

Mr. Weeden. I would like to ask another question, Will, and that is to the extent you do a transaction on the Pacific Coast Exchange or you do one on the Midwest Exchange, or a Third Market, in any one of those transactions that you do on the regional or on the Midwest or Pacific Coast or with a Third Market, do you believe that those transactions, published on a consolidated tape, would misinform or mislead the public in any way?

Mr. Weinstein. Only to the extent that they did not have access to those transactions prior to the said transactions taking place.

Mr. Weeden. You don't understand. I presume each time you deal on the Pacific or Midwest or in the Third Market that you are getting what you consider to be best execution?

Mr. Weinstein. Right.

Mr. Weeden. Therefore, there are no public orders on the book that are not being taken care of that ought to be taken care of; there are no better bids, in your estimate as a broker, and that you wouldn't mind having those transactions printed on a public tape?

Mr. Weinstein. You are putting words in my mouth.

――――――

Mr. Weeden. Steve or Will, do you think that in order to achieve what you think you mean by "equal regulation" that we ought to be forced to begin charging institutions more money, because we have to add a commission, than we presently are?

Mr. Peck. The answer to that is no. If I have to do certain things under a particular set of market-making circumstances, I want to be certain if I am competing with you that you have to do the same thing I do at all times. That is the kind of thing I am talking about. You have to have the same kind of capital that I do, you have to trade in blocks the same way I may or may not, and certainly you have to have capital and be hard on your quotes and all of those things, which you may do but not all of your competitors do.

I just want to be certain that everybody has to do the same things that I do, or conversely, I certainly want to be able to do the same things that other guys do or don't do, and I can't do that now.

Mr. Weinstein. To go a little further, I think if you feel it is good business judgment to charge nothing or to pay clients to do business with you, that is perfectly all right with me. That is not my problem.

My problem is that once they are in the arena that they be totally equal in terms of opportunity, lack of opportunity, and what you can and what you can't do.

For example, you belong to a couple of exchanges which allow you to purchase a security net in the Third Market and resell that security on the Exchange. Is that not true?

Mr. Weeden. That is right.

Mr. Weinstein. That is true. Now, to me, that is an unequal situation. Every transaction that Oppenheimer & Co., or any other member firm, is involved in is recorded on a tape. You can find out what price we bought the stock at and find out what price we sold the stock at. I can't find out any of the same information about you.

Mr. Weeden. That gets us back, I think, to the really fundamental difference that you are hearing here. We would like to print that transaction on the tape, and we are prepared to go forward with a consolidated tape before we resolve all of these other "unequal regulatory problems," which are, as Steve has mentioned, what kind of membership exchanges have, what kind of commissions they charge, what kind of floor brokerage commission they charge, what kind of reciprocal practices they have, all of those other problems that, in my opinion, are way, way down the line.

We think very clearly that, to the extent there are regulatory problems, you are going to be able to expose those, and to have a handle on them if you develop a consolidated tape and offer the opportunity to everybody, including the regulatory agencies, of seeing what is going on in every marketplace.

To the extent that you have to wait until you solve all of these other problems, then I think you are not going to have a consolidated tape.

In 1973, hearings also were held on S. 410 and HR 2519, titled the National Securities Market System Act of 1973. Similar hearings on HR 5050, a sister bill, also took place earlier. The entire industry participated, as well as institutional interests, representatives of small public investors and academics. Everyone had their say.

Not only did everyone from the industry have their "public" say, they were swarming over the office buildings housing members of the Senate and House. As Fred Bleakley wrote in an *Institutional Investor* Magazine article titled "The Lobbying Effort That Failed" in August 1973, Wall Street was "galvanized into a massive, unprecedented lobbying effort" to defeat S. 2519, HR 5470 and its predecessor HR 5050.

On one hand, the NYSE flip-flopped on the issue of negotiated rates, first agreeing to them if the bill included "eliminating the Third Market" and then withdrawing that offer when they realized that that was not going to happen. At the same time, the Securities Industry Association was pulling out all stops to reverse the move toward negotiated rates. As Paul Kolton, chairman of the AMEX, explained, "There was only one way to conduct our lobbying effort. That was through the grass roots." Lee Kendall and SIA Chairman John Whitehead, of Goldman Sachs, contacted brokers from the home states of each of the 16 senators on the Banking Committee. Also, as Bleakley reported, on April 2 and 3, the SIA's annual legislative committee session, more than 100 brokers from around the country fanned out on Capitol Hill to see their Congressman about any upcoming bills that would have an impact on the securities industry.

In July 1973, well more than 100 individuals testified before Congressman John Moss' subcommittee. More than 30 individuals represented exchanges, member brokers and broker associations. M.A. Schapiro was represented by a three-man team, while Jack and I spoke for Weeden.

I began my testimony by quipping that I was worried by a headline in the *New York Daily News* that morning: "Tape Dispute Goes To Court." I also referred to another disturbing headline which appeared in the *Washington Daily News* the morning we first testified before this committee: "Chou and Nixon Okay Exchanges." One can become a bit paranoid if he's not careful.

In my testimony, I not only supported both the Senate and House bills' emphasis on increased competition, but reaffirmed my own conviction that greater use of technology was essential to better markets.

> "This industry can only make real money on big volume. This country's capital market can best function on broad public participation. The best way to attract volume and to broaden the customer base is to lower costs."

In retrospect, as I look at the present 2-billion-share days in both listed and over-the-counter stocks and 3-cent-per-share commissions, we were more than right on.

After emphasizing our support of HR 5050, I introduced Jack as our resident expert on capital, computers and clearing. Jack was at that time chairman of the NASD Capital Standard Committee, a member of its Automation Committee and a member of the board of directors of the National Clearing Corporation. "Jack is one of the handful of people in our industry who understands the 'how' as well as the 'why' of a central market," I said.

When one reviews the list of other participants, Jack stands out as the only representative of a securities firm whose responsibilities involved the back office. It was his personal understanding of clearing and computers, combined with his knowledge of how markets actually functioned, that made him unique.

Later that year we testified before Senator Harrison Williams' Subcommittee on Securities on S. 2519. In these hearings, we said all the same things as we said before Congressman John Moss' subcommittee, while emphasizing the following:

> "We have no problem with accepting the concept of priority to the public order. We envision the National Market System as setting up a public book; any time prior to our dealing with any of our customers, whether they are institutional or whether they are public orders of non member broker-dealers or member broker-dealers to the extent that there is an equal bid or better bid in that public book on behalf of a public customer, that bid should take priority to our participation as a dealer in the marketplace."

We had made our points — we thought successfully. Jack and I went back to New York and began to plan for the coming National Market System.

Out of those meetings came the idea of building a National Market System on our own — not the crude system then employed by the NASD called NASDAQ, but rather one that linked markets, provided automatic execution, gave priority to public orders and electronically reported last sales to a consolidated tape. We believed that the industry could not do it as they had too many differences, but if we could show them one, and demonstrate it to the Congress, the SEC, member brokers and the public, we could win them over. Just like the semiconductor industry, all we need to do is reduce the cost of our product (trades) and volume would soar.

Unfortunately, what had been for us a bit of a love fest with Congress became in 1973 and 1974 more complicated and ended up giving us half a loaf where we thought we had won the battle hands down. I guess it was to be expected, considering the array of forces aligned against us. In the end, the legislation four years in the making was extraordinary in its call for change and an improved marketplace, but to our narrower perspective it abandoned the Third Market to the whims of the SEC, whose leadership and bureaucracy were inadequate to repulse the constant pressure from the NYSE.

Nevertheless, the concept of a National Market System was still firmly in place. Putting our money where our mouth was, we began to design and build its first prototype, with the intention of using the Cincinnati Stock Exchange to showcase its capability.

20

WHAM

Sometime in 1973, after reading the language in the proposed Securities Acts Amendments of 1974 (subsequently tabled and then altered in 1975), Weeden began designing and then building a screen-based trading system that would accomplish the objective of a National Market System. The effort was headed by my brother Jack. When it was completed in 1976, it came to be known as the Weeden Holding Automated Market (WHAM) System and was introduced on the floor of the Cincinnati Stock Exchange.

The system was very straightforward. Anyone with a screen could place bids or offers into the system, with size, and at the same time see bids and offers entered by others on the system. All bids and offers were firm, and a trade would occur when an offsetting bid or offer was entered at the same price. There would be strict time and price priority, with the exception of bids or offers entered as public orders, which would take precedence over market makers. The system would allow for multiple market makers who could be located either upstairs or on the floor of an exchange. A significant innovation in WHAM over the newly developed NASDAQ system was the ability of a market maker to see the inside market in up to 22 securities at the same time and to easily and quickly alter his quote in all those stocks whenever changes in the market called for it.

As I have already described, Weeden was the odd-lot specialist on the Cincinnati Stock Exchange in those stocks in which we made an off-board market. At our suggestion, the rules of the Cincinnati were altered so that any member could register as a market maker, have access to a screen and compete on an equal basis. Member brokers with orders could enter their market orders or limit orders through the exchange's screen and receive an execution immediately if it were a market order, or be given time and price priority if it were a limit order. Our system was termed a hard CLOB. It had the ability to incorporate other exchanges with their specialists' markets and public limit orders on an equal basis, as well as accommodate market makers registered with the NASD. Thus, it met all the requirements for a National Market System as envisioned by Congress.

Why did we do this? Was this just a further effort on my part to "stick it in their eye" (whoever "their" was)? Was I really in orbit, lacking all sensitivity to what the Street wanted? Needed? They certainly did not want further change on top of what was already taking place. Even at Weeden we were going through a tough time, losing gobs of money. There were opponents to WHAM within Weeden as well.

To me, it was very straightforward. In the same way we had felt it important to be part of Quotron, AutEx and Instinet, I felt that with the impending securities acts amendments some kind of system that included a CLOB was inevitable, and I wanted to make sure Weeden would be part of it.

And furthermore, I felt that any system that gave us exposure to small retail orders, and large orders from institutions who, for whatever reason, didn't want to do business directly with us, would be to our advantage. I also felt that our experience as a market maker, our direct knowledge of how institutions acted and how they handled orders, our long-standing relationship with them built on service and trust, and our comfort in taking risk would stand us in good stead relative to the specialist. We were used to competition and had done all right against the best in other securities like bonds and preferred stocks.

It was Jack who took the lead on designing our WHAM system. Jack was not only a tinkerer, he liked the detail. He was a perfectionist, and he knew computers inside and out. And when one started down the road of asking what was the ideal market structure, you ended up with WHAM.

At the time, the technology in use was fairly crude. Even NASDAQ was a primitive system when compared with what we knew was possible. On NASDAQ in 1974, an OTC market maker could view only one stock at a time. More important, he could only change one market at a time. This was unacceptable in times of rapid price movement, as it took too long to change the 20 or 30-odd markets you were following. You'd get calls from other market makers wanting to hit your bid or take your offering on those stocks where you had not gotten around to changing your market in time.

So Jack designed a screen that allowed a market maker to follow 22 stocks simultaneously and to change his market on every stock with one stroke on the keyboard. In addition, the system allowed competing market makers, direct access by brokers with agency orders, real-time execution (at a time when brokers could only execute via the telephone) and priority to public orders.

My guess is we spent around $2 million developing the software, and we had it ready for operation in 1976.

While Jack was putting the finishing touches to WHAM, the National Market Advisory Board was being formed to debate what a National Market System should look like, and my job was just beginning.

21

Fail-Safe

In the meantime, the NYSE had other ideas. When we thought the last battle had been fought over the Securities Acts Amendments, another front was opened. Out of the blue, a bill, S. 3126, was introduced on March 7, 1974, by senators Alan Cranston of California and William E. Brock of Tennessee. It was entitled "SEC Authority Over Third Market Trading."

The opening paragraph describes that the purpose of the bill was

"To amend the Securities Exchange Act of 1934 to authorize the Securities and Exchange Commission to prohibit brokers or dealers from trading listed securities otherwise then on national securities exchanges in the event the Commission determines that such trading is contrary to the public interest and the protection of investors."

Two days of hearings by the Senate Subcommittee on Securities were scheduled for March 27 and 28, 1974, before which Weeden & Co. was invited to appear.

In retrospect, it was a last-ditch effort by the NYSE to do away with the Third Market. It was threatening and certainly not to be taken lightly. Our prepared statement was aggressive and attacking. We had the Justice Department, the Treasury Department and even the SEC on our side. Their statements the day before all suggested changes in the language that would make it very difficult for the SEC to restrict our Third Market activity. Even so, we had a few zingers we wanted to throw at the opposition. Bob Beshar prepared the statement with his usual flair, which drew critical questions from the Committee and angry letters from Paul Kolton (chairman of the AMEX) and Gus Levy (senior partner of Goldman Sachs).

From our viewpoint, we felt the bill was just another ploy to divert the SEC and to delay the march toward negotiated rates and a National Market System, but it quickly became apparent that the NYSE saw this bill as more significant.

After his prepared statement, Jim Needham was asked by Senator Harrison Williams about just what kind of events would trigger the provisions of S. 3126.

> "Our position is that you shouldn't have to go through that agonizing procedure of trying to determine anything. The simple solution really is to require that all trading take place on an exchange; then you don't have to determine whether you want the investing public *skewered* 5 percent of the time or 10 percent of the time, or 15 percent of the time, which was being suggested earlier."

> "As soon as it (off-board trades as a percentage of the total) gets to be 6 percent (presently 5 percent), you just require everybody to go right back to where they were. It would be that simple."

"Back to where they were" referred to his prediction that most of the largest firms would leave the Exchange when negotiated rates came into effect.

> "We know that Merrill Lynch will leave. They have said it. We know that Goldman Sachs has said it; we know Paine Webster has said it (spelling of Webber as recorded)."

> "I am glad Senator (Joseph) Biden is back — and I put this question to you simply — I am concerned, I don't want to see the American public *skewered* 5 percent of the time or 10 percent of the time." ... Why won't they (the Third Market firms) do it? Why won't they cut the little guy in on their business? That is the question that this subcommittee has to get an answer to and no other. Senator Biden, all you have to decide is how many times you want the public to be *skewered*."

> "I would say that if the percentage (done in the Third Market) went

from 5 to 6 percent I would move if I were a commissioner of the SEC."

In his inimitable way, Jim had made it clear what they wanted from S. 3126.

Jim unfortunately had not done his homework when he cited the intentions of the major firms to leave the NYSE. Those very same firms had testified under oath in *Thill Securities Corporation v. New York Stock Exchange*. (The case involved a broker-dealer's challenge to the NYSE's anti-rebate rule, and the Antitrust Division of the Justice Department filed an *amicus* brief on behalf of Thill.) The firms' testimony in the *Thill* case made it clear that they intended to stay. Included was the testimony of Gus Levy:

> "Upon further reflection since that time (in 1968, when he stated that in the event of negotiated rates Goldman Sachs would seriously consider leaving the NYSE) ... I have rejected the view, and do not now believe that the advent of fully negotiated commission rates would be likely to cause my firm to leave the NYSE."

We didn't let the opportunity pass to point out this discrepancy in our prepared statement.

Levy, upon reading my quote by him, wrote Senator Williams: "I feel it is very important to inform you that Mr. Weeden's reference to my statement, *absent a proper analysis of what I know I meant by that statement, is, in my mind, most misleading*" (emphasis added).

Unfortunately, Gus Levy never had much regard for me. I had always regarded him as one of the giants of Wall Street who, as a young man in the late 1920s or early 1930s, came to Goldman Sachs willing to work for nothing until he proved himself. He then went on to become their most successful trader, a block positioner and eventually head of the firm. As a trading firm, we had great admiration for Gus Levy, as well as Sy Lewis at Bear Stearns, the Salomon Brothers firm and others who first responded to our Third Market making by taking positions themselves.

Gus had no reason to reciprocate that admiration and expressed his antagonism whenever he could. Particularly toward me. Even before this exchange, an incident occurred during a cocktail party given for those to be seated on the dais of some charity dinner. When I arrived (as told to me later), Gus noticed the fact, turned to the group gathered around him and said, "Who let that guy in?"

There were other snips from these hearings that are worth recording.

In my testimony I had said, "Already the word has gone out to slow up the computer research and program development and to resist all change and compromise on the consolidated tape."

I felt comfortable with that statement, as I was intimately involved in the progress toward a consolidated tape. While I was only a member of the Policy Committee, I sat in on all the meetings of the Operations Committee, chaired by Arnie Staloff representing the PBW exchange, and I was fully aware of the NYSE strategy of delay.

But Senator Biden, quite properly I might say, wanted to know who "put the word out," and I was unable to provide a specific name for him. It was the one part of our testimony that was weak and which might have undercut the impression we were attempting to make. Fortunately, Paul Kolton felt required to answer my accusation in writing and inadvertently supplied numbers showing that in August 1973 the monthly expenditures of the Securities Industry Automation Corporation (SIAC) on the development of the consolidated tape had dropped from $80,000 to $25,000.

Virgil Sherrill, a senior partner at Shields and Co., a major block positioning dealer, speaking as chairman of the Securities Industry Association (SIA), which represented 745 organizations from all parts of the country, did not hesitate to put the situation confronting this committee in the direst terms.

> "It is also generally agreed that any material erosion of the agency auction market would have serious repercussions for the American and *perhaps the world economy*" (emphasis added).

Mr. Sherrill admitted on questioning from Senator Edward Brook that the SIA had never polled its membership on this issue, and that a sizable portion of his membership included non-member brokers who gratefully used the Third Market daily as well as some 30 Third Market makers themselves. He went on to cite how Aunt Millie is ignored when blocks take place in the Third Market, but ignored the fact that a similar situation occurred when his firm took blocks to regionals for crossing, and never thought to point out that blocks on the NYSE ignored Aunt Millie's limit orders on other exchanges.

I have to say it was just such testimony that got me riled up and determined not to let them get away with it.

No doubt these men were decent people, but I was not used to the arrogance, hypocrisy and misstatements that resonated throughout their public testimony. My own testimony was not above sarcasm and pointed accusations, but I never said anything I didn't believe and I never colored our testimony with misleading or deceptive statements.

We would comfort ourselves after such hearings by saying that if we reacted as we did, then probably the committee members and their staffs would also see what we saw. And it must have been so, as the result of these two days of hearings was a watered-down amendment that would never affect our business.

22

The Securities Acts Amendments of 1975

What was meant to be the Securities Acts Amendments of 1974 was at the last moment mysteriously held up by action of the Rules Committee in the Senate and was only to become law in 1975. This made it coincide with the implementation of fully negotiated rates on May 1, a date still looked upon as one of the more traumatic moments in the history of the securities industry.

Although the market had recovered sharply from its 1974 lows, neither the prosperity nor the buoyancy normal to Wall Street had yet returned. At a spring meeting of some 50 industry leaders drawn to Scottsdale, Arizona for a weekend of discussion about the future, a poll taken by the sponsors made clear the continuing despondency and negativism held by most of the attendees. Negotiated rates would do nothing but exacerbate the recent lack of profitability. Institutional research would dry up, the industry would consolidate into a few large firms, the national distribution system of strong regional firms would collapse, institutional commissions would be subject to destructive discounts and the small investor would end up footing the bill in the form of higher commissions. And last, but not least, the exchange-based system of agency auction markets would be replaced by dealer markets as members would leave in force to engage in the more profitable business of acting as principal.

I remember how my own view of the future stood in stark contrast to the majority. I felt just the opposite would happen, and expressed it clearly in my answers to the survey.

My experience with the semiconductor industry, as a board member of National Semiconductor, had convinced me of the value of competition, cost-cutting and price reduction as the means of increasing volume. No better example of how the capitalist system can work to the benefit of the consumers was this new and vibrant industry unshackled by cozy agreements and monopolistic practices.

For Weeden, probably the one firm that should have been most affected by negotiated rates, our annual report for the year ending September 30, 1975 would say the following:

"Though negotiated commission rates allow brokerage firms to be more competitive with our firm, we have experienced no adverse effects attributable to negotiated rates."

This was followed by our September 30, 1976 statement, which read:

"The Weeden stock trading division was able to match its 1975 performance."

Knowing the feeling on Wall Street about the coming apocalypse, shared interestingly enough by many of the institutions who were good customers of ours, we tried to describe the positive side of the event: "Accentuate the positive, eliminate the negative." Our speeches during this period were filled with the benefits of a National Market System, but no one seemed to be listening.

It was Fred Siesel who found the solution: humor. We were sitting around my office discussing the impending May Day, and how to lighten the event. Fred had already produced "The Oft Bored Trading Rules" calendar using MGM photos of their leading actors and actresses. It was a take-off on the attitude of the NYSE toward the Third Market and was conceived when S. 3126 was being proposed in the Senate. Could we do one for the coming of negotiated rates?

Fred went out to lunch and came back two hours later with a handful of pictures of Hollywood personalities he found at the stationery store on New Street. He already had captions. Over the next couple of days we played with the captions, laughed uproariously, refined the wording and rushed into print the "May Day" calendar. It was early April. You can see it for yourself in the Appendices. It is still funny today, and it can often be found hanging on the wall of some trading room that dates back to those earlier times.

Back to 1974. The year-long delay in the Securities Acts Amendments caused two significant changes. Congress succumbed to the argument, plausible if not correct, that the exchanges would not survive the double whammy of negotiated rates and removal of Rule 394(b). After all, these were Keith Funston's two columns essential to keeping the exchange structure standing.

In committee of the two houses, the issue of 394(b) was deferred until the SEC had determined that a National Market System was in place — that meant when the consolidated tape and the composite quote were operating and an industrywide protection of public orders had been built.

The second change was to establish a National Market Advisory Board (NMAB) that would advise the SEC on the design and method for implementing a National Market System. The NMAB was formed in July of 1975, and I was invited by SEC Chairman Ray Garrett to be one of the 15 members representing the various viewpoints within the securities industry and also including knowledgeable representatives from the public.

This assignment came to absorb much of my time over the next two years and provided me with a further opportunity to voice my views and those of my firm on how a National Market System would work. Unfortunately, it diverted my attention from certain danger signals developing within Weeden that would culminate in our near demise.

23

The National
Market Advisory Board

The National Market Advisory Board (NMAB) was another brilliant ploy by the NYSE to delay, and eventually prevent, the creation of a National Market System. Their instincts were correct. While Congress clearly endorsed the concept of a NMS after extensive studies, hearings and debates, and was firm in its intent to see one evolve, their vision did not extend to the details. That should be left to the SEC and the industry. The NMAB would include representatives from all segments of the Street plus leading personages from each of the major user groups: banks, mutual funds, insurance companies, the corporate world, academia and the individual retail investor. The SEC would monitor the board's progress, study its recommendations and facilitate their implementation, while Congress would watch from a distance.

As the NYSE surmised, the SEC itself did not want to impose a design on an industry where there wasn't broad support, and the NMAB slowly would become the template for inaction.

While naturally honored to be chosen to serve on the NMAB, I was not happy with another committee going over old ground. I had no illusions that this blue-ribbon board would have any more luck at achieving consensus as had the several industry committees before. Nevertheless, it was necessary to participate and make my views known to a new audience who just might listen. Anyway, WHAM was about to go live. Weeden was continuing to grow, and we had right on our side.

The board's meetings began in October 1975. The members were to serve through September 1977 and were asked to meet every month for two days in Washington, D.C. SEC Chairman Ray Garrett had assembled a distinguished and knowledgeable group of individuals, including George Putnam, chairman of the Putnam Funds; John Scanlon, retired chief financial officer of AT&T; Milton Cohen, former head of the Special Study of the Securities Markets; and Jim Lorie of the University of Chicago Graduate School of Business, to name just a few of the non-industry representatives. The industry was also well represented with quality people. (A complete list of members is in the Appendices.)

Except for the retirement of John Leslie, chairman of Bache & Co., and his replacement by Bob Fomon, CEO of E.F. Hutton, the board remained intact. It was dissolved at the end of 1977 after better than 40 full days spent together discussing and debating National Market System matters.

In the beginning we were given a laundry list of seven issues, including items such as governance, the role of issuers, access to the system, membership, clearance and settlement. All of these issues generated discussion and resulted in some differences; although, to my memory, none seemed impossible to resolve. In the end, it was one issue — protection of limit orders — that fundamentally, and irrevocably, divided the group. As it turned out, we were divided not just in two, but into several camps.

Don Stone, a partner of Lasker, Stone and Stern, a NYSE specialist firm, and I were the only two who had served on prior industry committees concerned with market structure issues.

We had known each other for a long time, actually dating back to the early 1950s when he and my brother Alan rented in the same apartment complex on East 23rd Street in Manhattan. Through Alan we had become friends, and we co-roasted Alan at his 40th birthday party in 1964. I knew Don to be one of the stronger, better specialists, and he knew that our business of making markets and taking positions was very similar to his. There was a strong professional respect for each other, despite our differences.

To insure that our friendship would not be spoiled by the coming debates in which we both anticipated sharp words, anger and accusations, we decided to break up the two-day confrontation with some tennis doubles, cocktails and dinner together. Those tennis games included two other board members; Bob Swinarton from Dean Witter and I matched against Don and Rick Guerin from Mitchum, Jones & Templeton. This did the trick, as Don and I are still close friends and occasionally play a round of golf together with my brother Alan (we were much better debaters than golfers).

Two days a month over a span of two years is a lot of time together. There was much serious discussion, heated debate and the usual funny incidents that you would expect. Everyone on the board made a contribution, although at the center of most debates were Don and I, he representing the NYSE and I representing Congress' vision. The NYSE had absolutely no interest in a NMS. In their mind they were already the central marketplace, and had been for a hundred years, and they saw no purpose in sharing the role with anyone. The Martin Report said it all.

Don had the difficult job of seeing that little or no progress was made, and I have to say he did a brilliant job.

This was a powerful group of no-nonsense men and women who were there to get something done. They came to the meetings, they actively participated, and they helped decide many of the issues on the table. Jack Scanlon had taken over as chairman when John Leslie retired, and he did a yeoman job of bringing people together. Yet on the issue of a public limit order book, the lynchpin to a true National Market System, the board scattered to the winds.

Before I go into that, I mentioned that some funny incidents happened along the way, one of which I remember vividly.

Bob Fomon had filled the empty seat created by John Leslie's retirement. Bob arrived at his first meeting in Washington about three hours late. We all waited to hear his apology, or at least an "I'm glad to be here." Rather, what we heard was "I didn't come here to hear a lot of s--t."

This occurred about a year after the board's meetings had begun, and it was clearly directed at me. I had gained the reputation of doing a lot of talking and sometimes dominating the discussion. I guess Bob felt it was his role to put an end to it. Anyway, this particular meeting had been going on for three hours, with the SEC staff trying to move us forward on some issue, the NYSE group, led by Don, explaining why it couldn't or shouldn't be done, and I challenging their position.

After a few minutes, Bob suddenly interjected again, "Do we have to listen to Weeden all day long? I'm sick and tired of his ranting. He doesn't know what he's talking about. Professor Lorie, how do you feel about it?" Jim softly replied, "I happen to agree with Don."

I then remembered Nancy Belleveau's description of Bob from a recent article in *Institutional Investor*: "mercurial," a "street fighter" who "tends to shoot from the hip." She was right on.

I was quite pleased with Jim Lorie's reply to Bob, and, as Gordon Macklin recollects, "so was Lorie."

We heard little more from Bob after that. He quickly lost interest and attended few of the remaining meetings.

In late January 1977, the NMAB wrote a letter to the SEC commissioners on the subject of establishing a CLOB. The letter was in answer to Release 34-12159 (March 2, 1976) by the Commission, in which it stated its intention "to utilize its new powers under the Act ... to facilitate the development of a composite book."

The letter pointed out that the impetus for the Commission taking action arose from discussions concerning the removal of restrictions on off-board trading (Rule 394(b)) by members of national securities exchanges.

In Release 34-11942 (December 19, 1975), the Commission noted:

"Of all the arguments advanced in favor of retaining some form of off-board trading rule ... the most persuasive concerned the desirability of continuing protections for public limit orders .... *It is clear, therefore, that the only fair, realistic, and practicable way of mandating satisfaction of public limit orders ... is through the creation and development of a composite book and the imposition of a requirement that all transactions, wherever and by whomever effected, must clear that book*" (emphasis added).

The letter went on to note that the SEC "observed that a composite book would also enhance competition among market makers (both exchange and Third Market), link markets through communication and data processing equipment and provide for the more efficient handling of limit orders" (pp. 1–3, NMAB letter).

With what appeared as a strong endorsement of a CLOB by the SEC, the NMAB first explored reasons why a CLOB was not a good idea. Four problems were presented by representatives of the NYSE.

First, there was the concern that NYSE specialists would reduce their market making activity because they would no longer receive revenue for servicing brokers' limit orders.

Second, there was concern that a composite book would lead to a system providing for direct execution by the broker, in effect bypassing exchange floors.

Third, the costs of developing a composite book would exceed the value of any benefits that might accrue to the industry or the public.

Fourth, instituting any type of composite book would so radically restructure the securities markets that trading in listed securities would evolve into a multi-dealer type of market.

Having heard these arguments on prior committees, I took the lead in countering them.

Regarding the first, I pointed out that there were others doing the same thing as the NYSE specialists, upstairs and on the regional exchanges, who earned little or nothing from handling the book. A CLOB would, by allowing them equal exposure to limit orders, not only encourage them to increase their activity, but also bring additional market-making competition into the market. I also dismissed the threat of their getting out of the business as sounding the same as brokers threatening to get out of the brokerage business with the coming of negotiated rates.

New York's second point could be met with a system where the CLOB was only accessible through exchanges and registered market makers. The Regional Market System (RMS) sponsored by the Cincinnati Stock Exchange was the prototype. (The Intermarket Trading System (ITS) also accepted this solution.)

The cost argument was made by Bob Hall, CEO of the Securities Industry Automation Corporation, member of the NMAB Technical Advisory Committee and surrogate for the NYSE. He estimated that a CLOB might cost $5 billion or more to create. Of course, no one really knew, although examples of similar systems, like the Sabre system for airline reservations, suggested a far smaller figure. I pointed out that the WHAM system cost Weeden barely $2 million and let it go at that.

Argument number four not only represented the Martin view, it clearly exposed what the floor of the NYSE was fighting for: no competition.

Eight of the eleven members who participated in the debate and registered their opinion to the Commission voted for a CLOB in some form as necessary to a NMS. The remaining three voted for the NYSE proposal for an Intermarket Trading System.

Unfortunately, the majority of eight divided on the details. Two felt that the unlocking of competitive forces would bring about a CLOB without SEC intervention (RMS); four felt a soft CLOB (only market makers and specialists' quotes being allowed access to the CLOB) should first be established until more experience was gained; and two voted for a hard CLOB (RMS) straight away as being the most efficient, fairest solution, and which "would contribute the most to re-establishing the confidence of individual investors in the market process."

In a final report to the Commission in December 1977, the NMAB spelled out the next steps to be taken to facilitate the establishment of a NMS.

In rereading the December letter, it provides no clear path for the SEC to take toward a NMS. While all the non-industry members voted for a CLOB (soft or hard), the industry was still as divided as ever. Consequently, it was not surprising that the SEC would sidestep Congress' call for a NMS. Jim Lorie was one who saw things most clearly and was most unwavering. From the first meeting, Jim had pushed for a CLOB, a system that was open, highly competitive and designed primarily to protect the public investor.

I mentioned Jim earlier regarding his letter to Congressman Moss in opposition to William McChesney Martin's concept for a central marketplace. Jim very much reminded me of my uncle Norman: slight of build, soft spoken, laid back. But there was one difference: Jim had a repertoire of off-color jokes that were constantly at the tip of his tongue. He was a professor of finance at the University of Chicago and was a solid contributor to the conservative view of economics. My across-the-board support of competition and open systems using the best technology available put me squarely in his camp. Fortunately, our times together have been enlivened by the considerable differences between us when we discuss political and environmental issues.

In the end, a majority of the board voted for some sort of CLOB. But, as with Supreme Court decisions, the result was four different recommendations to the SEC, with the majority divided in the details.

Meanwhile, the leadership of the SEC was shifting with the retirement of Ray Garrett in 1975.

24

National Market System Abandoned

Rod Hills succeeded Ray Garrett as chairman of the SEC in the fall of 1975. I knew Rod very well, as we had been fraternity brothers at Stanford and shared a room for one year. Rod was a year behind me. He was a good football player, very likeable and able — one of many from southern California in the Zete house.

Rod was appointed chairman in October 1975, shortly after his wife Carla had been appointed Secretary of Housing and Urban Development by President Ford. They were the prototype of the very talented, upwardly mobile couples beginning to permeate the political and corporate world. Before coming to Washington they were partners together in the Los Angeles law firm of Munger, Tolles, Hills, and Rickershauser. Rod's field of law had been labor relations. Market structure was something he was not familiar with, although options and the futures market seemed to hold his interest.

We never discussed market structure, those few times we were together, because I was sensitive to a possible impropriety in doing so. And I think Rod's lack of interest was also a factor. Under Rod, the SEC left to the NMAB the responsibility for designing a National Market System and waited for its recommendations.

During this time, WHAM was completed and went into operation under the name Regional Market System (RMS). The Pacific, Midwest and Boston stock exchanges joined Cincinnati in the experiment.

The WHAM system actually worked. Cincinnati had changed its rules to allow access to its market to any NASD member in good standing who had $100 to spare. It allowed Merrill Lynch to be an upstairs market maker, on par with Weeden & Co., the established, and, until WHAM, sole specialist in 230 listed stocks. And it allowed the specialist on the floor of the Midwest, or any other stock exchange, to place his market in competition, real time, with instant execution and time priority over all his competitors. The only requirement on all market makers and specialists was to recognize a public order at the same price before he executed for his own account.

Its weakness was that it was too "ideal." It scared not only the NYSE but all the other exchanges, who saw their value in an increasingly electronic age diminishing to nothing. (The London Stock Exchange Big Bang became a good example. In 1986, when the London Stock Exchange converted from a floor-based market to a computerized screen-based system, our May Day Calendar was reproduced and distributed under the title "Big Bang.") WHAM even frightened the brokers, who saw that such a system could ultimately allow their customers to go into the market electronically without a broker involved. In fact, Instinet became just such a system by allowing institutions to trade with one another without the intervention of a broker.

The NYSE quickly countered with its own system, in cooperation with the Midwest exchange, called the Intermarket Trading System (ITS), which was designed to link exchange floors together but without provision for limit orders. It eventually attracted all the regional exchanges as it gave them direct, no-cost access to the New York floor. NYSE's assurance to the SEC that the ITS would be supplemented with some sort of CLOB never materialized, as the SEC under Williams increasingly indicated a hands-off attitude.

Rod Hills had been succeeded in April 1977 by Harold Williams, also from Los Angeles, where he had been dean of UCLA's Graduate School of Management. I had first met Harold when I had participated in a conference on market structure at UCLA some years before.

Harold was a very bright, careful chairman who was sensitive to the winds blowing along Wall Street and who determined that the SEC should do nothing that the majority of the industry did not want. His public statements appeared strong but gave clear signals to the exchange community that the SEC would no longer be confrontational and insistent on market structure issues.

Therefore, when the NMAB presented its potpourri of recommendations, the Commission backed off from its previous determination to
force a CLOB.

Over the next few years through and beyond 1981, when Williams
left the Commission, the two experiments for moving toward a National
Market System continued. The ITS gained ascendancy while the RMS
(later named the Multiple Dealer Trading System, MDTS) lost its appeal
— not only with the other exchanges, but also because it never
attracted broker participation beyond Merrill Lynch and Paine Webber,
both of whom did a little business in a few stocks.

Led by the NYSE, the Street was not ready for a CLOB and the ITS
became the preferred system. Efforts to rejuvenate the idea of a National
Market System, including a recent effort by former SEC Chairman Arthur
Levitt, continued to meet strong opposition.

Eventually, the Cincinnati Stock Exchange was allowed to join the
ITS, after which it sold its WHAM system to the Chicago Board Options
Exchange (CBOE), giving their floor traders direct access to the NYSE
floor.

If there was a lesson to be learned, it was the fact that the NYSE,
through its enormous resources, power and influence, was able to
stymie the mandate of Congress to see a true National Market System
for listed stocks.

My belief that a National Market System is in the public interest, that
it would make for a better marketplace and that it would result in
greater volume and profitability for the Street has not diminished over
the years. And from time to time, I have published an opinion along
these lines when an opportunity arose to do so.

25

Weeden Loses Control

Fiscal 1977 started badly for Weeden. Along with many of the primary dealers in government bonds, Weeden accumulated inventory in anticipation of further easing by the Federal Reserve. The economy was still weak and the prospects of more inflation seemed to be fully discounted. Unfortunately, the market failed to respond. The February 21 issue of *Business Week* ran an article titled "Bond Dealers Take an Icy Plunge," mentioning Weeden & Co.'s reported loss in the first quarter of fiscal 1977 (October–December 1976) of $1.9 million. Since we were a public company, it was incumbent upon us to report our situation. The Street was rampant with rumors on the severe losses being incurred by the bond houses.

As a trading house, we understood down markets, temporary losses and the opportunity to make it all back in spades when the market turned. Unfortunately, the stock market had turned down as well, and our increasingly large inventory added to our troubles.

Undeterred, under John Krause we continued with our expansion plans, in particular in the area of unit trusts. Unit trusts were a means whereby individuals with modest funds could acquire a diversified portfolio of bonds through a single purchase. Firms like Weeden would accumulate blocks of bonds, consisting of, say, all New York State issues; make up a package totaling $10, $15 or $25 million; and offer them to brokers, who sold them to individual investors. These were quite profitable to the accumulator (Weeden), as the firm earns the markup when packaging the trust as well as an additional cut from the resale. The trick is to accumulate at attractive prices and package as the market is rising.

Weeden had been very successful with our first unit trust fund, named the Empire State Trust Fund, and had aggressively expanded to a point later in 1977 when we were accumulating for five separate funds simultaneously.

Unbeknownst to me and the rest of the board, this program of stock-piling bonds for an increasing number of future unit trusts was aggravating an already-high ratio of inventory to capital. I say unbeknownst, because I cannot recall our focusing on this at the time. This is not meant to be an excuse, but somehow it got away from us just as other initiatives were drawing our attention. In July of 1977, we acquired William Reaves & Co., a firm specializing in research in utility companies, and then in October we acquired Wainwright Securities for some $3 million in convertible notes and equity. Both acquisitions were motivated by our belief that making markets alone was not enough to continue attracting institutional inquiry.

With May Day in 1975, the block trading firms like Salomon Brothers, Shields and Bear Stearns became much more competitive in price, and their effort to gain market share made them overly aggressive. Meanwhile, the research-only firms were suffering due to high overhead and little stomach for block positioning.

William Reaves had the best reputation for knowing the value of utility companies and complemented neatly our Third Market activity. Wainwright was almost without peer in the field of maintenance research, that is, in-depth reports (50 pages) but without a specific recommendation. A five-page write-up on Wainwright in *Institutional Investor* spoke of their 5,000 pages of reports annually that were must reading for most large and mid-size money managers. Our market making and their research seemed a good fit.

Meanwhile, Jack was opening offices to handle Dexter Securities' business of providing the small broker-dealers with execution and clearing services.

The Wainwright acquisition introduced us to Nomura Securities, which had become a 25 percent owner through a joint research effort in Japan. Nomura was the largest Japanese broker, with capital several times that of Merrill Lynch. They took Weeden's common stock for their interest in Wainwright and immediately began exploring ways of doing business with us. Our leadership in the Third Market impressed them, as did our overall expertise in all trading areas. They also became fascinated by our use of technology: the WHAM trading system, our inventory control system, our nationwide linkage with Merrill Lynch for the purpose of borrowing stock, and our efficient execution and clearing system for other brokers. By the end of 1977, we had six to eight Japanese technicians milling around our trading areas and back office trying to understand our systems.

All of this was going on when we transitioned to a new system for recording and controlling accounts payable. Late in November, John Krause and I left for a two-week trip to Tokyo to meet Nomura's top management. When we returned, we found a Weeden that was in deep trouble operationally and burdened with excessive inventory. Our efforts to integrate Wainwright's 125-man organization and several thousand accounts, and to reconcile their control system with ours, came just at the time that our new accounting system failed. We literally lost control of where we were — and most important, we did not know whether or not we met the minimum regulatory requirements for capital. On top of that was the issue of certain indiscretions by John involving excessive expense accounts. An internal investigation resulted in John's resigning as president and CEO and leaving the firm.

Who to replace John Krause? That was the question. Alan thought we should re-establish the "troika" arrangement as before. I was opposed, arguing that decisions would have to be made quickly and decisively by a single CEO. I offered to take on the job. Alan objected. As a third solution, Frank offered to return as CEO temporarily. That suggestion brought all three sons into agreement and was rejected. Frank then suggested Jack become CEO as a compromise. Jack had no interest whatsoever. This all happened the last week of December.

We were in very bad shape. The stock market had been down all year, volume had decreased and we were losing money in stocks after expenses. The bond market was close to a free-fall because of inflation fears, short-term interest rates had risen above long-term rates (see charts, Portfolio III, plates 7 and 8) and Weeden was up to its armpits in inventory. We had no idea what our inventory markdown would show. On top of this, we had lost control of where we were and were unable to determine our capital position with any accuracy.

In this environment, the board met to figure out how to go forward. The board consisted of the four Weedens (Norman Weeden had passed away in 1970) plus Reese Harris, retired senior officer of the Hanover

Trust Company, who had joined us in 1971.

It was a strange set of meetings, even for a family used to argument and confrontation at the dinner table. Alan had recently returned from his year-long sojourn around the world. Even before the indiscretions came to light, he had soured on John Krause, and was sorry he had pushed him for president of Weeden. There was Frank, still smarting from being kicked upstairs but still maintaining close interest in our daily business. Jack was in his own world of operations, and I, as Chris Welles put it, was still off crusading and leaving managing to others. Needless to say, in these circumstances strong words and violent emotions were expressed as we moved toward a decision on who should run the firm. If a vote had been taken, I believe it would have been Jack and I voting for me, and Frank and Alan voting for Alan's troika — that is, the three of us running the show as equals. Reese was the tie-breaker. After much discussion, Reese finally asked both Alan and me about our thoughts on whether the firm could be saved. Alan didn't think so. I did. Reese decided for me, and that was how it ended on December 31, 1977.

26

The Collapse of Weeden

The following figures give an inside view of what was happening at Weeden:

Revenues for Fiscal Year ending Sept. 30 (in 000's)

	1974	1975	1976	1977	1978
Bonds	$ 6378	$10561	$20459	$17519	$ 1367
Stocks	$11235	$15051	$14231	$ 5082	$ 4702

They show the buildup of Weeden's bond business through fiscal 1976 and the severe reduction in revenues from stock transactions in fiscal 1977, caused in large part by a stock market drop of almost 20 percent (see chart, Portfolio III, plate 7). While stock trading regained profitability in fiscal 1978 through cost reductions and improving market conditions, bond revenues continued their fall due to high inventories and a further deterioration in bond prices (see chart, Portfolio III, plate 8).

When 1978 began, we were still in the dark as to where we stood in filing our 10-K. We could not possibly meet the deadline of the 10th of January. The NASD gave us two weeks to put our act together or cease operations. Sunday evening, the 22nd of January, we held a board meeting at which it was concluded that we would not be able to satisfy the NASD the following morning. Our people continued to work through the night.

At 10 a.m. on January 23, nine examiners from the NASD arrived at our offices and were ushered into our board room. They were met by a full complement of personnel from operations tired from their around-the-clock efforts and wearing black t-shirts with NASDIES in bold letters across the front. (The takeoff on the word "nasties" was our way of lightening the mood; I'm not sure we succeeded.) In slow motion, Jim Avena, assistant manager for operations, pushed a two-foot-high pile of computer printouts across the table to the waiting examiners and stated that we were in capital compliance as of December 31, 1977 — ever so barely.

I further explained to the NASD examiners that since December 31 management had succeeded in reducing our year-end inventories substantially, and that whatever questions might be raised about our condition on December 31, we were, as of today, in full capital compliance.

The 24/7 effort by our operations people included many ex-Weeden employees who had come back at night and on the weekend to help. Walter Raquet stands out in this regard; he devised a very creative way of accounting for our inventory that caused the NASD to hesitate just long enough in their findings until we were clearly back in compliance and under control.

I was now in charge. We lost $16.6 million — more than half our capital — in the January–March quarter. More than that, we had begun a process of peeling off offices, departments and employees, sometimes by overnight decision and sometimes after much soul-searching, agony and heartache. It was a trying time.

Our first major decision, after a firmwide effort to reduce inventory, was what to do about Wainwright and its 125 employees. Since our acquisition in October they had been losing $100,000 a month, growing to $200,000 in January. Payment for their research in the form of orders never materialized as they projected, and their salespeople were finding a growing reluctance on the part of their clients to pay for their brand of research. Wainwright generated good, in-depth stuff, but clients wanted "recommendations," "ideas" packaged in short, concise language.

Jack, Frank and I met for dinner on January 31 at the Blarney Stone across from my apartment on 60th Street between Park and Lexington and talked over meatloaf and mashed potatoes. We knew our situation to be precarious, and something drastic had to be done. Jack and I went back to my apartment and went over the alternatives. It became increasingly clear that Wainwright had become a major albatross. What to do? They had called a meeting with me for 7:30 the next morning with a demand that we give their key people guarantees to stay. That, of course, was impossible to do. After midnight I called Mike Jeffers, our counsel, and asked him whether our agreement with Wainwright allowed us to close them down. Mike said yes, and I went into the meeting with Pete Morley and Steve Meyers, the number one and two at Wainwright, with that option available. I asked them how long they felt it would take to become profitable. Nine months and a further $1 million in losses, they said. I then asked if they thought someone would want to acquire them. They said, "In this climate — no."

I said, "Well then, it seems that we have no alternative but to close you down, since we cannot afford the $1 million drain in capital."

Pete Morley, to his credit, accepted the decision gracefully and as a real professional. He took the message to the gathering of analysts and salesmen waiting for an answer to their demand. I accompanied Pete and then made a statement explaining our position and my regrets. As soon as Pete spoke, one of the senior analysts left the room, as I learned later, to accept the offer he had already received from Merrill Lynch.

Unfortunately, not all my decisions were as dramatic or decisive. February began a slow, agonizing process of cutting here, cutting there, trying to keep the most profitable departments, the best producers, the most seasoned traders.

Many of our people demonstrated strong loyalty, but the diminishing prospects for the firm and the continuing loss of capital made it difficult for even the most loyal not to react to the opportunities being presented by a Street who well knew the talents of our people.

Adding to the problem was the bonus obligation we had with the municipal department for profits made in the year ending September 30, 1977. We argued that the losses since then were already greater than what they made in 1977, but they argued that that didn't matter. Another drain of capital. Our only profitable area in municipals was the dollar bond desk because they had the ability to short bonds and maintain a balanced exposure. When they accepted an offer from Bear Stearns for the entire unit, it was a very black day for me.

Compounding the rumors and then admissions by us as to the extent of our losses was a report by *Securities Week* that the SEC was investigating us for capital violation. Somehow the reporter had heard this from an unnamed source and asked me for verification, as the SEC would not comment on it. I said that I did not know of any investigation and that publishing the rumor about it would be quite harmful to our ability to continue doing business with our clients. *Securities Week* published the story anyway, which added to our woes.

It was the need to remain in capital compliance and how best to reduce overhead and our inventory that determined our course of action over the next few months. Our stock inventory was highly liquid, except for a few inactive utility stocks, and was brought down almost immediately. Bonds were another matter. We were still trying to dispose of some corporate and municipal positions when we finally merged with Moseley, Hallgarten and Estabrook early in 1979. Cutting overhead was trickier and involved deciding whether it was best to cut departments or offices. We ended up doing both. All this was with the objective of conserving capital. The London office was an immediate problem, because the savings in overhead were more than offset by the substantial severance payments required under English law. Attrition helped out until finally the benefits of closing outweighed the penalties.

Early on, Bob Beshar had floated the idea that we bite the bullet while we still had a fair amount of capital and close down everything at once. We could go out of business entirely, use part of our retained capital to negotiate out of lease obligations and termination needs, and pick the fifty "best and brightest" to restart the business focusing on our traditional areas of expertise. We estimated that we could end up with $5 or $6 million in capital, more than enough to re-establish ourselves. We were never up to making that kind of decision, and as a result we barely had $2 million in capital when we finally made our deal with Moseley, Hallgarten and Estabrook — and we still had further to go to reduce overhead.

The process involved a lot of unpleasant, hurtful, sad decisions as we chopped good people, closed offices and abandoned our 50 years of momentum and growth. Just writing this and remembering those times again is difficult.

(In the cover article in the June 1978 issue of *Institutional Investor*, titled "The Tragedy of Don Weeden," Chris Welles traces the history of the firm and family and what led up to our troubles. I thought the article was sensitive and revealing, although I was never comfortable with his description of my efforts over the years as noble but quixotic.)

Our public stance during this time was to get ourselves straightened out and in a position to continue as we had, although in a more focused, less expansive manner. Nevertheless, soon after the disastrous first quarter of 1978, I began to explore the possibility of a merger. Spear, Leeds & Kellogg, the large specialist firm on the NYSE, was the first I talked to. They knew our business, had respect for our reputation and talent, and expressed interest in expanding their dealer activities beyond the Exchange floor. Unfortunately, it didn't work out. I thought we would have made a good combination. Jefferies & Co., our largest competitor in the Third Market, was another logical possibility. They were doing more and more positioning at the time, had a complementary style and service, and had been contemplating expanding into fixed income securities. They did some serious due diligence but concluded at the eleventh hour that we still had too much baggage to get rid of in areas that they knew little about and weren't that sure they wanted to get into.

Early in September, out of the blue, a phone call came from John Bulkley, who had recently been made president and CEO of Moseley, Hallgarten and Estabrook, a holding company for an operating subsidiary in the securities business, a structure very similar to ours. Since the early 1970s, F.S. Moseley had been acquiring companies in some sort of distress, the last being an arbitrage firm, C.D. Richards. They were used to the process of absorbing companies, although Weeden was a bigger mouthful than they had handled to date. By the time we completed the final merger in February 1979, Weeden was down to two offices and 75 employees. In the previous 15 months we had racked up losses of more than $25 million that were available to the merged company going forward. Also, our standing in the municipal bond underwriting community elevated Moseley to the status of a major underwriter, an important but impossible advance for Moseley to achieve on its own.

The agreement to merge came perilously close to breaking down when our municipal department had a loss in October, as the merger was dependent upon our bringing a certain amount of capital to the table relative to their capital. It also made some of the Moseley management team quite apprehensive about our business.

At his request, John and I met for breakfast at the Racquet and Tennis Club on Park Avenue to determine whether or not the merger made sense anymore. Sensing they had made a tentative decision not to go forward, I offered a firm 74 percent/26 percent deal that was sufficiently attractive for John to change his mind. We shook hands and started the process of working out the details. Whatever disagreements I had with John later on, I never forgot his decision to accept my offer and to stick with it.

If anything proves the value of one person being in charge and able to make a decision on the spot, it was my ability during that breakfast to sense the deal slipping away and to come up with a proposal that saved the day. After that breakfast, I began smoking again and renewing my enjoyment of alcoholic beverages.

My relief in having avoided bankruptcy at the eleventh hour was shared by our few remaining employees as well as the whole Weeden family. But even more there was a feeling of sadness over seeing a fine company and its 57-year history relegated to the tail end of another firm.

The name Weeden had built in municipal bond trading, our leadership in pioneering the Third Market, the role we played in changing the rules of the equity markets ... the collection of "The best in our business" in trading, operations and technology had all but disappeared.

There was no joy in Mudville during those two remaining months while the merger was being finalized.

While the collapse of Weeden was accelerating, I still found some time to speak out for a National Market System, and Jack was working with the Cincinnati Stock Exchange to get the Regional Market System accepted and used. Unfortunately, our main energies were required at home. In many ways 1978 proved to be a difficult year.

SEC Advisory Committee for a comprehensive market disclosure system for listed securities, April 1972. Standing, left to right: Bill Lupien, Don Stone, John Lifton (SEC), William Clark, Helen Steiner (SEC), Peter Mero, Don Weeden, Sandy Lewis. Seated: Chairmen James Needham (NYSE), Gordon Teach (NASD) and William Casey (SEC).

When the *blue* chips were down.

The fourth quarter of 1973 was one of the most unsettled in stock market history. First the Dow Jones Industrial Average went up 50 points...then it plummeted 214 points...then rose again 67 points. During this difficult period, Weeden & Co., as market maker, bought and sold more than 50 million shares* of those 262 stocks that are traded both by Weeden and on the New York Stock Exchange. Here are the details:

Volume Leaders

Stock	WEEDEN Volume	N.Y.S.E. Volume	Weeden Volume Compared to NYSE Volume %
Texaco, Inc.	1,419,000	6,869,600	20.7
Exxon	1,184,600	4,941,400	24.0
Kresge, S.S.	1,128,300	4,697,500	24.0
General Motors	1,074,000	9,053,600	11.9
Federal National Mortgage	977,900	5,440,100	18.0
Mobil Oil	974,400	3,292,000	29.6
Alcan Aluminum Ltd.	908,400	3,540,300	25.7
Ford Motor	902,300	5,291,200	17.0
International Paper	844,500	3,563,700	23.7
First National City Corp.	835,400	5,526,700	15.1
Sears Roebuck Co.	826,700	2,498,500	33.1
Continental Oil	779,200	4,410,000	17.7
Gulf Oil	733,200	8,295,600	8.8

Market Share Leaders

Stock	WEEDEN Volume	N.Y.S.E. Volume	Weeden Volume Compared to NYSE Volume %
Sears, Roebuck Co.	826,700	2,498,500	33.1
Mobil Oil	974,400	3,292,000	29.6
Oklahoma Gas & Electric	138,500	505,600	27.4
J. C. Penney	395,300	1,469,900	26.9
Central & South West	532,800	1,980,400	26.9
Southern California Edison	584,800	2,195,000	26.6
Inland Steel	160,000	601,900	26.6
Florida Power & Light	372,700	1,420,100	26.2
Unionamerica	136,300	524,200	26.0
Alcan Aluminum Ltd.	908,400	3,540,300	25.7
Consumers Power	213,400	835,600	25.5
International Nickel	461,600	1,829,400	25.2
Caterpillar Tractor	610,900	2,431,700	25.1

Breakdown of our Volume by Customer

	Total Shares	Percent of Total
Banks	19,421,449	35.3
Mutual Funds	3,041,063	5.5
Other Institutions	9,469,448	17.2
Brokers — Exchange Members	16,635,648	30.3
Brokers — Non Exchange Members	4,962,677	9.0
TOTAL Market-maker volume	53,530,285	97.3
N.Y.S.E. Transactions for our own account	1,483,400	2.7
TOTAL VOLUME	55,013,685	100.0

Breakdown by Transaction Size

		Shares	%	Number of Transactions	%
Odd Lots	(1-99)	1,412,385	2.6	37,880	34.3
Round Lots	(100- 499)	7,396,600	13.8	50,291	45.5
	(500- 999)	4,934,400	9.2	9,284	8.4
	(1,000-4,999)	17,723,400	33.1	10,338	9.3
	(5,000-9,999)	11,024,800	20.6	1,994	1.8
Blocks	(10,000 & Over)	11,038,700	20.7	794	0.7
		53,530,285	100.0	110,581	100.0

If you're interested in best execution, whether the market is turbulent or calm — come to Weeden. Our markets are available to all brokers, banks and other financial institutions.

Weeden & Co.
specialists in competition

New York • Boston • Chicago • Houston • Los Angeles • Philadelphia • San Francisco • London

A list of securities in which we maintain markets is available upon request. Contact: J. D. Weeden, 25 Broad Street, New York, N.Y. 10004 or (212) 344-2300.

*Weeden Volume consists of market-maker activity on regional exchanges plus Third Market volume. In our volume above, we have included our purchases as principal in addition to our sales as principal and agent, as we will when reporting all transactions on a common tape.

The Third Market.
The 12 billion dollar stock market competition built.

Volume Figures—Year 1971 (Source: SEC)

	Dollar Value of Share Volume		Share Volume
New York Stock Exchange	$147,098,395,502		4,265,279,018
American Stock Exchange	17,663,735,896		1,049,317,475
Third Market (Including Weeden & Co.)	**12,383,965,000**		**297,850,000**
Midwest Stock Exchange	7,443,310,823		215,649,958
Pacific Coast Stock Exchange	6,962,107,700		206,327,097
Weeden & Co. Market–Maker Volume			
Third Market	$ 4,478,248,757	100,583,141	
On Regional Exchanges	318,797,707 **4,797,046,464**	7,831,348	**108,414,489**
Phila.-Balt.-Wash. Stock Exchange	4,265,040,613		114,490,321
Boston Stock Exchange	1,090,360,609		26,493,334
Detroit Stock Exchange	350,727,467		9,571,263
Cincinnati Stock Exchange	93,398,555		1,979,994

Weeden & Co. is registered with the SEC as Third Market market-maker in 265 issues under SEC rule X-17A-9, and is listed with the New York Stock Exchange as such on these same issues for the purposes of NYSE rule 394(b).
Weeden & Co. assumed specialist responsibilities on the Cincinnati Stock Exchange on June 15, 1970, and the Detroit Stock Exchange on March 1, 1971.
Weeden & Co. assumed market-maker responsibilities on the Phila.-Balt.-Wash. Stock Exchange on July 12, 1971, and the Boston Stock Exchange on October 2, 1971.
Our markets are also available through NASDAQ and Over-The-Counter to brokers, dealers and financial institutions. We subscribe to AutEx and Instinet.

Our volume is built on offering best net price.
We invite you or your broker to check our market
prior to execution of your order.

Weeden & Co.
specialists in competition

New York · Boston · Chicago · Houston · Los Angeles · Philadelphia · San Francisco · London

New York Stock Exchange Chairman James Needham on cover of *Institutional Investor* Magazine, "The Big Board Takes the Offensive," March 1973

One of the largest markets in listed securities is a firm.

Volume Figures—Year 1972 (Source: SEC)

	Dollar Value of Share Volume (in thousands)	Share Volume (in thousands)
New York Stock Exchange	159,700,186	4,496,187
American Stock Exchange	20,452,646	1,103,222
Third Market (Including Weeden & Co.)	13,580,785	327,031
Midwest Stock Exchange	8,427,981	228,751
Pacific Stock Exchange	8,023,893	248,490
Weeden & Co. Market-Maker Volume	**5,622,599**	**128.913**
PBW Stock Exchange	5,274,083	143,105
Boston Stock Exchange	1,562,151	38,472
Detroit Stock Exchange	362,390	9,808
Cincinnati Stock Exchange	103,439	2,324

Weeden & Co. is registered with the SEC as Third Market market-maker in 269 issues under SEC rule X-17A-9, and is listed with the New York Stock Exchange as such on these same issues for the purposes of NYSE rule 394(b).

Weeden & Co. assumed specialist responsibilities on the Cincinnati Stock Exchange on June 15, 1970, and the Detroit Stock Exchange on March 1, 1971.

Weeden & Co. assumed market-maker responsibilities on the PBW Stock Exchange on July 12, 1971, the Boston Stock Exchange on October 2, 1971, and the Pacific Stock Exchange on November 11, 1972.

Our markets are also available through NASDAQ and Over-The-Counter to brokers, dealers and financial institutions. We subscribe to AutEx and Instinet.

The firm of Weeden & Co. ranks among the leaders because of our ability to offer best net price. We invite institutions to check our market directly or through their brokers prior to executing an order.

Weeden & Co.
specialists in competition

New York • Boston • Chicago • Houston • Los Angeles • Philadelphia • San Francisco • London

Weeden & Co. trading floor, Jersey City, New Jersey, 1976

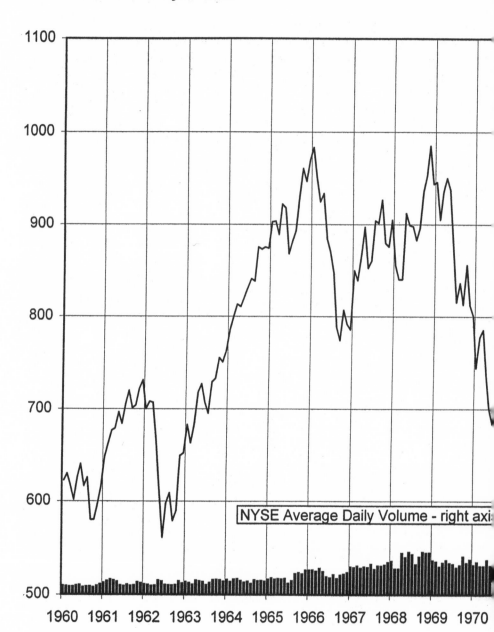

DJIA Monthly Close

NYSE Average Daily Volume - right axis

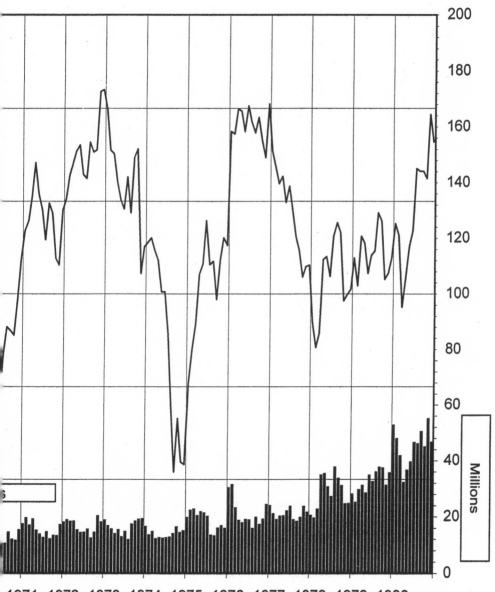

200

180

160

140

120

100

80

60

40

Millions

20

0

1971 1972 1973 1974 1975 1976 1977 1978 1979 1980

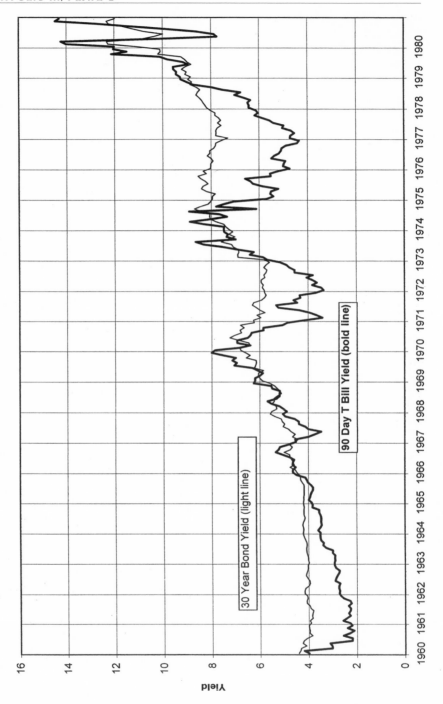

90 Day Bill vs. 30 Year Bond Yield

Reprint of folder cover, "Cincinnati/NMS, an invitation to participate," 1978

Cover of *Institutional Investor* Magazine featuring article "The Tragedy of Don Weeden," June 1978

27

MHEW, 1979–1985

On February 16, 1979, the shareholders of Moseley, Hallgarten and Estabrook Holding Corp. received shares in Weeden Holding Corp. equivalent to 74 percent of the outstanding shares upon completion of the merger. The remnants of Weeden's bond trading desk were integrated into Moseley's bond desk, with my brother Alan sharing the responsibility for running it with Bernie van Ingen. Over time the arrangement did not prove satisfactory to Alan, and he decided to retire from the company. Jack was given some operational responsibilities but eventually left for Instinet, where for three years he was in charge of operations.

Weeden's Equity Trading Division, as it was now called, was now part of a member firm and no longer in the Third Market. This presented a problem for the Moseley management, as our list of accounts included customers of various Moseley offices and individual brokers. While their business in most cases was a fraction of what Weeden had been doing, they nevertheless did not want to give up their coverage. The result was the establishment of two block trading desks in Moseley's newly constructed trading room at One New York Plaza. We were successful in convincing Moseley that "Weeden" had brand-name value and that they should allow us to continue to answer the phone with "Weeden." Also, our confirmations should read "Weeden Equity Trading, Division of Moseley, Hallgarten, Estabrook & Weeden" (MHEW). Whether we fooled anyone on this, who knows or cares. The fact remains that we acted as an independent group within MHEW.

I was exhausted from the events of the past year, and both elated and depressed by the results. I began the new arrangement, frankly, out of touch with our day-to-day trading activity. Steve Gladstone had been instrumental in getting our department through the transition and beginning our new role in a profitable manner. Lou Barail, who had been Weeden's director of personnel, made the transition to MHEW and became part of our group, running sales and providing management oversight. Lou was well liked by everyone and was key to establishing an accurate and favorable method of accounting for our revenues, expenses and profitability. This was very important because our deal, worked out with John Bulkley, Moseley's president and CEO, was a 50-50 split of bottom-line profits before bonuses. This arrangement was made before we actually came under their tent and at a time when the Moseley management was skeptical that much, if any, profit would be forthcoming from the stock desk.

It's my belief that their willingness to accept a 50-50 split was due to their intentions to get rid of us as soon as their tax lawyers gave the okay. Tax law at the time allowed for a corporation with new ownership to benefit from any prior losses as long as the activity which created the loss continued to exist. Weeden's losses in 1977–78 came to more than $26 million. That figure would have more than offset any profits for the next five years based on Moseley's projections and in their thinking was the key value of Weeden at the time of the merger. Consequently, they had to be careful not to dump us too fast.

There were other reasons for not wanting us around. I mentioned the duplication of institutional coverage, which rankled some of their most productive salesmen. Another reason was their aversion to risk. Moseley, Hallgarten and Estabrook was a collection of brokerage firms servicing high-income clients, charging agency commissions. Their OTC department mainly processed agency orders and their municipal department was hesitant to position. The inventory that Weeden's Third Market desk was used to carrying was totally inimical to their agent-only philosophy. This would change in time, as it did with many brokerage firms, but when we arrived it was of concern.

Probably the most troublesome thing to Moseley about our equity trading desk was its attitude. We were young, talented and confident, bordering on cocky, and because we began to do well, we were disdainful of those around us. Our more casual dress code separated us from the rest, and our relationship to our superiors was more Western

(Weeden) than those Boston blue-bloods were used to.

MHEW's new trading room took up almost the whole floor at One New York Plaza. It was open and noisy, and we usually provided the noise. If we had a big trade we'd bring in a case of Heineken at the close to celebrate — something that was unheard of. It got so bad that when John Bulkley would stride into the trading room upon occasion, he would carefully avoid our section — a difficult thing to do, since we were in the center of the room.

John's dilemma was that we started to make good profits from the very beginning. Lou Barail and Steve Gladstone had been the key negotiators in our 50-50 deal, and Lou was the one who made sure that our expenses were not overstated. I sat on the Moseley board and had most of the contact with John and the rest of its management. He soon realized that our business was for real and that we could generate consistent profits without undue risk. The trading desk managed our inventories so they remained within Moseley's limits, and the overall operation ran smoothly under Lou. We began to develop a talented group of salesmen and traders, in particular Barry Small and Tim McDonald, who became key to our future success.

It wasn't long before John wanted to change the deal, and the burden of talking him out of that idea fell to me. In a crazy way, the more money we made the more uncomfortable John was with me, and somewhere along the line he found a reason to ask me to resign from the board.

At the time, my contribution to the desk was minimal. Besides dealing with the internal politics within Moseley and visiting their various offices explaining who we were, I continued my activities in Washington, although to a much lesser degree. Rule 394 was still on the table, with a divided SEC debating its future. The Regional Market System (RMS) experiment had been approved, with MHEW and Merrill Lynch joining in the test. It was hard for me to let go even though Weeden was now part of a member firm. I'm sure the team would have preferred me spending my time more productively, but I was afraid to ask.

The most traumatic experience we had together was the sudden death of Lou Barail in an automobile accident late one night out at the end of Long Island. Lou not only ran the division, he was genuinely loved by everyone inside and outside our group. His loss could have caused our group to break up, but people like Tim McDonald, Bob Weppler and Barry Small decided to stick it out.

We continued to do well, but it didn't change the antagonism that underlay our relationship with the rest of the firm. Suggestions by me to John and Fred Moseley that they issue options to our people, as they were doing throughout the firm, were met with "You guys got too good a deal already." As a group we continued to be "fish out of water," and neither side made much effort to correct the situation.

It was during this time that I first came to know Steve Leuthold. In 1980, he had published a book, *The Myths of Inflation and Investing* (Crain Books), which traced the history of interest rates and inflation for the last 1,000 years, paying particular attention to their relationship to the U.S. stock market during the period from 1790 to the present. I read the book in 1981 at a time when inflation had risen sharply, short-term interest rates were approaching 20 percent and long-term Treasuries were yielding 13 percent. Steve made the point that inflation of this sort doesn't last indefinitely and that the risk of loss in buying long-term non-callable bonds or, even better, zero coupon bonds guaranteed by the U.S. government, was negligible, while the opportunity for capital appreciation was substantial. I wrote a memo to the MHEW management recommending they allocate $1 million of their capital to a position in long-term government bonds (the only suggestion I ever made to Moseley), while advising a similar investment strategy to several of my friends who had some spare capital.

What was important was not his or my timing but, rather, my getting to know Steve through a series of phone conversations we had at the time. We discussed his ideas and I told him about us. These discussions began a relationship that led to our partnering in late 1987 after Weeden had separated from Moseley.

Sometime during 1983–84 we began to consider leaving. My job was to explore opportunities on the Street where our expertise would fit in, be appreciated and be properly compensated. I remember talking to my father, Frank, about leaving, and he thought it was a good idea. "They never understood our business and were always uncomfortable with our presence," he said.

This was in the fall of 1984. Frank would soon succumb to prostate cancer, which had been brewing for 15 years. He was 91 and a half years old when he died, and he'd had a full and vigorous life for all but the last month. Even after his sons had kicked him upstairs and then allowed the business to implode, he was philosophical about it and maintained a close and friendly relationship with all of us. One of my sorrows was that he passed away before we left Moseley and reconstituted Weeden.

During this time I continued to serve on the Instinet board. Instinet had raised additional capital when Bill Lupien joined the company in 1983, but the pre-Moseley shareholders of Weeden still owned a good portion of the stock. At the time of the merger we valued the Instinet shares at $.17 per share. The market for Weeden was around $2.50 per share. Not until Bill Lupien joined did the Instinet stock do anything. Because of the pre-merger distribution there suddenly were a lot of shareholders, and a public market developed. I was still enthusiastic about Instinet's prospects, and when Nomura Securities wanted to sell their block of stock at $.10 per share, I encouraged the traders to buy it. They didn't like Jerry Pustilnik, Instinet's president, with his octagonal-shaped glasses, and passed, even though I offered them a six-month put at $.09 per share. They were all doing very well and didn't need any capital gains at the time. But the next time I came to them with a venture deal, after we sold Instinet to Reuters, they showed more interest. Bill Lupien turned Instinet around by marketing it as the way for the OTC market makers to show their bids and offers to one another anonymously at prices in between the displayed inside quote. This became widely used by the Street and began to attract the institutions to Instinet because they could execute at prices inside the quoted market and do it without exposing their interest.

This was the beginning of Instinet's ultimate success story. Unfortunately, more capital was required to gear up, and we were forced to sell the company to someone with deep pockets. Reuters was the logical suitor, and the acquisition for Reuters common stock took place in 1987 at a valuation of $125 million, or $9 per Instinet share.

My efforts to find a suitable partner for Weeden Equity Trading were not successful because it always turned out to be what I'd call a lateral move — we would still be part of a larger organization which would have control over us.

It was about this time that an old friend of mine from Minneapolis visited me at the firm apartment on the corner of Third Avenue and 65th Street, just across from the Sign of the Dove. Chuck Kelly and I had met as incoming freshmen at Stanford in the fall of 1947. We both swam on the freshman swim team and became good friends. Each summer I would stop off at his home on Lake Minnetonka on my way back to Stanford after working the summer in Weeden's New York office. We would then drive Chuck's new forest-green convertible across the country to Stanford. One year it was a Plymouth, the next year a Buick.

After graduation, we both entered Yale Law School and roomed together until I entered the U.S. Air Force pilot training program. We continued to keep in touch after the Air Force (he was in the JAG Corps). Both of us were now married and living in New York.

Chuck eventually returned to Minneapolis, where his mother still lived and where he continued to have many friends well placed in the leading corporations headquartered there.

He listened to our success story at MHEW and our desire to go out on our own. He felt there were people in the Minneapolis area who would help finance us — he had Cargill and the Weyerhaeuser family in mind — and helped put together a 12-page description of our business.

The numbers were very impressive, as the following chart shows:

(in 000's)

	1980	1981	1982	1983	1984
Gross Revenues	$6256	$5029	$8058	$10263	$11000
Pre-tax Income	$1500	$ 721	$2054	$2963	$2900
Est. Pre-tax Return on Equity	66%	46%	76%	108%	78%

The return-on-equity calculation was an approximation, based on the capital that would have been required to operate the department. We felt they were conservative, as the numbers included interest expense, which would disappear in the new company.

Presentations by me and Chuck over a three-month period resulted in our obtaining commitments for more than $5 million from investors in the Twin Cities area. We raised a total of $10.5 million, the bulk of the remaining capital coming from individuals on our trading desk through borrowings from Morgan Guaranty Trust Co., and the rest from the Weeden family and close friends. The loans from Morgan were unusual, as they were collateralized only by our signatures, our record while at MHEW and their past experience with the Weedens.

Moseley was not happy with our intention to leave and eventually exacted a warrant to buy 10 percent of the new company. We in turn gained the use of the name Weeden & Co.

Moseley soon after ran into capital problems, and sometime in 1987 they went into bankruptcy. Their last remaining asset was the Weeden warrant, which was purchased by the Richardson family (Richardson-Merrill, Vicks VapoRub), who exercised it in 1989.

Our last day at Moseley was December 30, 1985. On January 2, 1986, we were up and running on the 29th floor of 180 Maiden Lane under the name Weeden & Co., Inc.

At about the same time, my personal life was undergoing significant change. My marriage of more than 30 years had been falling apart for some time. Our four children were now grown, and Vera and I separated and eventually divorced. In the interim, I met a wonderful woman through my involvement with the Charles Ives Center for the Arts in Danbury, Connecticut, where I had recently become chairman of the board and a major contributor. Pat and I soon fell in love, and we married in April of 1987. Between us, as of this writing, we have seven children and 13 grandchildren.

28

The New Weeden

Leaving MHEW and going on our own was successful from the first trade. There were only five of us — Steve Gladstone, Tim McDonald, Barry Small, Bob Weppler and me — who had approached Moseley with our intentions to leave. But we knew we had the whole division behind us and anxious to make the move. On January 2, 1986, 26 of us opened up for business as Weeden & Co., Inc.

By this time, Bob Cervoni had joined us full time and became an important addition. Initially, Bob was induced to moonlight for us while we prepared for our move. We had no one who knew the administrative, regulatory and compliance requirements of an independent firm, and Bob's accounting background with Oppenheim, Appel, Dixon & Co. made him perfect for the job. Chuck Kelly also joined us, a director and vice president in charge of investment banking.

Our enthusiasm over leaving Moseley was contagious. Also, it helped that we didn't miss a beat from Friday to Tuesday over the long New Year's weekend. All of the credit goes to Bob Cervoni, Barry and everyone else who participated in making the move seamless. From the very beginning, Barry was assuming management responsibilities that eventually would gain him the formal title of senior managing partner.

Naturally, one of our critical decisions had been where to relocate. I had the misguided impression that everyone wanted to minimize fixed costs, and so after much effort I guided the four others to a sublet located next to a vacant lot on the corner of 23rd Street and Sixth Avenue. It was in the Iron Triangle district, which at the time was very marginal — but cheap (it began to attract upscale tenants in the late 1990s). The five of us went there one afternoon after the close of the market, looked the space over and then went to a coffee shop across the street to discuss the idea. Bob Weppler summarized the feelings of the group when he observed, after stepping around the homeless man sleeping outside the restaurant and another sleeping at the table next to us, "This neighborhood isn't for me." We ended up on the 29th floor of 180 Maiden Lane, a brand-new Class A building overlooking the South Street Seaport. Shortly after our move, I bought a telescope from Abercrombie & Fitch in order to monitor the goings-on at the Seaport.

We started the firm with practically everyone having a seat on the board: the five of us who initially left Moseley, Chuck Kelly, plus Ted Weyerhaeuser, Ben Jaffray and Joe Bennett representing the investors from the Twin Cities. Nine seems like a lot for the board of a brand-new 26-employee firm, but it worked out well. The balance between insiders and the older, more widely experienced outsiders proved remarkably compatible. John Driscoll, also part of the Weyerhaeuser family, was an invited guest at all meetings because his directorship of a bank precluded his formal participation.

A key addition occurred early on when we hired Keith Balter, whose father, Lee Balter, was the head over-the-counter trader at Tucker Anthony, R.L. Day. From the first moment Keith joined us, he and later his expanding department were profitable. If he had a loss day once every quarter I was surprised. His control of inventory and his daily consistency in producing a profit were something that I, who had lived with the daily ups and downs of the old Weeden, had never seen before. Keith was not that good in his relationship with customers — even with his peers on the Street — but Barry provided Keith with the kind of support and buffers that have made him the premier trader at Weeden over the past 15 years.

We did much better in our first year than we had dared hope: some $25 million in revenues and a nice bottom-line profit. We did well enough, in fact, to encourage us to change our corporate structure to a limited partnership at the end of 1986. The next year, 1987, was even better. Fortuitously, we had almost no overnight inventory going into October 19 (the day the Dow dropped 508 points), allowing us to avoid the big losses others incurred and take advantage of the chaotic and volatile market.

In 1987 Chuck Kelly reintroduced me to Steve Leuthold. Steve was located in Minneapolis and ran a very successful research firm, the Leuthold Group, with more than 200 institutions as clients. His appeal was in his objective, quantitative review of the relative value of financial markets: stocks, bonds, currencies, foreign. He also prepared sector and individual stock analyses based on similarly objective and clearly defined criteria.

A tentative relationship was established, through which we hoped to benefit from Steve's strong contacts with money managers and research analysts. In turn, he would benefit from our professional execution of his soft-dollar orders (see Glossary) from those institutions who subscribed to his work. This relationship began well and has grown stronger and closer over the years, although not without some differences. We were two strong-minded, independent and successful teams that needed time and good management to meld together. Time has shown that this was accomplished to everyone's satisfaction.

In the midst of this period of growth and profitability for the new Weeden came the Black Monday crash of October 19, 1987. I don't know whether Weeden would have survived under our old policies of maintaining large overnight positions and highly leveraged capital. Fortunately, the attitude of our partners running the trading desk regarding inventory and exposure was disciplined and conservative.

In October 1987, the structure of the listed market was quite different from the way it was in the 1970s, setting the stage for more violent and unpredictable price swings. To begin with, the group of Third Market firms who had previously provided two-sided markets in the major listed stocks of interest to institutions had all but disappeared. And the member-firm block positioners, absent any incentive or encouragement from either the Exchange or the SEC, felt no compulsion to "step up" and provide needed liquidity in times of stress. Thus the market was dependent solely upon the specialist. This situation was exacerbated throughout October 19 and 20 by the lack of timely information on what was occurring at the "post." As a consequence, participation by other liquidity providers was minimal while the violence lasted.

Thus, in those listed stocks that were "market leaders," the entire responsibility for holding back the invasion of panicky sellers, led by the portfolio insurance strategists, fell upon a highly undercapitalized group largely out of touch with the outside world. It was an impossible task, and one which elicited oft-told stories by specialists of their hero-ism and sacrifice. To describe the situation in military terms, the absence of a National Market System caused the Street to have only one soldier protecting the beach from sudden invasion.

Not surprising, as a group they survived and actually prospered from the excessive volatility that occurred. While several studies sought an explanation for what I call "clear-air turbulence" — inasmuch as there were no economic storm clouds in sight and because it was so short-lived — none suggested that the excessive volatility occurred because of the absence of strongly capitalized, highly competitive firms ready to provide liquidity.

It is interesting to compare the "monopoly structure" of the listed market to that of the OTC market. Here the major criticism was the fail-ure of the "competing" market makers to answer their phones, thus sug-gesting that they reneged on their responsibilities to the public investors. While it is true that phones were not answered when the computer system broke down due to locked markets, the numbers actu-ally suggest something quite different was happening. At the end of October 19, long inventories held by OTC market makers increased substantially, and the market as a percentage move had declined less than 60 percent of the decline on the Big Board. This was contrary to the normal occurrence in markets, where the highest quality exhibits less volatility and attracts more capital.

What happened was that the market makers, mostly brokerage firms with many in-house accounts, took care of their own retail while declin-ing to answer phone calls from their competitors. By having multiple market makers active in most stocks, the avalanche of sell orders was distributed over many firms whose capital was considerably in excess of the specialist community. If the listed market would have had the same capital available, the drop in the market would have undoubtedly been smaller.

I suggested in an op-ed piece I wrote for the *Wall Street Journal* (see Appendices) that October 19 offered a good reason for revisiting the idea of a National Market System in listed stocks.

While our arrangement with the Leuthold Group was developing nicely, our efforts in the area of investment banking proved unsuccess-ful. It had been my strong contention that the old Weeden had erred in not taking advantage of our preeminent Third Market position (as Salomon did in the bond area) in order to force entry into the new-issue underwritings of those corporations whose stock we actively traded. Now I felt there was an opportunity for Weeden, with its strong institutional ties, to bring to the public market smaller, institutional-quality companies whose modest needs for capital kept them below the major investment bankers' radar screen.

Chuck and I gave it a try, but neither of us had the necessary experience in corporate finance to make a go of it. Chuck left to do other things, and we brought aboard someone who had had experience in running a successful banking operation at a small firm in San Diego. Unfortunately, we had more failures than successes, and after another year of trying we got out of the business. It was apparent that I was not good in overseeing this activity, and my partners had no further stomach for the attendant costs and the distraction.

I then turned to running Weeden Capital Partners, which raised $6 million to invest in Silicon Valley technology. Here we had better luck and ended up providing a modest return to the individual partners who participated. At one point, the firm felt it necessary to play investment banker for one of our venture investments called Cymer, Inc. (CYMI). We succeeded in raising $6 million just at the moment their technology (deep ultraviolet light for photo equipment used in semiconductor manufacturing) was beginning to gain acceptance by the industry. The capital gain accruing to the firm and many of the partners was very rewarding and helped to re-establish my credibility.

In 1992, our head count had grown to about 60 and revenues were $38 million, giving us a little more than $600,000 in revenue per employee. "Partner" is a better word than "employee," as everyone had some partnership units. By this time, a majority of the ownership was in the hands of our active employees, with no one person owning more than 9 percent. As we grew, our policy from the beginning was to issue units to the newcomers and increase the ownership of others who deserved it.

It always had been the policy of Weeden, going back to 1922, to encourage employee ownership. We kept salaries low, paid bonuses when the profits were there, and felt that ownership created additional incentive to work hard and watch the expenses.

In the early years we built up our capital to where we felt we could manage whatever inventory requirements were placed on us by our customers, at which point we began a policy of distributing all of our excess profits back to the unit-holders.

Sometime in 1993, a lease renewal, tax considerations and lifestyle factors started us thinking about moving out of New York City. After considering New Hampshire (no taxes), North Carolina (great golf) and Sun Valley (why not?), we settled on Greenwich, Connecticut because it was close enough to the city to allow every one of our 54 New York personnel a reasonable commute.

Morale wise, it was the best decision we've made — next to that of leaving MHEW — and contributed to keeping our key producers and essential support people. In July 1994 we made our move to 145 Mason St. in Greenwich, and we've never looked back.

It was also in 1995 that Barry Small and I agreed the time had come to formally announce that he was running the firm. We had talked about it for some time, as Barry had been assuming that responsibility from the very beginning. Barry wanted to make sure he was up to doing it while still remaining on the desk during the trading day. I was ecstatic, as it meant a commitment by Barry to accept this responsibility on a long-term basis and to put all his effort into building a company of young talent that could survive in an increasingly competitive environment. The company was now formally in the hands of someone my father would have appreciated, had he still been around.

It was not long afterward that Barry unleashed a series of initiatives that greatly broadened the team involved in management. Not only in the area of sales and trading, but throughout the firm's operations a structure developed for analyzing, reporting and executing that crossed over the several disciplines in the firm.

Barry's formal education hardly predicted these emerging talents. As an undergraduate at Colgate, his major was economics — but as part of a traditional liberal arts curriculum. He also played soccer, and did well enough to be voted captain of his team and be recognized as an All-American in his senior year. After two years playing professional soccer in Dallas and New York, he came to Weeden & Co. in 1977, where he worked as a management trainee in operations.

It was also sometime after our move to Greenwich that Barry and Bob Cervoni began to develop a technology team that would put us on the forefront of the communication and computer revolution that was beginning to catch the eye of Wall Street. Shades of the old Weeden.

Through a combination of home-grown system development and the best available from third parties, we kept up with the major Wall Street firms in providing linkages with the markets, the institutional investors and the information providers. Barry was the driving force and Bob brought all the necessary pieces and players together. (Incidentally, Bob was another of modest background, hard-working and with unique management skills, who came out of nowhere to put together and administer the operational and financial side of the business.)

The third leg of our management team became Tim McDonald, whom I can only describe as a great salesman — if not the greatest institutional salesman on Wall Street today.

Tim came to us literally off the boat — a commercial fishing smack that worked out of Montauk. It was at Keeler's Anchor marina that Tim met Lou Barail and Steve Gladstone back in our early days at MHEW. Tim comes from a large Irish family in Albany. His father was tax commissioner and important in the Democratic Party. Tim graduated from Albany Business College and the SUNY Institute of Technology in Utica before going off to do the things he liked to do. The transition from fisherman to salesman was instant. Big, good-looking and naturally gregarious, Tim lives by attention to detail, a strong work ethic and a simple business code that the customer is always right. His production at Weeden has been a mainstay of our annual revenues and an inspiration to all the other salesmen. The rapport between Tim the salesman and Barry the trader has been key to our developing and maintaining a strong relationship with our accounts.

Thus, throughout Weeden's history, the firm was being guided by men who fully understood the marketplace and customer service while at the same time were taking a strong interest in all the nitty-gritty details of running a tight ship. It is this attention to detail that has provided Weeden a return on capital attained by very few Wall Street firms.

From 1992 to the present, Weeden's revenue has reflected the overall increase in activity in both the listed and over-the-counter equity markets. Because of close attention to expenses, year-to-year profits have tended to exceed industry averages.

In the middle of this period, Weeden became entangled in a major class-action lawsuit and investigation of the over-the-counter market charging conspiracy among the major market makers to keep the inside spreads on NASDAQ artificially wide.

Right from the beginning, we strenuously objected to being included in the case, as we knew that we had not participated in any conspiracy to disadvantage our customers. Dealing solely with institutional investors, we did no internalizing of order flow and provided no service except best execution. More than 30 percent of our trades were done on Instinet because it often had better prices than NASDAQ, and our overall spread was less than $.06 between purchase and sale. We were indignant at being included, but learned to our dismay that the rest of the participants were willing to agree to the billion-dollar settlement (our share being $5 million) and were not willing to consider our request to be excluded. We felt like a dolphin inadvertently caught in the fisherman's giant net.

Our non-role in the conspiracy was vindicated when the Justice Department decided to drop us from their own investigation. But this happened only after a strongly worded and, I must say, emotional speech to a roomful of skeptical antitrust lawyers in a meeting at the Justice Department. I pointed out Weeden's past role in ending fixed commissions, our long fight for more competition, and our support of technology (AutEx and Instinet) to make the markets more transparent, more accessible and less expensive to use. Being dropped by the Justice Department saved our small firm considerable expense by not having to monitor for any future antitrust violations.

As time went on, I found myself being asked to participate as a speaker or panelist at various conferences and give my views of trends in the marketplace. As "President Emeritus" of the Third Market, my partners let me say whatever I wanted to while reminding me that Weeden was now an electronic member of the NYSE. I always made the point when speaking publicly that my remarks reflected my own thinking and opinions, and not necessarily those of my firm. During these years, *Institutional Investor* Magazine was good enough to recognize my past role in the industry, and the Chicago Stock Exchange once named me their Man of the Year.

In 1998, the idea of a Super Regional Stock Exchange began to receive serious attention as a way of improving the regional exchanges' ability to compete with the NYSE. I felt so strongly that it was not a good idea that I wrote a letter to the *Wall Street Journal* outlining my views, hoping it might be reprinted on their op-ed page. While this didn't happen, the ideas it contained are still valid.

I started the letter by saying that while a Super Regional Stock Exchange was a bold idea, it would only perpetuate the second-class status of the regionals. Unless the Intermarket Trading System was altered to include a central limit order book (CLOB), regional specialists would continue to operate with one arm tied behind their backs.

"At present, a specialist on the regionals must guarantee the execution of limit orders in order to attract market orders, which are the lifeblood of all market makers. This means he must buy or sell for his own account on the wrong side of the market, jeopardizing his profitability and his willingness to commit capital. This is the main reason why regionals have difficulty in developing well-capitalized specialist operations on their floors."

"A central (or composite) limit order book would create a level playing field by allowing limit orders to receive equal exposure and execution no matter which exchange they were sent to."

"For the public investor, a CLOB would provide maximum protection for their limit orders, would increase liquidity by strengthening the regional specialists and would heighten competition among exchanges, all of which would be to their advantage."

"Unfortunately, a CLOB is not in the cards as the ITS requires a unanimous vote to change its rules. New York quite understandably opposes a CLOB, recognizing that its 'book' is the critical element distinguishing it from the other exchanges. To share the book through a CLOB is inimical to their interest."

"With the present pace of technology, narrowing of spreads and desire for greater access by the public, the playing field must be leveled in order to give the regionals a fighting chance."

"Without SEC pressure or Congressional action on this issue, the future of regional exchanges is in jeopardy."

With the arrival of decimalization, the disappearance of payment for order flow, lower access fees by DOT (the NYSE Designated Order Turnaround System) and other NYSE initiatives to capture order flow, the future of the regionals as a viable market for listed stocks is even more in jeopardy.

Since its inception in early 2001, decimalization has been a mixed bag. For small retail traders, penny spreads have lowered their costs of entering and exiting the market. For retail brokers, it has shifted compensation from spreads and paybacks to commissions with minor effect on their bottom line. For market makers in the highly competitive NASDAQ marketplace and on the regional exchanges, it has been a disaster. For institutions with large orders and the brokers servicing them, it has caused the market to become more opaque and volatile. For the franchised specialist on the NYSE, it has been a bonanza.

These few excerpts from a letter to our clients by Barry Small, who sits daily on the trading desk, give an idea of the present frustration.

"The objective of recent changes in market structure should be to incent and encourage all market participants to join in price discovery and create a more efficient place. ... I feel as if the rule changes (decimalization) were made to close down informal flow to all market players except the specialist. The specialists' already sky-high profit margins will increase, as observed in a recent blurb on January 29, 2001 in the *Wall Street Journal* quoting an unnamed specialist: 'Specialists are going to need wool pockets to hold all the cash they are going to make off conversion to decimals.'"

"Limit orders are severely compromised and at risk to be penny-jumped with little downside to professional traders and specialists. I don't care what the NYSE is saying, this is a major, major problem. ... Since limit orders are disincented, then market orders are encouraged, which will increase the velocity and volatility of executions. This will result in higher costs for everyone involved."

"The SEC and NYSE have succeeded in closing the markets by pulling information away from the very participants who are the market. ... The specialist gets the only real look and can act instantaneously, while we can only react weakly to trades unforeseen. Liquidity will continue to shrink, velocity and volatility will increase, transaction costs will soar and general confidence in the fairness of the markets will erode. No one will trust the process as the special-ist lines his wool pockets and Goldman Sachs continues to invest heavily in the Exchange it lobbied against so aggressively last year."

Barry doesn't say it, but the root problem is that the market structure in NYSE-listed stocks does not allow for other dealer capital to effec-tively provide competition to the specialist. The reason? The Intermarket Trading System (ITS) stands between the NYSE floor and all other mar-ket centers. In almost every other market — options, NASDAQ, U.S. government bonds, futures — there exist multiple dealers with regu-lated responsibility to make markets. These dealers have equal access to the center of the market and provide a competitive environment in which the investor can choose with whom to deal. If one market maker is hesitant to make a good market, or has used up his available capital, or tries to take undue advantage of incoming inquiry, the investor has clear alternatives. If Weeden doesn't do a good job for our client, we may never hear from him again. Competition is the regulator and pro-vides integrity to the market.

The ITS, by not providing for real-time linkage and a neutral site for exposure of limit orders, prevents other dealers and regional specialists from providing strong sources of competition to the NYSE specialist.

There is a solution to all of this, if the SEC is strong enough, focused enough and determined enough. It is found in a simple reconfiguration of the ITS to enable it to advertise public orders to the other partici-pants. A simple requirement should be added giving time and price pri-ority to all public orders so displayed.

29

Weeden Today

As we move through the ninth decade of Weeden, I find Dickens' famous opening line from *A Tale of Two Cities* most appropriate: "It was the best of times, it was the worst of times."

"Worst" in the sense that our industry is experiencing an extended period of declining markets, lower volume, disappearing profits and a demoralized customer base. While the general mood on Wall Street is as bad as I can remember, history can be useful to regain a more balanced perspective on the future. After the great crash of 1929, the markets also rallied, but then resumed their downward trend. Only after major changes in market structure and time — lots of time — did the markets recover and resume their upward trend.

While I'm not old enough to remember the crash of '29 (being born in June 1930, I have always speculated that if the October crash had come in September I might not be here), I have seen markets in every succeeding decade that declined sharply and then recovered. I am sure the same will happen again.

The 1990s were very good to Weeden, and I see no reason why these "best of times" should not continue. Our management team is very good, if not better than at any time in the past 80 years. They are all young, talented and energetic. They are very focused and disciplined. During the recent bubble, they stuck to what they did well and avoided "looking over the fence." They understand that survival today will depend on controlling costs, and that technology is the wave of the future.

Since we moved to Greenwich in 1994, our employee count has doubled. Besides adding salesmen and traders, much of the increase was in the computer, communication and software sections, as Barry Small aggressively built out our ability to interact both internally and with our customers.

Nevertheless, the '90s were a difficult time to recruit, as we were not of the mind to offer large signing bonuses or guarantees. We had to rely on our location in Greenwich, a good working environment, a special camaraderie from top to bottom and the opportunity for everyone to become significant owners of the firm. Our ongoing program of moving ownership into employee hands has been critical to our ability to attract and retain the best talent on Wall Street and maintain profitability.

It was in this environment that I found myself increasingly underemployed with plenty of time to work on a history of Weeden. For those who have read this far, I hope you found it interesting. I had fun revisiting those interesting times and remembering all the good people I came to know.

30

2002:
Still No National
Market System

When I started this book, I had in mind writing only about those years when Weeden & Co. was a principal player in the market and an active force for change on Wall Street. Those years began in 1963, when our Third Market activity became publicly known, and lasted until 1978, when Weeden lost its identity through merger with another firm. I soon found this inadequate, because to understand the forces at play one had to know more about the Third Market, where it came from and why. And to understand why Weeden was involved meant explaining how our business developed.

But even more, it required describing the Weedens themselves, where they came from and what made them tick. Because if you think about it, we probably could have avoided the whole conflict that developed between ourselves and the NYSE.

Some firms quietly backed off from making markets in listed industrial stocks. Others ended up becoming members of the NYSE, while still others kept quiet and accommodated themselves to the majority view.

Looking back, I think that the firm — the family — did the right thing, and I have no apologies for the stand we took and the things we said. What happened to Weeden is another matter. There I feel badly, and still do. We had a great thing going and lost it through neglect. That part of the story had to be told as well.

Then there was the six years in the penalty box while at MHEW. This period of time gave us the opportunity to think about what happened, regroup into a profitable operation and reconstitute ourselves into a smaller, more focused, better-managed Weeden than before. This part of the story was needed also to provide a happy ending to a firm that had its origin in San Francisco some 80 years ago.

Telling the story of those times during the 1960s and '70s makes it clear, at least to me, that we did make a difference and that difference helped almost everybody.

The changes that occurred prepared the industry to handle the enormous growth of demand for our services and our products during the 1980s and '90s, and ushered in an unprecedented period of prosperity for Wall Street.

Weeden was not alone in bringing about these changes, but we were certainly important. In the area that we were especially interested — the market for listed stocks — our presence was essential to effect many of the improvements that took place. I don't believe the Securities Acts Amendments of 1975 would have turned out the way it did without our being there to explain, educate and counter the arguments of the vocal majority.

What I do regret is the fact that the problems at Weeden diverted our energies from seeing the National Market System through to its final development. We had to step out of the ring. And there was no one left to fight the good fight.

As this book goes to press we still do not have a National Market System in listed stocks. In fact, all signs point to our going in the opposite direction. The NYSE has recently made it clear that they want to get out of the Intermarket Trading System (ITS). It serves no useful purpose for their interests and complicates their execution of trades in their own market. They would rather have regional orders flow into them through their DOT system, where they have better control. They have also indicated their desire to go it alone on reporting their sales to the public. They have always felt that the revenue-sharing arrangement made in 1975 was biased toward the regional exchanges, whose trades were smaller in size and number and anyway in their mind not important in establishing price levels for the public.

Meanwhile, the NYSE is bringing on line several new initiatives to divert more order flow away from the regionals and into their market directly, including charging less to the brokerage community for the use of DOT, offering the public a better look at their "book," and Institutional Express, whereby the institution can talk directly to the specialist. NYSE seems determined to capture a sufficient percentage of public orders directly so as to effectively take the other market centers out of the picture.

This trend is being fueled by other events affecting the economics of market making on the regional exchanges. With the coming of decimalization, spreads in all equity markets have narrowed and profits after expenses have become very marginal. For regional specialists, it has eliminated the use of payment for order flow, a method which had been effective in bolstering their business. It has also made the practice of guaranteeing limit orders totally unattractive. Consequently, regional specialists are migrating their capital to more productive uses, like options and OTC stocks. The final elimination of Rule 390 has done little to excite upstairs market making because of the way ITS works to prevent them from competing effectively with the New York specialists, the result being no additional liquidity providers. The combination of disincentives to compete and NYSE's more aggressive program to capture all the order flow puts the handwriting clearly on the wall.

With the events of September 11, 2001, the significance of this "great leap backward," to use Don Farrar's description of William McChesney Martin's central marketplace, has escalated from an intra-industry power struggle into a national security issue. If the NYSE had been the central target, our listed stock markets would have been out of commission indefinitely. A structure that centralizes most of the physical activity and concentrates the communication linkages into a single place would have had to be replaced from the ground up, just as the World Trade Center will be.

A National Market System would have avoided the consequences of such an attack by having decentralized the market into dozens of centers, tapping into myriad pools of capital and telephone linkages throughout the country as diversified as our interstate highway system.

Thus, the questions to be asked 37 years after the Securities Acts Amendments of 1975 are several:

- Are we seeing a classic move toward a natural monopoly, and should this be of concern?

- Was Congress (and everyone else) wrong in opting for a National Market System that provided for competing markets and priority to public orders?
- Is there something wrong with the structure that allowed this trend toward a single market to occur?
- Has the SEC exercised its responsibilities properly and used its powers effectively to insure the creation of a National Market System, as Congress mandated?
- Are there national security issues to be considered since the events of September 11?

Ultimately, it will be up to Congress to review what has happened and renew its determination to create a National Market System, if it wishes. Normally that will happen only when a crisis occurs and public opinion calls for action. That crisis might occur from one of the following:

- Regional exchanges find that they can no longer compete.
- A growing misuse of monopoly power by the NYSE specialists.
- Further terrorists attacks.

I hope that we will not have to wait for any of these to happen. The SEC has the authority to bring about a National Market System. But past experience suggests that it will not use that power without some additional prodding by Congress. I still believe after 27 years that the benefits of a National Market System are just as compelling today as they were in 1975, and since September 11 they've become even more so.

WEEDEN & CO.

INCORPORATED

IN REESTABLISHING AN INDEPENDENT WEEDEN & CO., WE CONTINUE THE TRADITION OF THE ORIGINAL WEEDEN & CO. FOUNDED IN SAN FRANCISCO MORE THAN A HALF CENTURY AGO.

THE FIRM WAS FOUNDED IN A COMMITMENT TO QUALITY IN ITS BUSINESS RELATIONS AND IN THE CHARACTER OF ITS PEOPLE. IN THE SPIRIT OF THE WEST, THE FOUNDING PHILOSOPHY ALSO INCLUDED A CONVICTION THAT COMPETITIVE MARKETS AND REALISTIC PRICES MEANT BETTER BUSINESS FOR EVERYONE.

THROUGH THE EFFORTS OF DEDICATED PROFESSIONALS OVER THE YEARS, WEEDEN & CO. ACQUIRED A REPUTATION FOR INNOVATION AND LEADERSHIP. THE WEEDEN NAME HAS LONG BEEN ASSOCIATED WITH POSITIVE CHANGES IN THE SECURITIES INDUSTRY.

WE ARE PROUD OF THIS TRADITION AND, TODAY, WE IN A NEW WEEDEN & CO. REAFFIRM OUR DEDICATION TO THESE PRINCIPLES.

JANUARY 6, 1986

Weeden & Co. tombstone, 1986

WEEDEN & CO.

INCORPORATED

DONALD E. WEEDEN
CHAIRMAN AND CHIEF EXECUTIVE

BARRY J. SMALL
MANAGING DIRECTOR - CAPITAL COMMITMENT

STEPHEN S. GLADSTONE
MANAGING DIRECTOR - TRADING

ROBERT G. WEPPLER
MANAGING DIRECTOR - SALES

TIMOTHY J. McDONALD
MANAGING DIRECTOR - SALES

CHARLES J. KELLY, JR.
MANAGING DIRECTOR - INVESTMENT BANKING

JOSEPH C. BENNETT
DIRECTOR;
MINING ENGINEER AND PRIVATE INVESTOR

BENJAMIN S. JAFFRAY
DIRECTOR;
TREASURER AND DIRECTOR, CARGILL INC.

FREDERICK J. WEYERHAEUSER
DIRECTOR;
DIRECTOR: AFRICA PROGRAM WORLD WILDLIFE FUND

ADVISORY BOARD

W. JOHN DRISCOLL
CHAIRMAN, FIRST NATIONAL BANK IN PALM BEACH
DIRECTOR, ST. PAUL COMPANIES; GOULD INC.;
FIRST NATIONAL BANK, ST. PAUL; WEYERHAEUSER CO.
NORTHERN STATES POWER INC.

Weeden & Co. board of directors, 1986

Don and Pat Weeden, 1996

The Weeden & Co. trading floor, Greenwich, Connecticut, 2002

Weeden & Co. advertisement: Reprint from *Pensions & Investments* describing results of a U.S. equity trading survey using the Plexus Broker Universe for the four quarters ending September 30, 2001

Acknowledgments

This book is not an academic treatise with hours spent in the library and careful footnotes. It is simply meant to be my personal account of Weeden & Co., the Weeden family and our time spent on Wall Street, with all the warts and inaccuracies one would expect from someone in his seventies.

True, I had a lot of help. First of all from my brothers, Alan and Jack, both older than I and therefore subject to the same infirmities of age. They made sure I spelled everyone's name correctly and didn't stray too far from the facts about the family and what went on at Weeden.

Books about those times, especially Joel Seligman's *The Transformation of Wall Street: A History of the Securities and Exchange Commission and Modern Corporate Finance* (1981) and Chris Welles' wonderful, but slightly premature *The Last Days of the Club* (1976), were freely used and quoted from, with permission of the authors. Ten years of *Institutional Investor* Magazine (1968–78) provided a treasure trove of articles, portraits and interviews, snippets of which appear throughout the book. Also helpful were old files containing speeches, articles, annual reports and clippings of one sort or another.

I'm indebted to Joel Harnett, who was chairman of the New York City Club when I was its president. He introduced me to Gary Avey, my editor, and together they have helped enormously in guiding me through this process of writing a book. There were others, too, like Bob Beshar, Chuck Kelly, Fred Siesel and Kate Welling, who read early drafts and commented on content, style and tone. Christine Roux, an English teacher in Seattle — also my daughter — helped in many ways to make the text more readable and clear. All of the above will be quick to deny any credit for the result.

Jim Lorie, who also read an early draft, felt he could help the reader by contributing a short foreword explaining what the book is all about. My thanks to Jim as well.

I also wish to thank freelance editor Deborah Paddison, whose eagle eye for detail was invaluable in turning a raw manuscript into a finished book, and my secretary, Jane Mitchell, who loyally retyped draft after draft. Last but not least, I'm grateful to my wife Pat, who patiently read or listened to some chapters more than a dozen times.

Writing this book turned out to be an engrossing task which I enjoyed, but am happy to have finished. I hope someone will read it, but that is not so important. The fact is, it is done. I have meant no harm to anyone and apologize to any who might feel affronted or wrongly described.

Appendices

Reprint of a Letter Submitted

to the

SECURITIES AND EXCHANGE COMMISSION

By

DONALD E. WEEDEN

Executive Vice President

WEEDEN & CO.

DECEMBER 19, 1969

WEEDEN & CO.

INCORPORATED

NEW YORK   SAN FRANCISCO   BOSTON   CHICAGO   HOUSTON   LOS ANGELES   LONDON

December 19, 1969

Securities and Exchange Commission
500 North Capitol Street
Washington, D. C. 20549

Gentlemen:

The securities industry, buffeted by change, faces a less than certain future. Many of the problems and conflicts confronting the industry are either presently before the Securities and Exchange Commission for decision or soon will be. The final disposition of these problems and conflicts will determine the shape of the industry for years to come.

We write the Commission as a major Third Market firm in order to expose a particular point of view concerning the issues before it. In Part I we discuss factors bearing on the future structure of the industry with special emphasis on the concept of a Central Market Place. In Part II we answer some of the charges recently directed at the Third Market by representatives of the New York Stock Exchange. In Part III we urge on the Commission a specific course of action.

Part I

Considerable restructuring of the securities industry must inevitably take place in the next few years. The forces compelling this change stem largely from the overwhelming increase in institutional business in common stocks acting upon archaic and inflexible rules maintained by the industry's principal stock exchange.

The resulting pressures have already brought about the growth of the Third Market, the advent of member firm block positioners and demands for public ownership of member firms to meet the increased capital needs of the Street. Increased institutional participation in the market place has raised the following important issues:

1. An equitable stock exchange commission structure; or whether minimum commissions in some instances are necessary.

2. Institutional ownership of stock exchange firms.

3. Institutional access to the exchange markets.

4. Access of non-member dealers to the exchange markets.

5. Access of member firms to off board markets.

The hard truth is that the economic interests of the institutional investor are better served by a negotiated market than by an auction market. The institutional investor prefers to control his own order; he wants direct access to the market makers; and under normal conditions he would rather avoid paying an unnecessary commission to a broker interpositioned between himself and the market maker.

The increase in institutional block business has drastically reduced the effectiveness of the specialist, not so much because the specialist lacks capital resources, but because he has lost contact with the market. The large ticket market has increasingly moved off the floor of the Exchange. Because New York Stock Exchange rules preclude the specialist from dealing directly with the public, he has found it impossible to obtain direct exposure to the full sweep of institutional inquiry. Consequently, he is flying blind and is understandably unwilling to risk his capital on large positions.

Into this vacuum has come first the Third Market, and more recently the member firm block positioners. Both groups have more access to the ultimate buyers than the specialists. The transition would have come earlier and with more dramatic suddenness were it not for the convenient uses that many institutions find for commissions in paying for research, rewarding depositors, and in the case of mutual fund management companies, repaying efforts by dealers to sell their fund shares.

The New York Stock Exchange's persistence in perpetuating the monopolistic position of its specialists, in fostering its members' isolation from other market places, and particularly in maintaining a commission structure for block business that greatly exceeds the cost of executing and processing that business, has resulted in tortuous distortions in the securities industry. The Commission Rate Hearing disclosed the elaborate and devious methods by which institutions are rebated commissions and fiduciaries use commissions generated on funds for which they are responsible to discharge their own obligations to others. We have witnessed institutions entering the securities business as broker-dealers with no other purpose than to reduce their commission charges. We have seen the New York Stock Exchange promulgate rules that would permit its members to sell stock to the public, while at the same time prohibit to institutional customers the right of membership; and we have noted with interest the Justice Department's reaction to these proposed rules. We have observed New York Stock Exchange members long identified as brokers being forced to take up the burdens of a dealer solely because the specialist system is not equipped to handle the large imbalances of institutionalized markets. We question whether the inherent conflict of interest between acting as broker and dealer in the same transaction is healthy for our industry. We submit that such distortions and others in our industry are at least in part the result of New York Stock Exchange practices. Continuation of these practices in the New York Stock Exchange version of a "Central Market Place" would, in our opinion, simply exacerbate the distortions and reinforce the devious devices related to them.

The Central Market Place Concept

We are not opposed to the Central Market Place Concept. We give it our wholehearted support. However, the N.Y.S.E. version of the Central Market Place is truncated and self-serving. By building a wall around its own special privilege, the Exchange has kept out the capital, the inquiry, and the participation of other market makers, and restricted its own members from seeking better markets away. The result is that the N.Y.S.E. is itself fracturing the Central Market Place.

The Central Market Place today is no longer a geographical concept. It is a communications concept. With today's electronic miracles available to the industry, all market makers wherever located could be combined into a central, interrelated market for fast and efficient access by investors to all of its segments. The true Central Market Place demands access to all available pools of positioning capital for maximum liquidity.

The New York Stock Exchange would have the Commission assist it in blocking this development of the Central Market Place. The Exchange's response to the massive need for more liquidity is to speak of supplementing scarce specialist capital by permitting partnerships with positioning brokers —a short-term expedient which, in our opinion, involves conflict of interest between the broker function and the dealer function. Were such partnerships permitted, Exchange rules would still make it difficult for a member broker to deal with outside market makers. Thus, a broker would be forced to deal with a competing broker acting, in this case, in partnership with a monopolistic specialist. Once again the Central Market Place is fractured by the New York Stock Exchange.

The New York Stock Exchange claims that its restrictive version of the Central Market Place protects the investor and, therefore, is a justified restraint of trade. While history and common sense rule that full and free competition best protects the investor, or any consumer for that matter, the Rules of the New York Stock Exchange say no. Specialist posts have long since been non-competitive on the floor of the Exchange; and the Special Study in 1963 stated that a return to competition in this regard was a practical impossibility. The Minimum Commission Structure and Rule 394, once stated to be the cornerstones of the New York Stock Exchange by its President, also restrain competition. Nothing in the New York Stock Exchange testimony at the Commission Rate Hearing, in its present proposals before the Commission, or in the anticipated content of future proposals, indicates anything but a continuation of policy directed towards reducing competition from other market makers and regional exchanges. For these reasons, we believe the New York Stock Exchange, not its competition, is fracturing the Central Market Place.

The New York Stock Exchange claims, as an important strength in its version of the Central Market Place, that, for better or worse, all inquiry is centered now in one place. A careful reading of the Commission Rate Hearing belies that claim. Testimony by the Chairman of the Board of Governors of the New York Stock Exchange with regard to block trades shows clearly that the specialist is often the last person shown a block inquiry from an institution, and many times is never exposed to it at all.

The Central Market Place will come to exist through freedom of access, not elimination of competing markets. There is no reason why all inquiry in listed stocks cannot be centered in an up-to-date version of the Central Market Place, involving computers and electronic display panels such as envisioned in the NASDAQ system. Such a system could be enhanced by a "public" ticker tape capable of reporting trades in all market places, including all exchanges, on a real time basis.

We reiterate that the present New York Stock Exchange proposals before the Commission and everything we hear rumored about its forthcoming proposals lead us to the conclusion that the New York Stock Exchange is attempting to maintain the present barriers between itself and the competitive forces in other areas of the industry, with the calculated hope that it will be more difficult for these competitive forces to survive. We believe that much of what the Exchange is doing and proposes to do is illegal under the anti-trust laws. We also believe that what the Exchange is trying to do will be extremely harmful in the long run to the entire industry.

Left to their own devices, without concerted action by the New York Stock Exchange, markets in listed stocks should logically evolve into a simple combination of the present auction market servicing broker-handled executions of public orders and a negotiated market of well-capitalized market makers catering mainly to institutions. This is the direction that the corporate bond market took in the 1930's and 1940's when increased institutional trading in those securities demanded something more than just an auction market. What evolved was a combination market place that preserved the auction market while at the same time encouraged the growth of market makers, both inside and outside the exchange structure. This system protected the individual investor and the brokerage function related to that type of business, yet was capable of providing the liquidity and depth necessary for expanded institutional trading.

We believe the market in institutional grade listed stocks will evolve into something quite similar. The extent of that evolution will depend largely on the balance that is struck between the participation of the individual investor and the institution in the ownership of such stocks. If, as we are told, "stocks are merchandised, not bought," an important determinant of this balance will be the level of commissions charged on small transactions relative to those charged on the larger trades and on sales of mutual fund shares.

We believe that the market makers in such a system will want to deal at net prices. The Commission Rate Hearing showed that member firm block positioners view the minimum commission as only a component in arriving at what is the actual net bid or net offer. A mandatory commission is an obstruction to a market maker and where present, permits the type of distortion exemplified by the give up. In addition, it creates a misleading price to the public to the extent that the transaction is publicized on the tape.

We consider it essential in such a system that all broker-dealers, including exchange members, have access to all market makers directly, without restriction, when handling orders over a certain minimum size or when in their judgment their customer is better served by going off board. Exchange members could act either as a market maker in the negotiated market or as a broker in the auction market. Non-member market makers could deal directly without commission with member market makers or member brokers on transactions over the established minimum size but would, of course, have no access to the auction market as a broker. However, some form of net trading between exchange specialists and non-member market makers should be encouraged. In the final analysis, the essential new ingredient of a combined system—the sine qua non of the true Central Market Place—is increased competition through greater access to all market makers by all participants.

Part II

The New York Stock Exchange in trying to preserve its concept of the Central Market Place has made a concerted effort through public utterances and letters to regulatory agencies to discredit the Third Market by charging that it is unregulated, as compared to the New York Stock Exchange, lacks adequate standards for reporting to the public, and assumes no responsibility in market making.

While we view these efforts as nothing more than an attempt by the New York Stock Exchange to preserve an illegal, monopolistic method of controlling trading in listed securities, we do recognize the impact that constant reiteration can have. Therefore, we would like to discuss these matters at some length with the Commission.

Reporting

One of the arguments that the New York Stock Exchange is using to protest the growth of the Third Market and inhibit the evolution of a combined system of auction and negotiated markets for listed stock is the absence of a stock ticker to report trades in the Third Market. The Exchange's argument is that the public interest is protected by the reporting of each sale and that any departure from this reporting is somehow malevolently clandestine.

We have always viewed the New York Stock Exchange ticker as primarily a sales device to induce trading, with any protective regulatory purpose as secondary. If its principal purpose were regulatory or in the public interest, then one would think the New York Stock Exchange would insist that all trades entered into by its members be printed on the tape for the benefit of the public, including transactions crossed by member firms on the regional exchanges, special purchases and sales by specialists made away from the Floor, off board transactions in exempt securities, and the few Rule 394(b) trades that take place. The New York Stock Exchange's lack of consistency in its application of principle puts in question the principle itself.

As a major Third Market maker, we are not adverse to the daily reporting of our trades in some manner to the public if the public is interested or if the Commission feels such reporting serves a regulatory purpose. Such publicity could be accomplished by publishing markets and volumes in the daily papers, much as O-T-C stocks are handled. If the Commission were to conclude that the ticker tape has a true basis as a public information vehicle and not as a merchandising tool, we would be happy to join the entire industry in reporting trades on a tape that was available to all market places. However, we point out that institutions are finding that the last sale on the New York Stock Exchange ticker is less and less a guide to the price at which they can buy or sell large blocks. Too often, there is a large disparity between the last sale of 100 or 200 shares and the price at which a large block is eventually liquidated. More important to the institutional buyer than the last sale is the present bid and ask price of the market maker and the size of his market. This fact should be taken into account in considering any industry-wide system. Perhaps, the auction market should continue to report actual last sales while the negotiated market reports bids, asks and size with a summary of volume and range at the end of the trading day. Such reporting would exceed the present reporting in the corporate bond market where only the auction market trades are reported on the New York Stock Exchange ticker tape.

Regulation

Absence of regulation in the Third Market has been cited by the President of the New York Stock Exchange and others in the Exchange community to discredit the Third Market and to support the Exchange's own restrictive policies. We discuss these charges here at some length because regulation of the auction market and regulation of the negotiated market and the interrelationships of such regulation should be thoroughly understood.

To begin, our firm is not adverse to any regulation of the Third Market by the Commission or by the N.A.S.D. if it appears that such regulation is necessary to curb questionable practices or to protect the integrity of the market. However, we are not anxious to be burdened with the expense and inconvenience of reporting under regulations that are unnecessary to the public interest.

Mr. Haack testified in the Commission Rate Hearing that, "third market makers are subject only to the fraud and anti-manipulative rules of the S.E.C. which relate to all brokers and dealers." He then went on to cite the ways in which a specialist is "regulated," some of which are totally unrelated to Third Market operations and some of which he errs in assuming that there is no Third Market equivalent. For instance, he ignores the capital requirements and the obligation to make a continuous market imposed on a Third Market dealer who registers as such with the Commission under

Rule X-17A-9. He states that the specialist cannot "walk away" from a market without Exchange sanction, thereby implying that Third Market makers can and often do. In this respect, we cite the specialist's monopolistic position as reason for his regulation in this area. We may have the ability to "walk away" from a market-making responsibility, but our competitive desire to keep our customers precludes our exercising this option very often. Our increased activity during times of market turmoil also suggests that "walking away" is not our regular practice.

Mr. Haack makes the point repeatedly that Third Market makers are not required to be a stabilizing influence on the market. We agree—we are not so regulated. Nor is the specialist in any effective way. By the nature of our business in a negotiated market place, we are almost certain to get more sellers in a falling market, and thus buy more; and more buyers in a rising market, and thus sell more. Our firm's conduct during the weeks surrounding the market break of May 1962 was specifically reviewed by the Commission. We are proud of that record for it shows inventory changes generally counter to market movement and increased, not decreased, activity. The small amount of business we do with other market makers and our policy of never selling stock through a broker on the New York Stock Exchange virtually eliminates the likelihood of our market-making being an unstabilizing force. Here again we say if investigation by the Commission reveals a defect, we are ready to talk of remedies.

Mr. Haack points out that Exchange regulations prohibit short sales below the market and that no comparable prohibition exists in the Third Market. He is right in theory, but wrong in fact. To the extent that an institutional client wishes to buy stock, we may short to him in the process of filling his inquiry. In such a case, there would be no reason for us to sell at a price lower than the last published market price, as our price to him is net of commissions. To our knowledge, we have never sold stock short to anyone below the last published sale.

Third Market firms, of course, could not legally go short on down ticks through sales on the New York Stock Exchange even if policy permitted them to sell on the Exchange, which ours does not. However, there does exist the possibility that a client might sell short to a Third Market firm stock which the client can borrow elsewhere for the purpose of making delivery. Such a sale would not affect the price on the New York Stock Exchange unless the stock were resold on the Exchange. Were it resold on the Exchange, there is a theoretical possibility that such stock could be sold on a down tick. We point out, however, that this possibility exists through any intermediary, including a New York Stock Exchange member, who accepts short stock from a customer who has his own sources for borrowing that stock to make delivery.

The primary cause for most of the regulation of the specialist is the fact that the dealer function in the Exchange market has become an exception to the American way of free enterprise and open competition. On the Exchange, the market-maker function has narrowed to the point where a monopolistic grant is given to a single specialist in each security. This specialist enjoys an exclusive franchise to make a market in his stock while, at the same time, he is exposed to the flow of public inquiry in that stock and charged with keeping the order book. In our opinion, most current regulation of the specialist and of the Exchange Floor has evolved through obvious need illumined by past abuse. Just as monopolies in public utilities have been subjected to regulation not bestowed upon other businesses, so the specialist must accept special regulation along with his privileged position.

The Third Market on the other hand is part of the huge O-T-C negotiated market place for bonds and stocks where regulation of the market maker has traditionally and successfully been achieved through open competition between independent dealers vying for the business of brokers, banks and other knowledgeable institutions entering the market with orders to place.

In the evolution of the Central Market Place for listed stocks, combining both auction and negotiated markets catering to institutions, we see no reason for the Commission to impose identical regulations on each segment. Such identity would be meaningless and illogical given the differing structures of those markets and the varying degrees of competition. It is no coincidence that institutionally dominated negotiated markets are the most competitive and the least regulated of all in the securities industry.

Responsibility

The New York Stock Exchange has questioned the wisdom of permitting the Third Market to operate without a formal charge of responsibility for maintaining fair and orderly markets and for maintaining minimum standards of business conduct.

Here again, should N.A.S.D. regulations be held insufficient, we have no objection to formally committing ourselves to the responsibility for maintaining fair and orderly markets similar to that which exists in the New

York Stock Exchange regulations. Nor would we object to any surveillance or reporting that the Commission deemed necessary to determine whether minimum standards of responsibility are being met.

On the other hand, we are convinced that free and open competition is the best regulatory force available and that such competition imposes a level of responsibility far higher than minimum standards formally stated.

Furthermore, we find it very hard to take the New York Stock Exchange seriously in this regard. Mr. Haack stated recently that, "competition in market places should be decided on the basis of depth and liquidity and overall performance and not on gimmickry or disparate regulation." We agree completely. We are willing and, we believe, able to compete on these terms. However, it is the New York Stock Exchange which has imposed Rules 394 and 394(b) upon its members, thus acting to protect its Floor from effective competitive bids and offers from the Third Market, thus placing its member brokers in the position of not being able to exercise their primary fiduciary responsibility of securing the best execution for their customer. We have for years been urging the Commission to encourage an obviously unwilling New York Stock Exchange to change these two rules. We suggest that the New York Stock Exchange review its defense of Rules 394 and 394(b) and read the Staff Recommendations on those rules prior to further questioning of "responsibility" and "minimum standards" in the Third Market.

Part III

The combined system for trading listed stocks which we envision should be more efficient and less expensive than the present system since it would reduce the number of high-cost hands through which an institutional block order must travel. A lot of the fat in the present system would be eliminated, and along with it, the unnatural compensation that accrues to many individuals and firms. Marginal producers and well-established firms, including ours, might find the going so rough that merger or liquidation becomes their only course. It is understandable that this spectre causes some firms to seek a return to the past. It is less understandable or defensible that the New York Stock Exchange lends them support through its policies and actions. The system the Exchange seeks to perpetuate is moribund. The forces acting on the market place for listed stocks are irreversible and will ultimately prevail.

We urge the Commission to resist the temptation to compromise in favor of the status quo. Compromise will only perpetuate present barriers and increase fragmentation of a growing market. Worse still, it will magnify the many distortions that presently plague the industry, distortions that grow harder to eliminate the longer they remain. Why prolong the process of adjustment? How much more responsible in the long run for the Commission to set free the forces of competition and permit a reasonably quick adjustment to the reality of institutional dominance in the listed stock market—a needed adjustment that would not increase the burden of regulatory surveillance of the true Central Market Place.

Yours truly,

s/ DONALD E. WEEDEN
Executive Vice President

Some of us are wondering
about May 1.

Others are more than
wondering.

Some think there will
be confusion.

Others think it's just
what the doctor ordered.

Some think it will lead
to dealer markets.

Some think it will
improve liquidity.

Some may offer
barebones execution...

and others boutique services.

There could be some
tough negotiating…

and some not so tough.

Some institutions…

might even be out for blood.

But whatever happens...

at the Weeden Market...

our service will continue
to be best net price.

Happy Mayday.

The Weeden Market is available
through our offices located in:

NEW YORK	212-344-2300
BOSTON	617-423-4710
CHICAGO	312-641-0615
HOUSTON	713-224-6184
PHILADELPHIA	215-864-7270
LOS ANGELES	213-489-2642
SAN FRANCISCO	415-362-3050
LONDON	628-6281

National Market Advisory Board Members
(1976–77)

Milton E. Cohen is a partner of the firm of Schiff, Hardin & Waite, Chicago, Illinois. He served as a member of the Advisory Committee to the Commission's Institutional Investor Study and as Director of the Commission's Special Study of the Securities Markets. His law firm is general counsel to the Midwest Stock Exchange, Inc., the Chicago Board Options Exchange, Inc. and the Options Clearing Corporation.

Aaron R. Eshman is President and Chief Executive Officer of Stern, Frank, Meyer & Fox, Inc., Los Angeles, California. He is also a former Governor of the American Stock Exchange and a Director and Executive Committee Member of the Securities Industry Association.

Robert M. Fomon is President and Chief Executive Officer of E. F. Hutton & Company Inc., New York, New York. He is also a former Chairman of the Pacific Stock Exchange.

John P. Guerin, Jr. is Chairman of New America Fund, Inc., and Mitchum, Jones & Templeton, Incorporated, Los Angeles, California. He is a former Chairman of the Pacific Stock Exchange and serves as Director of a number of public companies.

James H. Lorie is professor of Finance at the Graduate School of Business at the University of Chicago. He was the author of the U. S. Treasury Department's statement on "Public Policy for American Capital Markets", submitted in February 1974 and is a former Governor of the National Association of Securities Dealers, Inc.

C. Rader McCulley is President of First Southwest Company, Dallas, Texas. He has served on various committees of the National Association of Securities Dealers, Inc. and has been a member of its Board of Governors. He has also been a member of the Commission's Advisory Committee on Model Compliance Program for Broker-Dealers and the Advisory Committee on the Implementation of a Central Market System.

Donald B. Marron is President and Chief Executive Officer of Mitchell, Hutchins, Inc., New York, New York. He is also a Director of the New York Stock Exchange and a Director of the Securities Industry Association.

Joane H. Miller is an individual investor residing in North Redington Beach, Florida. She attended the University of Tennessee and is a graduate of the New York Institute of Finance. She has been a registered representative of a New York Stock Exchange member firm and currently serves as Treasurer of two Florida Gulf Coast Symphony Boards.

James W. North is Executive Vice President of the Chase Manhattan Bank, N.A., New York, New York. He is a former President of the Trust Division of the New York State Bankers Association and President of the Trust Division of the American Bankers Association.

George Putnam is Chairman and President of the Putnam Funds and Chairman of the Putnam Management Company, Inc., Boston, Massachusetts. He is also the Treasurer of Harvard University and Chairman of the Harvard Management Company.

Ralph S. Saul is Chairman, President and Chief Executive Officer of INA Corp., Philadelphia, Pennsylvania. Previously, he was Chairman of the Executive Committee of the First Boston Corporation and President of the American Stock Exchange. He was also Director of the Commission's then Division of Trading and Markets and a member of the Commission's Advisory Committee on Market Structure.

John J. Scanlon is a retired Executive Vice President and Chief Financial Officer of the American Telephone and Telegraph Co., New York, New York. He serves as Director of a number of public corporations including Avis, Inc., Browning-Ferris Industries, Inc., Harvey Hubbell, Inc., National Distillers and Chemical Corp., and USLIFE Corp. He is also Adjunct Professor of Finance at the Wharton Graduate School of Business of the University of Pennsylvania.

Donald Stone is a senior partner of Lasker, Stone and Stern, New York, New York, specialists on the New York Stock Exchange. He has served on the Advisory Committee to the Commission's Institutional Investor Study and as a member of the Commission's Advisory Committee on Market Disclosure and Advisory Committee on the Implementation of a Central Market System.

Robert W. Swinarton is Vice Chairman of Dean Witter & Co., New York, New York. He is also Chairman of the Board of Governors and Chairman of the Executive Committee of the National Association of Securities Dealers, Inc. and Chairman of the Board of NASDAQ, Inc.

Donald E. Weeden is Chairman of the Board of Weeden & Co., New York, New York. He was a member of the Commission's Advisory Committee on Market Disclosure. Weeden & Co., which is a member of most regional stock exchanges, is the leading third market firm, and is the only registered odd-lot dealer on the Cincinnati Stock Exchange. Weeden & Co. also owns a substantial share of Institutional Network Systems (Instinet).

Introducing Cincinnati/NMS—
"The Exchange without walls"

The Cincinnati Stock Exchange has aptly been described as "an Exchange without walls" partly because we welcome all brokers to our marketplace and partly because we have brought our market to the broker wherever he is located. Now, through our Multiple Dealer Trading System called the Cincinnati/NMS, the CSE provides a method whereby competing dealers, specialists and market makers can equitably and efficiently participate in our market—we have brought the marketplace to the dealer. In effect, we have developed the largest "floor" of any securities market in the country to go with our nonexistent walls. Our floor stretches from ocean to ocean. It is paved with computer core rather than oak planks but it serves the same function as any exchange floor—it provides a meeting place for buyer and seller—broker and dealer. Participants located anywhere in the country can personally participate in our auction.

The most advanced mechanism
in operation today

On our floor, all auction principles are not only preserved but enhanced: the broker has the ability to meet broker within the dealer spread, the broker has the ability to show his order to a national crowd, priority is given to public orders. In addition to these auction characteristics, the Cincinnati/NMS has provided the most advanced and sophisticated mechanism in operation today to allow multiple dealers to compete for the public order flow in a fair and equitable manner.

Computer Age efficiencies result
in lower operating costs

Not only does the Cincinnati/NMS bring the efficiencies of the computer age to the securities industry, it also has the capability of dramatically lowering the broker's cost of execution. While the system's capacity is limited to trading some 50 issues, the primary purpose of the Cincinnati/NMS is to demonstrate the potential benefits of an efficient computer-assisted trading market so that the industry can more easily perceive, design, build and bring to fruition the benefits which will flow from a truly National Market System.

The heart of a traditional exchange market is the action which occurs at the specialist's post. At this location the specialist maintains and represents the limit orders which have been left in his book. The specialist also acts as market coordinator to the extent conflicts arise between orders in his book, orders represented in the crowd and his own desire to buy or sell inventory.

On the Cincinnati/NMS the specialist's post is moved into a computer and the function of maintaining the "book" is assigned to the computer. This means that the entry of limit orders and retrieval of limit order information, both by the entering broker and by other users of the market can be handled in a much more efficient manner. The role of coordinator, the determination of who has preference in cases where there are multiple buyers or sellers, is also assigned to the computer. This reduces to zero any confusion as to priorities. Within the Cincinnati/NMS priority is assigned first to price and within price to time of receipt of the order. Within price, absolute priority is given to public orders, regardless of time of receipt, over bids or offers by dealers for their own account.

Text from "Cincinnati/NMS, an invitation to participate"

The clear, concise and impartial implementation of trading priorities through computer programs combined with a complete audit trail of transactions, gives the Cincinnati Stock Exchange not only the most advanced and complete but also the most inexpensive surveillance capability over floor activity of any exchange in the country.

Cincinnati/NMS—
It's what the ideal National Market should be

To understand the sophistication of the Cincinnati/NMS one should compare what our prototype encompasses when compared with the one other tentative approach towards a National Market System, the New York Stock Exchange's I.T.S. program.

The I.T.S. is but one of the four component parts which industry sources generally agree will eventually constitute a National Market System. These four components are:

1. A composite quote system.

2. An order routing system capable of routing orders to all markets and, perhaps, even the best market.

3. An inter-market communication system.

4. A central limit order file.

Whereas I.T.S. represents a tentative beginning of Item #3 above, capable of serving all listed issues traded on multiple exchanges, the Cincinnati/NMS encompasses all four component parts. It is a complete prototype of what an eventual National Market System might be. Although limited in capacity to some 50 issues, the system does have the capacity to interconnect all exchanges as well as many dealers, market makers and brokers.

The two approaches, I.T.S. and the Cincinnati/NMS, are not incompatible with each other. In fact, the Cincinnati Stock Exchange has requested representation on the I.T.S. system and we would welcome NYSE participation in our experiment. Our concern with the I.T.S. approach is that the step by step progression toward the ultimate system is not spelled out, the ultimate market structure is hazy at best and the cost of developing each of these components, the cost of interfacing them as they come on line and the cost of operating them when completed is nonexistent. The

most important of all these unanswered questions is the latter—how efficient, how labor intensive, will the ultimate market be. In the answer to that question lies the key to the ultimate profitability of the broker segment of our industry and the variety and cost of services the broker will be able to offer his customer.

We believe that hard data developed from actual operation of our prototype National Market System will hasten completion of the ultimate system and reduce the cost of trial and error development. At the same time our activity in a few issues in no way threatens the existing primary market structure. In effect, we are offering the industry a working laboratory model with which it can experiment with a market designed for the 21st century at a user cost projected to be less than the current out of pocket cost of execution on the NYSE.

Your opportunity to participate

The Cincinnati/NMS is truly a giant step towards the creation of the oft discussed National Market System. The industry's involvement is important if not essential. As a broker or dealer you stand to lose nothing through participation. On the other hand, noninvolvement simply means you are denying yourself the opportunity to increase your knowledge, comprehension and understanding.

There is room for all brokers, dealers, specialists and marketmakers on our Exchange without walls. You are cordially invited to participate.

For further information as to how your orders can best be executed in our market please contact: Ms. D. Rosemary Goodrich, Executive Secretary, The Cincinnati Stock Exchange, 205 Dixie Terminal Building, Cincinnati, OH 45202 (513) 621-1410.

THE WALL STREET JOURNAL, TUESDAY, APRIL 12, 1988

October Crash Proves Need for National Market System

By Donald E. Weeden

Fundamental to the Exchange Act of 1975 was establishment of a national market system for exchange-listed stocks. Thirteen years later, such a system is not yet in place. Would it have made a difference on Oct. 19 if there had been one?

An answer to this critical question should be sought by those studying the October crash. Yet nowhere in the Brady commission report nor in the voluminous study by the Securities and Exchange Commission is there any mention of a national market system or even of the Exchange Act itself.

If the answer to the question is yes—or even maybe—the second question is: What should Congress, the Securities and Exchange Commission, the securities industry or others do to bring one about? Also, just what is a national market system? Its final structure was never precisely drawn, but Congress had something clear in mind when it mandated to the SEC the job of guiding the industry toward building one.

First and foremost, Congress contemplated that any securities firm wanting to make markets and compete for the public's business should be allowed to do so, and the way to do it in a centralized system was to link such firms electronically. It was Congress's intent that a public customer, wherever he entered the system, would find equal access to market information and timely execution. For those with limit orders (orders left with a specialist to sell or buy when a stock reaches a certain price) a central limit order book that pools the limit orders of all exchanges into a composite book would give priority

to public orders. Suitable regulation over all participating dealers could be established by the SEC to ensure adequate protection for the public.

Certain elements of a national system were obvious and quickly made their way into use. The first was a composite tape that brought information from various market centers onto one ticker tape. A composite quotation display system soon followed, allowing customers and brokers to see quotes from all markets on a single screen. And an Intermarket Trading System allowed orders coming to one exchange to flow from one exchange to another quickly, easily and at no cost.

What was not accomplished was the final step of interlinking all the firms that might want to make markets in listed stocks. This was the most difficult step because it seemed to threaten the very existence of exchanges.

Would this last step have made a difference last October? I think so. One thing is clear: More money made available to individual firms for market making through a national system would have been welcome. On Oct. 19 and 20 it might have significantly damped the volatility and greatly moderated the negative psychological and economic reactions.

Several weaknesses in the market structure (both listed and over the counter) added greatly to price volatility on Oct. 19 and 20. Insufficient capital in specialists' hands was cited by the Brady report and the SEC study. This was particularly critical in those stocks considered market leaders.

It's not clear how much market-making

capital would be attracted to New York Stock Exchange stocks under the open-access rules of a national system. The government bond and over-the-counter markets provide some clues. There, unobstructed, dealer capital tends to gravitate to securities with high volume and continuing customer interest.

My best guess is that almost every firm currently seeking business with institutional investors would participate to some degree and probably would be joined by most of the retail firms. Eventually, as the national system took on international positions, every major firm around the world would participate.

Another problem in October was the deficiency in critical instantaneous information. No one but specialists had a clue (and even they were uncertain) as to just how much selling pressure there was. A national system could have informed widely scattered dealers of order imbalances. The Intermarket Trading System could be easily expanded to include institutional trading desks and modified to include a central limit order book. This would automatically consolidate and publicize imbalances in orders as well as limit orders.

Some progress, especially in market access, is being made. The inadequate linkage between market makers in Nasdaq (the National Association of Securities Dealers Automated Quotation system) will be eliminated soon—or substantially corrected—by the introduction of user-friendly terminals. Combined with new rules requiring maintenance of markets and their timely update, this should go far to make the market more responsive and responsible.

The exchanges seem less focused in their reaction to Oct. 19, tending to complain about one another's use of the Intermarket Trading System, concentrating their criticism on the trading practices of certain customers, and trying to make derivative markets the fall guy. There is some recognition by the New York Stock Exchange of the imperfect nature of the specialist system, but it is limited to replacing one monopolist with another.

One positive fact coming out of the studies so far is recognition that the marketplace and those within it do not have a responsibility to prevent downturns. It is possible only to minimize the violence and reduce the volatility.

In the early '70s, Wall Street had a paper-crunch crisis that led to many failures of firms and losses to their customers. Out of that came the congressional hearings that resulted in the Exchange Act of 1975 and legislation creating the Securities Investor Protection Corp., a federal and industry agency that provides limited insurance to customers of failed brokerage houses.

There is an analogy between that crisis and the one in October. It was never suggested then—nor should it be today—that the solution was in putting restraints on customers. Rather, the job of the securities industry is to improve its capability to serve the customer and thereby help prevent another Oct. 19.

To the amazement of most, the Exchange Act catapulted the securities industry into its greatest period of growth, profitability and customer satisfaction. Oct. 19 pointed out some deficiencies still existing in market structure.

A national market system as envisioned by Congress is a worthy goal, even moreso today than 13 years ago. The coming public hearings on the October crash would be an appropriate time to determine how to finish the task.

Mr. Weeden is chief executive officer of a New York securities firm.

Chronology of Events
1922–2002

1922   Weeden & Co. is formed in San Francisco by brothers Frank
and Norman Weeden. The firm's initial business is dealing in
seasoned California bonds.

1927   Weeden & Co. incorporates, precluding it from becoming a
member of the NYSE. The firm opens additional offices in Los
Angeles and New York.

1948   Weeden adds a small number of industrial common stocks listed
on the NYSE, in which the firm quotes a two-sided market.

1957   The NYSE institutes Rule 394, ending the practice of allowing
member firms to execute customer orders in listed stocks with
non-member dealers and away from the specialist.

1959–63 The United States Supreme Court finally rules in favor of
Municipal Securities Co. in the case *Silver, dba Municipal
Securities Co., et al. v. New York Stock Exchange.* The issue was
whether the Sherman Antitrust Act was violated when the
NYSE ordered its member firms to collectively pull all direct
telephone connections to Municipal Securities without notice.
Weeden visits the Justice Department and obtains their inter-
vention on behalf of the plaintiff.

1961–63 Congress commissions the Special Study of the Securities
Markets, independent of the SEC. In the study's report, the
over-the-counter market for listed securities is first detailed to
the public and given the title of the "Third Market."

1964–66 Chase Manhattan Bank lists on the NYSE, causing M.A.

Schapiro, the largest bank stock trader, to challenge Rule 394 as being in violation of the Sherman Antitrust Act, since it prevents owner Morris Schapiro's long-standing customers from using his market in Chase's common stock. Schapiro is supported by the Justice Department. The SEC arranges for a compromise titled Rule 394(b), which proves ineffective. A study by the SEC supporting Schapiro and the Justice Department is kept under wraps for six years.

1967 Management of Weeden & Co. is turned over to three of Frank's sons, Alan, Jack and Don, with Alan becoming president and CEO.

1968 The Justice Department writes the SEC and questions various practices in the securities industry as being violations of the Sherman Antitrust Act, including the minimum commission rates. Representatives of Weeden & Co. appear at the subsequent SEC hearings, describing in detail the firm's role in the Third Market and arguing for the removal of NYSE Rule 394 (b).

1969 Weeden & Co. writes a letter to the SEC describing the effect of institutional activity in the marketplace and the effect of new technology on the structure of the market. Weeden coins the phrase "The central marketplace today is no longer a geographical concept. It is a communications concept."

Weeden supports new communications technology through investments in AutEx, a computerized display of buy and sell interest between brokers and institutions, and Instinet, a computer-based system allowing institutions to trade directly among themselves.

1970 NYSE President Robert Haack creates furor among his members when he publicly calls for the end of fixed commissions.

Frustrated by SEC inaction on NYSE Rule 394(b), Weeden & Co. joins the Cincinnati Stock Exchange as their odd-lot specialist and later joins the Detroit, PBW, Boston and Pacific stock exchanges as an alternate specialist.

Donaldson, Lufkin & Jenrette incorporates and becomes the first NYSE member firm to go public. Shortly thereafter, Weeden & Co. raises $20 million in two public offerings managed by Bache & Co., a NYSE firm.

Under NYSE pressure, the NASD reverses its policy and excludes listed stocks from appearing on its NASDAQ system, due for startup in 1971.

Congress responds to Wall Street's paperwork crunch, NYSE Wednesday closings, the demise of numerous brokerage firms and resultant losses by public investors by calling for a "study of the securities market, the securities industry and the public investor."

1971   A report by William McChesney Martin commissioned by the NYSE calls for, among other issues, "elimination of the Third Market."

President Richard Nixon appoints William Casey chairman of the SEC. Two months following publication of the Martin Report, Casey calls for SEC hearings on market structure.

1972   An SEC "Statement on the Future Structure of the Securities Markets" rejects the Martin Report's proposal to abolish the Third Market and reaffirms the SEC's commitment to market making competition.

Studies by both houses of Congress call for a National Market System that would include the Third Market and would include a consolidated tape, a consolidated quote system, priority to public orders and elimination of barriers to competition.

With more than $30 million in capital, Weeden becomes one of the top 25 firms on Wall Street and begins a major expansion in fixed income trading.

1973   Jim Needham, recently elected chairman of the NYSE, begins a campaign to "eliminate" the Third Market, with full-page ads in the *Wall Street Journal* and the *New York Times*.

An SEC white paper on the structure of a central market system reaffirms its support for including all markets, eliminating barriers to competition and protection of public orders through a centralized book.

1974 Separate bills are submitted to the U.S. Senate and House of Representatives to amend the Exchange Act of 1934, among other things calling for a National Market System. The bills are buried in the Senate Rules Committee and are resubmitted with important changes in 1975.

An effort by the NYSE to have Congress establish criteria for the elimination of the Third Market is made meaningless by the intervention of the Justice Department, Treasury Department and the SEC.

Under the direction of Jack Weeden, Weeden & Co. begins to design and build an electronic trading system meeting the criteria established by Congress for a National Market System.

1975 The SEC ends all fixed commissions on May 1, and Congress passes the Securities Acts Amendments of 1975. President Gerald Ford signs them into law.

The National Market Advisory Board is formed at the request of Congress, and Don Weeden is one of 15 members appointed by SEC Chairman Ray Garrett. The board's mission is to recommend to the SEC the details for implementing a National Market System.

1976 Alan Weeden leaves on a 15-month sabbatical and John Krause is elected president and CEO of Weeden & Co.

Weeden completes its Weeden Holding Automated Market (WHAM), which allows for competing market makers and exchange specialists to participate, and turns over the system's operation to the Cincinnati Stock Exchange. The Midwest,

Pacific and Boston stock exchanges join with the Cincinnati to create a Regional Market System trading in a limited number of stocks.

Newly formed Weeden Holding Corp. creates Dexter Securities for the purpose of executing and clearing trades for non-NYSE-member firms. The NYSE retaliates with a new rule that prevents Dexter Securities from joining the NYSE.

1977   A combination of events — including overexpansion, bad markets and in-house difficulties — results in severe losses for Weeden & Co. In late December, Don Weeden replaces John Krause as CEO.

The SEC under Chairman Harold Williams effectively ends all progress toward a National Market System.

1978   Losses at Weeden & Co. continue, forcing the firm to merge with Moseley, Hallgarten and Estabrook in February 1979. The new firm is called Moseley, Hallgarten, Estabrook and Weeden (MHEW).

1979   Prior to the merger, Weeden sells its WHAM system to Control Data and distributes its 70 percent interest in Instinet to its shareholders.

1986   The Weeden Equity Trading Division leaves MHEW and re-establishes Weeden & Co., Inc. with $10.5 million in capital.

1987   Instinet is sold to Reuters for $125 million in stock.

1994   Weeden moves its New York office to Greenwich, Connecticut.

1995   Barry Small is formally appointed managing partner and CEO of Weeden & Co., Inc., a position he held unofficially for several years.

2001   Weeden & Co., Inc. reports an average pretax annual return on revenues of 21.8 percent for its first 15 years.

The events of September 11 introduce a national security issue into the debate over the need for a National Market System.

2002   Weeden & Co., Inc. continues to use its knowledge of the marketplace and the best in technology to service the institutional investor. There is still no National Market System.

Glossary of Terms
& Acronyms

AMEX—American Stock Exchange, the second largest stock exchange in New York City.

ASEF—Association of Stock Exchange Firms. Merged with the Investment Bankers Association of America in 1972 to form the Securities Industry Association (SIA).

auction market—Trading securities through brokers or agents on an exchange, where buyers compete with other buyers and sellers compete with other sellers for the best price.

"Aunt Millie"—A fictitious person representing all small retail investors of concern to the SEC, Congress and Wall Street that her interest in the market be properly protected.

AutEx—A computer system allowing multiple broker-dealers to communicate buy and sell interest to multiple institutions simultaneously. Developed by Alan Kay.

BAS—Block Automation System. Developed by the NYSE to compete with AutEx.

blue-chip stock—Refers to stocks of companies considered by investors as high quality and safe.

book—In which specialists record public limit orders.

broker-dealers—Firms in the business of buying and selling securities, registered with and regulated by either an exchange, the NASD or both.

cage—That part of the operational end of the business, or back office, where securities and money were handled and made secure through limited access.

CBOE—Chicago Board Options Exchange.

CLOB—Central (or Composite) Limit Order Book. A central repository that would contain bids and offers of market makers and specialists as well as priced limit orders from the public. There would be a requirement for all dealers and exchange floors to satisfy orders in the CLOB at a given price before executing in their own market. A "soft" CLOB refers to one where there is no difference in priority between market maker and specialist bids and offers and those placed in the CLOB on behalf of a public customer. A "hard" CLOB gives priority to public orders at a given price regardless of the time the public order was entered.

CMP—Central marketplace. Also National Market System (NMS).

commission—The broker's basic fee for buying or selling securities or property as an agent.

Composite Quotation System (CQS)—A system for collecting bids and offers from competing markets and displaying them in a centralized manner.

consolidated tape—A single tape that collects trades from all competing marketplaces and displays them in time sequence.

CTA—Consolidated Tape Association. An industry group formed to establish and administer a consolidated tape.

DISCOB—Dealers in Seasoned California Bonds (Weeden & Co.).

DOT—Designated Order Turnaround System of the NYSE (1976). Now SuperDOT (1984), capable of handling daily volume exceeding 2 billion shares.

electronic display boards (1966)—Used by several companies to display market information on a real-time basis. Normally had recall capability and supplemented the ticker tape as the preferred system for receiving information.

floor—The large trading area where stocks are bought and sold on a stock exchange.

fragmentation—Several market centers executing trades in the same security.

"Gadget"—A system for giving shipping instructions to the various Weeden offices receiving bonds from customers in advance of delivery in order to reduce interest costs connected with late deliveries.

give-up—A practice where member firms would "give up" to another firm a portion of the commission earned on a trade, even though that firm performed no service, usually at the request of the customer paying the commission.

"Guerilla Group"—Refers to several municipal bond houses active in the secondary market who teamed up to bid on new issues.

IBA—Investment Bankers Association of America. Merged with the Association of Stock Exchange Firms to form the Securities Industry Association (SIA).

Instinet—An electronic system allowing broker-dealers and institutions to expose their buy and sell interest to others on the system and to effect trades immediately or after negotiation. First operated in 1969; went public in 2001.

institutional investor—An organization whose primary purpose is to invest its own assets or those held in trust by it for others. Includes pension funds, investment companies, insurance companies and banks.

Intermarket Trading System (ITS)—An electronic linkage that enables the various U.S. exchanges and registered market makers in listed stocks to display their markets and execute trades between one another.

Investment Bankers Code Committee—Industry group formed in early 1930s to work with Congress in designing the Exchange Acts of 1933–34.

limit order—An order to buy or sell at a specific price, different from what is available in the market. It can be a price inside the available quote or outside it.

listed stock—The stock of a company that is traded on a securities exchange.

LOIS—Limit Order Information System.

Maloney Act—Passed by Congress in 1938. Established the National Association of Securities Dealers (NASD) to govern broker-dealers who were not members of any exchange and to regulate stocks that were not listed on any exchange.

market—The means through which buyers and sellers are brought together to facilitate the transfer of securities.

market maker—A term used to describe the business of quoting two-sided markets, either on an exchange as a specialist or in the over-the-counter market.

market order—An order to buy or sell at the best price existing in the market at the time the order is entered into the market.

Martin Report—A study of market structure commissioned by the NYSE and prepared by William McChesney Martin.

May Day—May 1, 1975, the day commission rates became fully negotiable.

MCLOF—Market Center Limit Order File.

MDTS—Multiple Dealer Trading System. Approved by the SEC in 1981 to operate as one of two pilot projects demonstrating a National Market System.

member firm—A securities brokerage firm with at least one member of the NYSE who is an officer or employee.

Multiple Trading Case (1940)—The SEC disapproved the NYSE rule that prevented its members from dealing for their own account in NYSE-listed securities on other exchanges.

municipal bond—A bond issued by a state or one of its entities (county, city, district or authority) where the interest paid is exempt from federal taxes.

NASD—National Association of Securities Dealers (see Maloney Act).

NASDAQ—An electronic system for the centralizing and publishing of dealer markets in over-the-counter stocks. Began operating in 1971.

NIRI—National Investor Relations Institute.

NMAB—National Market Advisory Board.

NMS—National Market System.

NYSE—New York Stock Exchange.

odd lots—Stock transactions that involve less than 100 shares.

off-board—Refers to transactions over the counter in unlisted securities or to a transaction of listed shares that is not executed on a national securities exchange.

OTC—Over the counter. A market for securities made up of dealers who may or may not be members of a securities exchange. The OTC market is conducted over the telephone and deals mainly with stocks of companies without sufficient shares, stockholders or earnings to warrant listing on an exchange.

PBW—Philadelphia Baltimore Washington Stock Exchange.

rights—Temporary securities given to existing shareholders of a company that entitle the holder to buy additional shares at a discount to the present market.

RMS—Regional Market System.

SEC—U.S. Securities and Exchange Commission.

secondary market—When stocks or bonds are traded or resold, they are said to be sold on the secondary market. Most securities transactions take place on the secondary market.

Securities Acts Amendments of 1974—Failed to pass in Congress; was postponed and modified into the Securities Acts Amendments of 1975.

Securities Acts Amendments of 1975—Amended the Securities Exchange Act of 1934 and, among other things, called for the creation of a National Market System in stocks listed on exchanges.

Securities Exchange Acts of 1933–34—Congressional acts establishing the U.S. Securities and Exchange Commission and empowering it to regulate activity of stock exchanges.

Sherman Antitrust Act—Passed by Congress in 1890 to eliminate restraints on trade and competition.

SIA—Securities Industry Association.

SIAC—Securities Industry Automation Corporation, an independent organization established by NYSE and AMEX to provide automation, data processing, clearing and communication services.

soft dollars—A term that applied to the practice by institutional money managers to use commissions paid to brokers for the execution of stock orders for research and other services.

specialist—A market maker who is a member of the NYSE or another exchange.

Special Study of the Securities Markets—An SEC study of issues involving the securities markets. Led by Milton Cohen and Ralph Saul, it was begun in 1961 and issued its report in 1963. See Chapter 4 ("The Special Study").

stock loans—When a brokerage firm lends to another brokerage firm or to its customers stock that is in its possession or control (usually stock owned by its customers), either to cover a short or to facilitate a delivery.

Third Market—Trading of stock exchange–listed securities in the over-the-counter market by non-exchange-member dealers.

ticker—A real-time flow of information on trades taking place on the floor of an exchange or a consolidation of trades taking place in various markets.

"Troika"—Russian for "a group of three." Used by Frank Weeden referring to Alan, Jack and Don Weeden.

WHAM—Weeden Holding Automated Market, a trading system developed by Weeden & Co.

Index

N

P